'TIS PITY SHE'S A WHORE

A Critical Guide

Edited by Lisa Hopkins

continuum

Continuum

The Tower Building
11 York Road
London SE1 7NX

80 Maiden Lane, Suite 704
New York
NY 10038

www.continuumbooks.com

British Library Cataloguing-in-Publication Data
A catalogue record for this book is available from the British Library.

ISBN: 978-0-8264-9932-5 (Hardback)
         978-0-8264-9933-2 (paperback)

Library of Congress Cataloging-in-Publication Data
A catalog record for this book is available from the Library of Congress.

Typeset by BookEns, Royston, Hertfordshire
Printed and bound in Great Britain by CPI Antony Rowe, Chippenham, Wiltshire

Contents

Series Introduction

The drama of Shakespeare and his contemporaries has remained at the very heart of English curricula internationally and the pedagogic needs surrounding this body of literature have grown increasingly complex as more sophisticated resources become available to scholars, tutors and students. This series aims to offer a clear picture of the critical and performative contexts of a range of chosen texts. In addition, each volume furnishes readers with invaluable insights into the landscape of current scholarly research as well as including new pieces of research by leading critics.

This series is designed to respond to the clearly identified needs of scholars, tutors and students for volumes which will bridge the gap between accounts of previous critical developments and performance history and an acquaintance with new research initiatives related to the chosen plays. Thus, our ambition is to offer innovative and challenging guides which will provide practical, accessible and thought-provoking analyses of Renaissance drama. Each volume is organized according to a progressive reading strategy involving introductory discussion, critical review and cutting-edge scholarly debate. It has been an enormous pleasure to work with so many dedicated scholars of Renaissance drama and we are sure that this series will encourage to you read 400-year old playtexts with fresh eyes.

Andrew Hiscock and Lisa Hopkins

Timeline

12 April 1586: John Ford baptized at Ilsington, Devon, second son of Thomas Ford and Elizabeth Popham, the niece of Lord Chief Justice Popham.

25 March 1601: A 'John Ford Devon gent.' who was almost certainly the dramatist matriculates at Exeter College, Oxford.

16 November 1602: Enters the Middle Temple.

Hilary Term 1605: Officially expelled from the Middle Temple for failing to pay his buttery bill.

1606: Publication of *Honour Triumphant*, a prose piece linked to the chivalric entertainments proposed for the visit of James I's brother-in-law Christian IV of Denmark, and of *Fame's Memorial*, an elegy on Charles Blount, Earl of Devonshire, husband of Penelope Devereux (Sir Philip Sidney's 'Stella').

10 June 1608: Formally readmitted to the Middle Temple.

1610: Death of Ford's father. Ford receives an inheritance of £10.

1612–13: Possibly writes a now lost play, *An Ill Beginning Has a Good End*.

1613: Publication of *Christ's Bloody Sweat*, a long religious poem, and of *The Golden Mean*, a neo-Stoic treatise in the vein of his maternal cousin Sir John Stradling's translations of Justus Lipsius.

1615–16: Ford contributes various writings, some of which have not survived, to the collective laments for his fellow Middle Templar Sir Thomas Overbury, murdered by the wife of James I's favourite the

Earl of Somerset. The idea that noble titles are not enough but that the aristocracy must also *act* nobly is a recurrent one in Ford's writings.

1616: Death of Ford's elder brother. Ford receives an inheritance of £20.

1617: Ford may be one of a group of 40 members of the Middle Temple who protested against wearing their caps in hall.

1620: Publication of *A Line of Life*, another neo-Stoical treatise.

1621: Collaborates with Thomas Dekker and William Rowley to write *The Witch of Edmonton*, a domestic tragicomedy based on a true case.

c. 1623: Collaborates with Dekker again on *The Welsh Embassador* and with Middleton and Rowley on *The Spanish Gipsy*. Also possibly works with Fletcher on *The Laws of Candy*.

1624: Collaborates with Dekker on a 'moral masque', *The Sun's Darling*, and on *The Fairy Knight* and *The Bristow Merchant*, both of which are now lost. In conjunction with Webster and Rowley, Ford and Dekker also co-write *The Late Murther of the Son Upon the Mother*, a now-lost domestic tragedy. Around this time Ford may also have written another lost play, *The London Merchant*, this time apparently on his own.

1626: Perhaps collaborates with Fletcher on *The Fair Maid of the Inn*.

1628: Publication of *The Lover's Melancholy*, Ford's first surviving independent play.

1633: Publication of *The Broken Heart*, *Love's Sacrifice*, and *'Tis Pity She's a Whore.*

1634: Publication of *Perkin Warbeck.*

1638: Publication of *The Fancies, Chaste and Noble*. The prologue to this says of the author 'he's farre enough from home', apparently implying that Ford was travelling.

1639: Publication of *The Lady's Trial*. Ford seems to have seen this through the press, but there is no further evidence of any activity on his part and no record of when he died.

1653: Anonymous publication of *The Queen*, a tragicomedy now generally attributed to Ford. Its publisher, Alexander Gough, had acted in *The Lover's Melancholy*.

9 September 1661: Samuel Pepys sees a performance of *'Tis Pity* but thinks it 'a simple play and ill acted'.

1691: Gerard Langbaine's *An Account of the English Dramatic Poets* offers the first literary appreciation of Ford.

1808: Publication of Charles Lamb's *Specimens of the English Dramatic Poets who Lived About the Time of Shakespeare* prompts a new interest in Ford.

1811: Publication of Henry Weber's two-volume edition of Ford's plays.

1816: Publication of Lady Caroline Lamb's *Glenarvon*, which refers to a number of Ford plays including *'Tis Pity*.

1827: Publication of Gifford's three-volume edition of Ford.

1894: Maurice Maeterlinck's adaptation *Annabella* is performed in Paris.

28–29 January 1923: The Phoenix Society gives two private performances, bringing the play to the the English stage for the first known time since the seventeenth century. The text was heavily cut.

30 December 1934: A private performance at the Arts Theatre Club, London.

1935: Publication of M. Joan Sargeaunt's *John Ford*, the first monograph on the playwright.

13 May 1940: Directed by Donald Wolfit at the Cambridge Arts Theatre.

18, 23 January 1941: Directed by Donald Wolfit at the Strand Theatre, London.

1962: Radio version produced by Martyn C. Webster broadcast on the *Third Programme*.

1970: Radio version produced by John Tydeman broadcast on the BBC.

1971: Release of the film version directed by Giuseppe Patroni Griffi.

1972: Separate productions by David Giles for the Actors' Company and by Roland Joffé at the National Theatre.

1977: Directed by Ron Daniels for the Royal Shakespeare Company.

1978: *Toch zonde dat 't een hoor ist*, directed by Dré Poppe and Jaak van de Velde, shown on Belgian television.

1980: A made-for-television version, directed by Roland Joffé, shown on British television.

1982: Tom Stoppard's *The Real Thing* includes snippets from an imagined performance of *'Tis Pity*.

1988: Directed by Alan Ayckbourn at the National Theatre and by Philip Prowse for Glasgow Citizens' Theatre. Publication of Angela Carter's short story 'John Ford's 'Tis Pity She's a Whore'.

1989: Release of *The Cook, The Thief, His Wife and Her Lover*, directed by Peter Greenaway, which is influenced by *'Tis Pity*.

1990: Directed by JoAnne Akalaitis at the Goodman Theater, Chicago.

1991: Directed by David Leveaux for the Royal Shakespeare Company. Release of *Close My Eyes*, directed by Stephen Poliakoff, which glances at *'Tis Pity*.

1992: Directed by JoAnne Akalaitis for the New York Shakespeare Festival's Public Theater.

1997: First screening of 'The Killings at Badger's Drift', the pilot episode for the TV series *Midsomer Murders*, which drew on the plot of *'Tis Pity*.

1999: Directed by David Lan at the Old Vic.

March 2002: Directed by R. J. Tolan for the Women's Shakespeare Company at Speeed, off Broadway.

2005: Directed by Edward Dicks at the Southwark Playhouse.

Introduction

Lisa Hopkins

Ford has always been a difficult writer to categorize, eluding or straddling a variety of different possible classificatory models. In the first place, he is a difficult writer to pin down chronologically. Born in 1586, he is in some sense an Elizabethan – he was almost 17 when the queen died, and had already moved to London – but an unusually late start means that all of his surviving independent dramatic writing seems to be firmly Caroline, after a period of collaborative authorship during the reign of James. Nevertheless, though the eight surviving plays which have been more or less securely ascribed to him seem probably all to have been written after 1625, it could reasonably be said that they are not Caroline in feel, since they all to a greater or lesser extent hark back to a considerably older model or models of drama. *Perkin Warbeck* in particular is a positive throwback, a late and solitary flowering of the once mighty and vigorous growth of the Elizabethan history play, and it is liberal in its glances back at Marlowe's *Edward II* and Shakespeare's *Richard II*, written four decades before. Not for nothing is *Perkin Warbeck* dedicated to William Cavendish, Earl of Newcastle and patron of Jonson and Brome, whose own play *The Variety* has a hero, Manly, who expresses his nostalgia for a bygone age by dressing as the Elizabethan Earl of Leicester.

Others of Ford's plays hark back in similar fashion, if not always to the same degree. Both *Love's Sacrifice* and *The Lady's Trial* consciously revisit *Othello*: in *Love's Sacrifice*, the twist is that the Dedesemona-figure, Biancha, did actually love the Cassio-figure, though she is not guilty of actual infidelity with him, and in *The Lady's Trial* it is that the Iago-figure, Aurelio, is genuinely mistaken, or at least self-deluded, and really did believe the Desdemona-figure to be unfaithful, while the Othello-figure, Auria, chooses to hear and accept his wife's explanation of her innocence and successfully arranges a happy ending, complete with multiple marriages. *The Lover's Melancholy*, with its mad father and cross-dressing daughter, combines echoes of *King Lear* and *Twelfth Night*; *The Fancies, Chaste and Noble* recalls aspects of *Women Beware Women*; and *The Queen*, which does not bear Ford's name on the title page but is now generally accepted as his, is another play to pay homage to *Othello* and also, as Lesel Dawson has recently argued, seems to remember the Essex Rebellion,[1] which by the time Ford wrote had taken place nearly 40 years earlier. *The Broken Heart*, meanwhile, revisits both the love story of Sir Philip Sidney, dead since 1586,[2] and, as Verna Ann Foster and Stephen Foster have convincingly argued, the accession of James I in 1603.[3]

Indeed so extensive is Ford's engagement with older plays that he could in some sense justly be termed an early critic of Renaissance drama, particularly of Shakespeare, whose plays he revisits and reworks almost obsessively. His special favourites are clearly identifiable, and it is instructive to note both what he takes from them and also what he does not. *King Lear* clearly lies behind the father/daughter relationships of *The Lover's Melancholy*, but *The Lover's Melancholy* has no trace of the battle on which the fate of nations depends, and, unusually for Renaissance drama, no interest either in bastardy or its possible effect on characters. *Othello* lies behind *Love's Sacrifice*, *The Lady's Trial* and perhaps the jealousy scene of *'Tis Pity*, but it is solely the love story and the accompanying jealousy which fires Ford's imagination; he shows no interest at all in the ethnic difference of Othello from those around him, and when he writes about human bodies it is only ever about what is inside them, never about skin colour. These differences help us to see that Ford's focus is love, not society, which indeed tends to exist only as a frame for human activity, edging and constraining it in ways which are always potentially unhelpful and sometimes actually so. Ford's great-uncle, Lord Chief Justice Popham, rubbed shoulders with some of the most famous names of the period, and Ford himself dedicated his works to a number of aristocrats of varying degrees of power and influence, but this public sphere is not where his real interest lies: he is – in every sense – a dramatist of the heart, and *'Tis Pity* is perhaps the supreme example of that.

'Tis Pity She's a Whore itself is shaped and conditioned by a number of previous plays. Most obviously, it looks back at *Romeo*

and Juliet. Romeo and Juliet are young, idealistic lovers; each is clearly the best possible partner that their society has to offer for the other, but the feud between their families means that their union is too radically exogamous for the small Italian city in which they live. Annabella and Giovanni are young, idealistic lovers; each is clearly the best possible partner that their society has to offer for the other, but the fact that they are brother and sister means that their union is too radically endogamous for the small Italian city in which they live – even though that city, Parma, had historically been ruled by members of the Habsburg family, who used intermarriage between uncles and nieces as a political tool. Moreover, like Romeo and Juliet, Annabella and Giovanni turn for advice to a friar and a nurse, and Bergetto's death is not unlike Mercutio's.

'Tis Pity She's a Whore is also influenced by other plays. Like the later *The Fancies, Chaste and Noble*, it clearly resembles Middleton's *Women Beware Women*, whose sub-plot of an incestuous relationship between Isabella and her uncle Hippolito is closely echoed in *'Tis Pity*'s incestuous relationship between Annabella and her brother Giovanni, with the foolish Ward and his sidekick Sordido in *Women Beware Women* also foreshadowing the foolish Bergetto and his sidekick Poggio in *'Tis Pity*. As Cyrus Hoy pointed out long ago, Ford also seems to be thinking of Marlowe, since Giovanni starts the play sounding like Faustus and ends it sounding like Tamburlaine,[4] and that is something I explore further in my own chapter in this volume.

I think it is also worth considering the possibility that *'Tis Pity* was also influenced by another Shakespeare play which has strong intertextual connections with *Romeo and Juliet*: *A Midsummer Night's Dream*. At first sight, this may seem a ridiculous suggestion, since the two plays are so different from each other. However, *A Midsummer Night's Dream* seems to have been a play in which Ford was interested, and which, moreover, he associated with *Romeo and Juliet*, since Huntly in *Perkin Warbeck* speaks scornfully of his daughter and son-in-law as 'King Oberon and Queen Mab'.[5] The perception of a connection is spot on, since *Romeo and Juliet* and *A Midsummer Night's Dream* are, indeed, linked. Quince's insistence that there will be a prologue to *Pyramus and Thisbe* and that 'it shall be written in eight and six'[6] recalls the 14-line Prologue of *Romeo and Juliet* and the sonnet which the lovers complete between them when they first meet, and the play-within-the-play, with its tragic little tale of 'Pyramus and Thisbe', could almost be seen as a knowing glance back at *Romeo and Juliet*, in something of the same spirit as Mozart in *Don Giovanni* having his hero dismiss a tune from *The Marriage of Figaro* on the grounds that he has heard it before. *A Midsummer Night's Dream* takes us to Athens, represented in *The Broken Heart* as a home of learning and something of a distant dream for Sparta-bound Orgilus; it pits city against wood, with the latter represented as salvific, while *'Tis Pity* makes a point of being confined to the city; and there are also, as I discuss in Chapter 8, other correspondences between the two plays. An audience would, of course, be at liberty to ignore this if they wished – the visceral rather than culturally specific nature of the incest taboo means that the play is readily comprehensible to audiences who have no recollection of *A Midsummer Night's Dream* or *Romeo and Juliet* – but awareness of such parallels can significantly inflect the responses of those who do spot them. *'Tis Pity*, then, is a play radically constituted by the drama of Ford's youth and early manhood, meaning that it cannot readily be pigeonholed as Caroline.

Moreover, the date of *'Tis Pity* is in any case mysterious. It is sometimes suggested that because *The Broken Heart* and *The Lover's Melancholy* were Blackfriars plays, while all Ford's other extant, independent works were acted by Christopher Beeston's companies at the Phoenix, it therefore seems likely that *The Broken Heart* and *The Lover's Melancholy* were the first of Ford's independent plays, a theory which seems to be supported by the indisputable fact that *The Lover's Melancholy* was the first of the plays to be published, in 1628. Thus Ronald Huebert states confidently that 'Ford's early association with the King's men comes to an end in 1630, after which he contributes his remaining plays to the repertoire of Queen Henrietta Maria's company'[7] (though Ford's last known play *The Lady's Trial* was in fact acted not by the Queen's Men but by Beeston's Boys). Irving Ribner,[8] G. F. Sensabaugh,[9] H. J. Oliver,[10] Una Ellis-Fermor,[11] Kenneth Muir,[12] Donatella Ravignani[13] and R. F. Hill[14] all place *The Lover's Melancholy* first in the order of composition, as Bawcutt is also cautiously inclined to do.[15] T. J. B. Spencer, however, thought that the evidence was inconclusive,[16] and there is a peculiarly puzzling statement in Ford's dedicatory epistle to *'Tis Pity She's a Whore*, addressed to the Earl of Peterborough, which appears to some critics to conflict sharply with the theory that *The Lover's Melancholy* is the earliest of the plays. There Ford refers to *'Tis Pity* as 'these first fruits of my leisure'. Whether he is speaking of a particular period of leisure, such as one of the holidays between law-terms, or whether he is saying that this is his first play – whether he is in fact even telling us that it predates *The Witch of Edmonton*, his first collaborative play – there can be no way of knowing. Partly because of this strange statement and partly because of its vigour, its style and its extraordinarily Jacobean character, *'Tis Pity* is the main rival of *The Lover's Melancholy* for the title of Ford's first independent play. Leech remarks that 'it is likely that *'Tis Pity* was one of his earliest independent plays', and later adds that it is indeed 'perhaps the first that he wrote independently'.[17] Derek Roper, in his edition of the play, seems inclined to consider it as Ford's earliest independent drama. He even puts forward the tantalizing suggestion that *''Tis Pity* may have been written at virtually any date before 1633, or, if Rosset is accepted as a source, between 1613 and 1633. It may quite easily have been a Jacobean play in fact as well as in spirit'.[18] Gamini Salgado also remarks that *'Tis Pity* 'may date from any time between 1615 and 1633',[19] and E. H. C. Oliphant suggests that both *'Tis Pity* and *Love's Sacrifice* 'were considerably earlier in date than 1621'.[20] Bawcutt, however, in his introduction to the play, points out that 'the title-page [. . .] states that it was "Acted by the Queenes Maiesties Servants, at the Phoenix in Drury-Lane". This suggests that the first performance took place between 1626, when the Queen's Company came into being, and 1633, the date of publication'.[21] Nevertheless, F. S. Boas feels that *'Tis Pity* is at least earlier than *The Broken Heart*,[22] and if it precedes *The Broken Heart* then we are left with no reason why it should not also precede *The Lover's Melancholy*, since we are no longer supposing that Ford wrote first for the Blackfriars and then for the Phoenix. H. W. Wells puts forward a tentative dating of *'Tis Pity* to 1627, *The Lover's Melancholy* and *The Queen* to 1628, *The Broken Heart* to 1629 and *Perkin Warbeck* to 1633,[23] and Felix Schelling rather less tentatively offers exactly the same dates and sequence but omits any mention of *The Queen*.[24] Finally, Robert Davril proposes 1626–27 for *'Tis Pity*, 'précédant de peu *Love's Sacrifice* (1627–28)' ('predating *Love's Sacrifice* by a little time'), 1628–30 for *The Queen* and the now lost *Beauty in a Trance*, 1630–32 for *The Broken Heart*, and 1633–34 for *Perkin Warbeck*.[25]

If Ford is difficult to pin down in chronological terms, he also poses problems when it comes to questions of generic classification. *Perkin Warbeck* is clearly a history play, and *The Broken Heart* and *Love's Sacrifice* are certainly tragedies, but his other plays are more difficult to categorize. *The Lover's Melancholy* is perhaps best described as a melancholy comedy, while both *The Lady's Trial* and *The Fancies, Chaste and Noble* read rather like two separate plays, with an intrusive and unsatisfactory comic sub-plot grafted in each case onto a main plot which is comic in structure but elegiac in tone and feel. As for *'Tis Pity*, it, like its models *Romeo and Juliet*, *Dr Faustus* and *Women Beware Women*, is obviously a tragedy, but it might well seem more profitable to consider it, like Ford's earlier, collaborative play *The Witch of Edmonton*, under the specific rubric of *domestic* tragedy, a genre separated from revenge tragedy or tragedy of state by the fact that its main characters are private citizens rather than rulers and that the consequences of its events are thus confined to the private rather than the public sphere. Certainly this would seem to be part of the point of Hippolita's dismissal of Annabella as 'Your goodly Madam Merchant' (II.ii.49), as Verna Ann Foster explores in her illuminating article *"'Tis Pity She's a Whore* as City Tragedy'.[26] I have suggested in my own article 'Incest and Class: *'Tis Pity She's a Whore* and the Borgias' that we should definitely notice that incest has sometimes been tolerated in ruling families in a way that it never has in bourgeois ones.[27] It does not do to forget class when reading *'Tis Pity*: this is tragedy as the study of the specific rather than of the arguably universal, and indeed Corinne S. Abate argues in Chapter 5 that it is the town of Parma itself which is the real whore of the play.

Despite his debts to other authors, however, Ford broke new ground in his treatment of incest. This was a subject in which he was strongly interested, as evidenced by the fact that mention of it surfaces also in *The Broken Heart*, when Bassanes supposes the worst of Ithocles's desire to be alone with his sister Penthea. In fact, there had usually been an innocent explanation of incest in the plays preceding Ford. Incest begins to become increasingly important as a subject for drama during the early decades of the seventeenth century. It can be seen as early as Shakespeare and Wilkins's *Pericles*, where it is the explanation of the riddle involving the king and his daughter, and it also appears in Beaumont and Fletcher's *A King and No King*, but there, and in Middleton's *No Wit, No Help Like a Woman's*, the threat is defused at the last moment when one of the supposed siblings is revealed to have been swapped in the cradle. It comes still closer in *Women Beware Women*, but even there the niece, Isabella, is tricked into sleeping with her uncle Hippolito when her aunt tells her that Hippolito's brother was not in fact her biological father. In *'Tis Pity*, though, there is no escape, and no possible salve for the conscience: here, two people who rightly believe that they are brother and sister voluntarily choose to sleep together.

What motivated Ford to represent so stark a violation of the taboo against incest? This has been the central question around which discussions of *'Tis Pity* have revolved, but no definitive answer has ever been offered. It does seem clear that a narrative of incest allowed Ford to raise questions of class, and also offered excellent scope for further play on the twin terms of heart and blood, in which he showed himself obsessively interested throughout his career, and which are further inflected here by sustained exploration of the meaning and resonances of the verb 'to know' and its cognates. Ford is clearly also not averse to the sheer force of the gut reaction which the mention of incest provokes in most people. Nevertheless, that visceral horror is not quite a universal emotion: in 2007 the UK press reported on a German brother and sister who were challenging the law against incest in that country, noting that 'Napoleon abolished France's incest laws in 1810. Neither is it a crime in the Netherlands, Luxembourg, Belgium, Portugal or Turkey. Japan, Argentina and Brazil have also legalised it in recent years'.[28] As Kate Wilkinson discusses in her account of the play in performance (Chapter 2), the acceptability of incest between brother and sister is also explored in the popular UK television crime series *Midsomer Murders*, in ways which are obviously influenced by *'Tis Pity*. Perhaps our fascination with the topic of brother-sister incest in particular arises partly from the fact that there is not necessarily any inbuilt power relationship between brother and sister as there is between father and daughter, and the availability of modern methods of contraception removes the compelling genetic logic against incest. Moreover, modern research has brought to our attention the phenomenon known as genetic sexual attraction, whereby blood relatives who have long been separated may, when they meet, 'misinterpret' the sense of recognition they feel as a feeling of sexual attraction – and this is a paradigm which might well seem applicable to *'Tis Pity*, where Annabella's first question when she sees her brother, who has been away studying in Bologna, is 'What man is he, that with such sad aspect | Walks careless of himself?' (I.ii.133–34). At a crucial moment of *'Tis Pity*, the pursuit of Bergetto's murderer is brought to an abrupt halt when the Watch find themselves brought up short in the liminal space where civic power ends and the Cardinal's begins. In some sense, this emblematic border between the secular and the spiritual can stand for the experience offered by the play as a whole: as audiences, we find ourselves collectively at sea in the uneasy liminality where convention and rationality have said all they can and the dimmer voice of the taboo begins insistently to make itself heard.

However uncertain Ford's intention, there can be no doubt about the degree of his care and persistence in carrying it out: Derek Roper observes that the appearance of the quarto suggests that it was printed from a fair copy made by Ford's own hand, or at least under his close supervision. The chief evidence for this is a lavish use of italic type which is not characteristic of Okes's printing but which is found in most of Ford's other plays.[29]

Mark Houlahan and Corinne S. Abate both explore some of the effects of this in their chapters in this volume (Chapters 7 and 5). Ford seems generally to have seen his plays carefully through the press, and *'Tis Pity* is no exception: he cared about bringing us this play to read, and in doing what he could by means of pointing and typeface to guide our response to it.

What then are we to do with this text, so troublingly uncertain in intent and effect but so precise in execution? There can be no doubt that *'Tis Pity* is an eminently teachable text. It would be difficult to have no reaction at all to the idea of incest, and difficult too to read the play, watch the Patroni Griffi film, and then not have a view on the way that the one relates to the other. In addition, *'Tis Pity* is notably versatile, making a good pairing with a number of other plays including not only *Romeo and Juliet* and *Women Beware Women*, but pretty much any tragedy of state or city comedy.

The play also speaks to a range of issues. In the first place, since the publication of Jonathan Sawday's seminal book *The Body Emblazoned* in 1995, critics of Renaissance drama have been increasingly alert to the importance and far-reaching implications of the Renaissance interest in anatomy, especially since Sawday observes that '[t]he womb or uterus was an object sought after with an almost ferocious intensity in Renaissance anatomy theatres',[30] so that what Giovanni does to his sister can be seen as touching on an issue of acute interest in the period. Thus in *King Lear* the maddened king cries, 'Then let them anatomize Regan, see what breeds about her heart. Is there any cause in nature that makes these hard hearts?',[31] while in Chettle's *The Tragedy of Hoffman* Lorrique declares 'This is Hannce Hoffmans sonne | that stole downe his fathers Anotamy from the gallowes at *Leningberge*'.[32]

It is true that for Hoffman 'anatomy' appears to be effectively equivalent to 'skeleton', as we see when Lorrique tells Duchess Martha that

Prince Charles and I ecap't the wracke,
Came safe a shore to this accursed plot,
Where we met Hoffman, who vpon yon tree

Preseru'd his fathers bare anatomy,
The biggest of them two were those strong bones
That acted mighty deeds.

(I3r)

However, Lorrique's further words make it plain that something of
our modern sense of an interest in anatomy is present here too:

At length he tooke aduantage, bound my Lord,
And in a chayne tyed him to yonder rocke,
While with a burning Crowne he seard in twaine
The purple Veynes, strong sinewes, arteries, [n]erues,
And euery cartilage about the head.

(I3v)

Finally, Claridiana in *The Instatiate Countess*, finished by William
Barksted and Lewis Machin from an initial draft by Marston, tells
his wife, 'I had rather Chirurgeons' Hall should beg my dead body
for an anatomy than thou beg my life'.[33]

In *'Tis Pity*, Ford's obsessive use of the words 'heart' and 'blood',
on which so many critics have remarked,[34] clearly points to an
interest in the interior of the body, and Giovanni has been studying
at Bologna (I.i.49), which was famous as a centre for the study of
anatomy, something which surely bears on his Jack the Ripper-like
decision to make Petrarchan metaphor literal by cutting out
Annabella's heart.[35] (It is one of the play's many ironies that the
Friar, emblem of the spiritual approach to the human condition,
eventually returns to Bologna, home of a more physicalized
understanding of it [V.iii.66–67].) As Michael Neill points out,
Giovanni's action may in fact recall an actual anatomical enquiry,
the postmortem examination of the body of Elizabeth's Maid of
Honour Margaret Ratcliffe.[36] However, it also reflects a more
general interest in the subject, which was fed by the publication of
William Harvey's *Exercitatio anatomica de motu cordis et sanguinis
in animalibus* in 1628, announcing his discovery of the role of the
heart in the circulation of the blood, which opened up wider
questions about the relationship between body, mind and soul. In
her chapter on 'The State of the Art' in this volume (Chapter 3)
Sandra Clark notes the impact that the new interest in anatomy has
had on Ford criticism, and Catherine Silverstone and Mark
Houlahan both take this a step further in their contributions
(Chapters 4 and 7). Indeed in all Ford's plays there is a dangerous
potential separability between different parts of the body, which

seem disturbingly capable of independent action. Where then does this leave the very different forms of knowledge and understanding of the relationship between the soul and the body emblematized by Friar Bonaventure, whom Ford has named after the Franciscan theologian known as the Seraphic Doctor, author of the *Lignum Vitae*, whose title seems to be punningly glanced at in Ford's own neo-Stoical tract *A Line of Life*?

This question maps onto another growth area in criticism of English Renaissance drama, which is a growing interest in the survival of prohibited Catholic beliefs and practices in an England which was now officially Protestant. Inevitably, this, like all other aspects of Renaissance criticism, has centred on the figure of Shakespeare. Ever since the publication of Ernst Honigmann's *Shakespeare: The Lost Years* in 1985, there has been sustained interest in speculating either that Shakespeare did indeed spend some time in his youth at Hoghton Hall in Lancashire, where he would have been living among recusants, or that he was for other reasons well disposed to Catholicism. The indefatigable work of Richard Wilson in particular has explored all the possible Catholic links of Shakespeare's family and friends and the ways in which these may impact on readings of his plays. However, other writers have also received attention from critics interested in this area. Ben Jonson's well-known Catholicism, for instance, has attracted renewed interest, with the publication in 1999 of a double issue of the *Ben Jonson Journal* on the topic of Jonson and Catholicism, and a fresh flurry of inquiry into the possible identity of the Catholic priest who was known to Jonson and was apparently able to supply details of the Gunpowder Plot.[37] As Sandra Clark explores in her chapter on the 'State of the Art', since my own work in 1994 suggesting links between Ford and Catholicism, Ford too has been approached in such terms by, for instance, Laurel Amtower[38] and also, in this volume, by Gillian Woods (Chapter 6). *'Tis Pity* was dedicated to John Mordaunt, who had been at court most of his life and who had been created Earl of Peterborough in 1628. Mordaunt was the son of Henry, fourth Lord Mordaunt, who had been imprisoned in the Tower on suspicion of complicity in the Gunpowder Plot, although only for a year; his mother was Margaret, the daughter of Henry, Lord Compton, and she was a staunch Catholic – indeed in 1625 the head of the English mission was operating from her house – and for this reason she was deprived of the custody of her son, who, also in 1625, was converted to Protestantism. His conversion does not seem to have been taken very seriously, however, for his name is included in the *Petition Against Recusants in Authority* drawn up by

Parliament in 1626,[39] so Catholicism does seem to be a potentially relevant context for consideration of *'Tis Pity She's a Whore*. Thus we can see that though we may never be able to answer the question of what Ford meant by a discussion of incest which disturbs us by being so strangely passionate and dispassionate at the same time, discussion of the question is infinitely interesting, and bears on a number of questions of great interest to both his age and our own. It is those questions which this volume aims to explore.

We open with an account of the play's critical backstory, offering the highlights in scholarship relating to the text since the seventeenth century. There then follows Kate Wilkinson's account of the performance history of the play after it re-emerged from obscurity in a heavily adapted version in 1894, followed by Sandra Clark's broad overview of recent critical research on the play. There then follow five chapters of fresh research designed to develop a new horizon of inquiry for the reader. In the first of these, Catherine Silverstone discusses Ford and desire in 'Fatal Attraction: Desire, Anatomy and Death in *'Tis Pity She's a Whore'*; in the second, Corinne S. Abate, in 'Identifying the Real Whore of Parma' considers Ford and gender; in the third, Gillian Woods discusses Ford and Catholicism in 'The Confessional Identities of *'Tis Pity She's a Whore'*; in the fourth Mark Houlahan discusses 'The Deconstructing *'Tis Pity?*: Derrida, Barthes and Ford'; and the last of the five is my own *"'Tis Pity She's a Whore* and the Space of the Stage'*, which discusses Ford's representation of social and civic space and considers its implications. Finally, Rhonda Lemke Sanford places the text in the university classroom, reflecting examples of the ways in which institutions integrate it into their syllabi and reviewing the existing resources available. This chapter also offers a critical bibliography to those readers wishing to take their research further on the volume's selected play.

Notes

1   Lesel Dawson, 'Dangerous Misogyny: John Ford's *The Queen* and the Earl of Essex's 1601 Uprising', *Explorations in Renaissance Culture* 33.1 (2007), pp. 64–82.
2   See Stuart P. Sherman, 'Stella and *The Broken Heart*', *PMLA* 24.2 (1909), pp. 274–85.
3   Verna Ann Foster and Stephen Foster, 'Structure and History in *The Broken Heart*: Sparta, England, and the "Truth"', *English Literary Renaissance* 18.2 (spring 1988), pp. 305–28.
4   Cyrus Hoy, '"Ignorance in Knowledge": Marlowe's Faustus and Ford's Giovanni', *Modern Philology* 57 (1960), pp. 145–54.
5   John Ford, *The Chronicle History of Perkin Warbeck*, ed. Peter Ure (Manchester: Manchester University Press, 1968), III.ii.11.

6   William Shakespeare, *A Midsummer Night's Dream*, ed. Harold F. Brooks (London: Methuen, 1979), III.i.22–23.

7   Ronald Huebert, *John Ford: Baroque English Dramatist* (Montreal: McGill-Queen's University Press, 1977), pp. 182–83.

8   Irving Ribner, *Jacobean Tragedy: The Quest for Moral Order* (New York: Barnes & Noble, 1962), p. 155.

9   G. F. Sensabaugh, 'John Ford and Platonic Love in the Court', *Studies in Philology* 36 (1939), pp. 206–26 , p. 220.

10 H. J. Oliver, *The Problem of John Ford* (Melbourne: Melbourne University Press, 1955), p. 48.

11 Una Ellis-Fermor, *The Jacobean Drama: An Interpretation* (London: Methuen, 1936), p. 229.

12 Kenneth Muir, 'The Case of John Ford', *Sewanee Review* 84 (1976), pp. 614–29.

13 Donatella Ravignani, 'Ford e Burton: Riesame di un Rapporto', *English Miscellany* 17 (1966), pp. 211–47, p. 211.

14 John Ford, *The Lover's Melancholy*, ed. R.F. Hill (Manchester: Manchester University Press, 1985), p. 3.

15 John Ford, *'Tis Pity She's a Whore*, ed. N.W. Bawcutt (Nebraska: Regents Renaissance Drama, 1966), Introduction, p. xvii.

16 John Ford, *The Broken Heart*, ed. T. J. B. Spencer (Manchester: Manchester University Press, 1980), Introduction, p. 49.

17 Clifford Leech, *John Ford and the Drama of his Time* (London: Chatto, 1957), pp. 37, 49.

18 John Ford, *'Tis Pity She's a Whore*, ed. Derek Roper (Manchester: Manchester University Press, 1975), Introduction, p. xxiv.

19 Gamini Salgado, *English Drama: A Critical Introduction* (London: Edward Arnold, 1980), p. 127.

20 E. H. C. Oliphant, *The Plays of Beaumont and Fletcher: An Attempt to Determine their Respective Shares and Those of Others* (New Haven, CT: Yale University Press, 1927), p. 89.

21 John Ford, *'Tis Pity She's A Whore*, ed. N. W. Bawcutt, p. xi.

22 F. S. Boas, *An Introduction to Stuart Drama* (Oxford: Oxford University Press, 1946), p. 345.

23 H. W. Wells, *Elizabethan and Jacobean Playwrights* (New York: Columbia University Press, 1939), Supplement, p. 13.

24 Felix E. Schelling, *Elizabethan Playwrights: A Short History of the English Drama from Mediaeval Times to the Closing of the Theatres in 1642* (New York: Harper & Brothers, 1925), p. 314.

25 Robert Davril, *Le Drame de John Ford* (Paris: Didier, 1934), p. 71.

26 Verna Foster, ''Tis Pity She's a Whore as City Tragedy', in *John Ford: Critical Re-Visions*, ed. Michael Neill (Cambridge: Cambridge University Press, 1988), pp. 181–200, p. 185.

27 'Incest and Class: *'Tis Pity She's a Whore* and the Borgias', in *Incest and the Literary Imagination*, ed. Elizabeth Barnes (Gainesville, FL: University Press of Florida, 2002), pp. 94–113.

28 Kate Connolly, 'Brother and Sister Fight Germany's Incest Laws', *The Guardian*, 27 February 2007, p. 17.

29 John Ford, *'Tis Pity She's a Whore*, ed. Derek Roper, Introduction, p. lxiii.

30 Jonathan Sawday, *The Body Emblazoned: Dissection and the Human Body in Renaissance Culture* (London: Routledge, 1995), p. 222.

31 William Shakespeare, *King Lear*, ed. Kenneth Muir (London: Methuen, 1972), III.vi.74–76.

32 Henry Chettle, *The Tragedy of Hoffman* (London, 1631), B2v.

33 William Barksted and Lewis Machin from a draft by John Marston, *The Insatiate Countess*, in *Four Jacobean Sex Tragedies*, ed. Martin Wiggins (Oxford: Oxford University Press, 1998), V.ii.47–48 and V.ii.78–80. All further quotations from the play will be taken from this edition and reference will be given in the text.

34   See for instance Denis Gauer, 'Heart and Blood: Nature and Culture in '*Tis Pity She's a Whore*', *Cahiers Elisabethains* 31 (1983), pp. 45–57, and Terri Clerico, 'The Politics of Blood: John Ford's '*Tis Pity She's a Whore*', *English Literary Renaissance* 22 (1992), pp. 405–34.

35   For comment on this, see Christian Billing, 'Modelling the Anatomy Theatre and the Indoor Hall Theatre: Dissection on the Stages of Early Modern London', *Early Modern Literary Studies* special issue 13 (April 2004), online: http://extra.shu.ac.uk/emls/si-13/billing/index.htm, and Susan J. Wiseman, ''*Tis Pity She's a Whore*: Representing the Incestuous Body', in *Renaissance Bodies: The Human Figure in English Culture c. 1540–1660*, ed. Lucy Gent and Nigel Llewellyn (London: Reaktion Books, 1990), pp. 180–197, pp. 181–82.

36   Michael Neill, ' "What strange riddle's this?": Deciphering '*Tis Pity She's a Whore*', in *John Ford: Critical Re-Visions*, ed. Michael Neill (Cambridge: Cambridge University Press, 1988), pp. 153–79, pp. 155–57.

37   See for instance Frances Teague, 'Jonson and the Gunpowder Plot', *Ben Jonson Journal* 5 (1998), pp. 249–52, and Patrick Martin and John Finnis, 'A Gunpowder Priest? *Benedicam dominum* – Ben Jonson's Strange 1605 Inscription', *The Times Literary Supplement*, 4 November 2005, pp. 12–13.

38   Laurel Amtower, ' "This Idol Thou Ador'st": The Iconography of '*Tis Pity She's a Whore*', *Papers on Language and Literature* 34.2 (1998), pp. 179–206.

39   M.J. Havran, *The Catholics in Caroline England* (Stanford, CA: Stanford University Press, 1962), pp. 83, 64.

CHAPTER ONE

The Critical Backstory

Lisa Hopkins

To say that one works on John Ford, even in academic circles, can still sometimes lead to being asked what one thinks of *Stagecoach* or *The Quiet Man*. Ford has, perhaps, survived the passage of time better than Beaumont and Fletcher, Massinger or Marston, but I would estimate his level of celebrity as having always been quite considerably less than that of Webster, and in recent years Middleton too has almost completely eclipsed him. However, this has not always been the case. There have been various surges of interest in Ford at different periods: the coincidence in name between John Ford the director and John Ford the dramatist led Angela Carter to produce a short story retelling of the most famous work of the earlier Ford, *'Tis Pity She's a Whore*, in the style of the later, with her main characters Johnnie and Annie Belle living out their incest story in the Wild West. A similar retelling was later attempted in Stephen Poliakoff's film *Close My Eyes*, which also features an incestuous brother and sister (with the latter, Saskia Reeves, fresh from a stint at Stratford playing Annabella in *'Tis Pity She's a Whore*).[1] Dorothy Sayers, in *Busman's Honeymoon*, also alluded to Ford when she took a chapter heading from *'Tis Pity She's a Whore*,[2] while Robert Graves, in his novel *Wife to Mr Milton*, makes the heroine's sympathetic cavalier brother James speak of 'those whom I hold in reverence, as, among dramatic poets, John Ford and John Webster', to which Milton himself (presented in the novel as a character of supreme repulsiveness) retorts that 'stale comic hodge-podges or villainous ranting exhibitions of blood should be everywhere by law forbidden'. The book also contains a subsidiary character by the name of John Ford – a chronically nervous gooseherd – and a question addressed to the future Mrs Milton by her maid which is also strangely reminiscent of Ford: 'Well, my fine lady, and did no gentleman yesterday offer you his heart smoking on a pewter dish?'.[3] Perhaps most notably, *'Tis Pity She's a Whore* forms a sort of play-within-the play in Tom Stoppard's *The Real Thing*, as Kate Wilkinson discusses in Chapter 2, and also clearly lies behind parts of Peter Greenaway's fim *The Cook, The Thief, His Wife and Her Lover*.

There had also been earlier signs of interest in Ford. In his own day, his plays attracted commendatory verses from many of his famous contemporaries, including Shirley, Crashaw and John Donne's son George, and he was by no means immediately forgotten after the Restoration, as is shown by distinct echoes (and indeed possible re-use) of his work in Sir Robert Howard's *The Great Favourite, or, the Duke of Lerma*, which appears to be a palimpsest of which a Ford play might well form the base layer. The most famous of Restoration tragedies, Otway's *Venice Preserv'd*, makes lavish use of imagery of ripped hearts,[4] and at the end of the play Priuli wants to be enclosed forever in a room hung with black, with only one candle, just as Calantha at the end of *The Broken Heart* seeks a similar seclusion before her death. Aphra Behn's *Love Letters Between a Nobleman and his Sister* echoes the plot of *'Tis Pity*, and her use of the Agnes de Castro story leads her to share a source with Ford, who seems to draw on this in *The Broken Heart*;[5] and there are also echoes of *'Tis Pity* in another prose work much influenced by Jacobean drama, Richardson's *Clarissa*. The mother of Clarissa's friend Anna Howe is called Annabella, and it is possible (as in the 1991 BBC adaptation directed by Robert Bierman) to detect hints of incest in the close relationship between Clarissa's brother and sister; Lovelace certainly (though mockingly) suggests incest to his cousin Charlotte, and fantasizes about having a son by Clarissa and a daughter by Anna Howe who would sleep together. When Clarissa dies, Lovelace wants her body embalmed and kept by him, and her heart in a casket; such fetishization is reminiscent both of Giovanni's attitude to Annabella and Calantha's to Ithocles in *The Broken Heart*. At roughly the same period, Ford's name was also taken in vain in Macklin's forgery of a quarrel between him and Jonson, which led to the publication of a pamphlet entitled *Old Ben's Light Heart Made Heavy by Young John's Melancholy Lover*, but 'the whole affair was exposed by Malone as Macklin's fabrication for the sake of publicity'.[6] Other titles of the period sharing Fordian subject matter included Eliza Haywood's *The Arragonian Queen* and Sophia Lee's *Warbeck*.

The heyday of appreciation of Ford, however, undoubtedly came in the Romantic period: as T. J. B. Spencer puts it, 'Ford suddenly rose to a high reputation in 1808'.[7] Moreover, whereas interest in him both before and after this tended to centre on *'Tis Pity She's a Whore*, many Romantic writers responded most passionately to others of his works, most particularly *The Broken Heart* and *Perkin Warbeck*.[8] New editions were produced, first that of Weber, which was promptly savaged by Gifford in *The Quarterly Review*, and then, most notably, that of Gifford himself, which immediately found its way into important libraries such as that of Sir Walter Scott at Abbotsford and triggered critical responses such as those of Swinburne, Hazlitt and Havelock Ellis. Most especially, Ford and his works seem to have been of intense concern to two women connected respectively with Shelley and with Byron: Mary Shelley and Lady Caroline Lamb. This may, in part, have been owing to family connections which linked both the Byrons and the Shelleys to Ford's own family. Ford's grandmother was a Stradling, a member of the important South Welsh family, the Stradlings of St Donat's;[9] when he was growing up, the head of the family would have been Sir Edward Stradling, a prominent antiquarian, who was succeeded by Sir John Stradling, the translator of Justus Lipsius. Both these men married members of the Gage family, of West Firle, in Sussex, and the Gages had close connections with the Shelleys: Sir Edward Stradling's wife Agnes was the granddaughter of Sir John Shelley of Michelgrove, and Shelleys and Gages were linked in other kinship networks.[10] Moreover, Ford's play *Perkin Warbeck* took as its heroine Lady Katherine Gordon, daughter of the Earl of Huntly and, according to seventeenth-century historians, of his first wife Annabella Stewart, daughter of James I of Scotland. Lord Byron's mother, Catherine Gordon of Gight, was similarly descended from this marriage, and Byron is known to have had an interest in the historiography of Richard III and its associated issues – he ordered a copy of Sir George Buc's defence of Richard and began to write a poem on Bosworth, and his interest in the subject has been recently suggested as the possible spark for Mary Shelley's decision to write a novel about Perkin Warbeck: 'This family connection would not have been lost on Byron who was inordinately proud of his lineage on both sides. Nor would it have been lost on Mary Shelley'.[11]

Ford is certainly a crucial influence on Mary Shelley,[12] as is testified most obviously by her heavy reliance on him in *The Fortunes of Perkin Warbeck*, which uses quotations from him in its chapter headings, models much of its characterization on him, and, most importantly, relies implicitly on the alternative tradition of exoneration of Richard III at which Ford hints by his refusal to offer outright rejection of the Pretender's claims.[13] Perhaps, though, Ford's presence in Mary Shelley is not confined to this one work. In her novel *The Last Man*, the scene in which Perdita, having discovered her betrayal by Raymond, has to act the hostess with a breaking heart concealed beneath her mask of civility suggestively echoes the restraint of Calantha's celebrated dance; and Kenneth Branagh's recent film adaptation of *Frankenstein*, 'novelized' by Leonore Fleischer, certainly blends motifs from Ford into the scene towards the end where the Creature kills Elizabeth much as Giovanni had Annabella: '[b]efore she died, she uttered one long scream, but it was choked off, as the Creature pulled the living heart right out of her body. It lay pulsing in his hand [. . .] The Creature held the heart in his hand, offering it to Victor as one would a gift'.[14] Mary Shelley's twentieth-century afterlife has thus become inter-textually linked with Ford's Romantic one.

The most extended and concentrated example of indebtedness to Ford, however, comes in the work of Lady Caroline Lamb, Byron's cast-off mistress. She planned a novel which she never wrote called *The Witch of Edmonton*, and her third book, *Ada Reis*, made use of two of Ford's plays – and lesser-known ones at that – in the names of its heroines: Fiormonda is taken from the wicked sister in *Love's Sacrifice*, and Bianca Castamela joins the heroine of that play with that of *The Fancies Chaste and Noble*. Appropriately enough, Gifford, the editor of Ford's works and thus one of the very few people likely to spot the allusion to the unpopular *Fancies*, seems to have been Murray's reader for the book,[15] and both he and another distinguished Fordian, Hazlitt, feature in Lamb's *A New Canto*.[16] But it is Lamb's first book, *Glenarvon*, which offers the closest dependence on Ford. The heroine, Calantha, named after the Princess of *The Broken Heart*, is, like her, destined to marry her cousin, though, like her literary forbear, she discards the arrange-ment for a love-match. Calantha's likeness to her predecessor is overtly remarked upon, although she herself, in keeping with the utter artlessness of her character, is pointedly unaware of it:

'Have you ever read a tragedy of Ford's?' whispered Lady Augusta to Calantha, as soon as she had ceased to exhibit – 'a tragedy entitled *The Broken Heart*.' 'No,' she replied, half vexed, half offended. 'At this moment you put me vastly in mind of it. You look most woefully. Come, tell me truly, is not your heart in torture? and, like your namesake Calantha, while lightly dancing the gayest in the ring, has not the shaft already been struck, and shall you not die ere you attain the goal?'[17]

Nor is it only the mood of Ford's play that is evoked: the final stage-setting of Calantha's dance is also suggested very closely by the description of the surroundings of the Princess of Madagascar – '[a]t the end of a long gallery, two thick wax tapers, rendering "darkness visible", the princess was seated' (I, p. 248) – and the character of the Princess of Madagascar in turn also evokes another Ford play: with its insistent concern with mistaken and concealed identity, and its enquiries into the performative and charismatic elements of leadership, *Glenarvon* often comes close to the imposture theme of *Perkin Warbeck*.

Other Ford plays are also glanced at in the novel. Glenarvon's complicated love-life includes an episode similar in both plotting and nomenclature to *Love's Sacrifice*:

> The victim of his unfortunate attachment had fallen a prey to the revengeful jealousy of an incensed husband; but her death was not more sudden, more secret, than that of the tyrant who had destroyed her. Every one knew by whose hand the fair and lovely Fiorabella had perished; but no eye bore witness against the assassin, who, in the depths of night had immediately revenged her loss.
>
> (II, p. 83)

This, of course, also suggests *'Tis Pity She's a Whore*, and Ford's most famous play makes other appearances in Lamb's text. There is her use of the phrase 'ties of blood' (I, p. 266), a favourite of Ford's; more directly, there is the fact that Calantha's daughter is named Anabel, that Glenarvon invokes the fate of Ford's Annabella when he declares, 'They may tear my heart out from my breast' (III, p. 7), and that there is a clear hint of incest in the description of Glenarvon's feeling for Calantha as 'the attachment of a brother to the sister whom he loved' (II, p. 179).

This was, of couse, appropriate enough in the light of Byron's involvement with his half-sister Augusta, and was ironically made even more poignant when Byron – Don Juan/Giovanni – eventually married an Annabella of his own. This may perhaps have provided one of the key reasons why the plays of Ford should have been attractive to those in Byron's circle, for the revival of interest in Ford also saw a new wave of debate on the topic, already touched on by Langbaine, who objected that he 'paint[ed] the incestuous Love between *Giovanni* and his Sister *Annabella* in too beautiful Colours',[18] of whether Ford was too generous to his sinning characters, and, in particular, to the incestuous Giovanni and

Annabella; 'lubricious' is a favourite term employed for him by early critics. It is perhaps little wonder that women like Mary Shelley and Caroline Lamb, themselves living sensitive lives marked by sexual scandal and social disjunction, in a tightly organized group linked with a quasi-incestuous nearness, should be drawn to the most sexually daring of Jacobean dramatists, and the one in whose work the difficulty of reconciling sexual and social impulses is most strongly figured. Mary Shelley may also be hinting at this most famous of all Fordian motifs when she imagines, in *The Last Man*, that a pair of survivors somewhere might bring forth a brother and sister who together could repeople the earth, though Betty T. Bennett has suggested that this is primarily 'an irreverent reminder of the incestuous beginnings of humanity in the Judaeo-Christian tradition';[19] and there is also the faint sketching of an incest motif in the first version of *Frankenstein*, in which Victor and Elizabeth are cousins. As Jean de Palacio points out, incest formed an important topos for both Shelleys, featuring in *The Cenci* and *Mathilda*, and indeed Ford is cited in the preface to *The Revolt of Islam*,[20] in its earlier incarnation of *Laon and Cythna*, where Shelley's tolerance towards incest outdoes the wildest of the attitudes ascribed to Ford. *Mathilda* also comes very close to the language of *'Tis Pity* when the heroine's father, partially echoing Giovanni, suggests it would be better if 'you tore my heart from my breast and tried to read its secrets in it as its life's blood was dropping from it'.[21] Mary Shelley, however, generally makes a rather different use of Ford, drawing less on his notoriety than on his sensitivity. Trying to make a new and respectable life for herself under the eagle eye of her disapproving father-in-law Sir Timothy, she noticeably draws overtly only on *Perkin Warbeck*, the one Ford play which does not centre on some form of sexual impropriety. Suggestively, she borrows, too, one of his most virtuous characters; but she also, as so often in her work, created the antithesis of that character. She invests her emotional energy both in a fallen woman, Jane Shore, and a respectable wife, Lady Katherine Gordon, who is obviously meant as the type of herself, but whose very name carries such strongly Byronic associations that we are inevitably reminded of the period in Mary's life when she, too, was a 'fallen woman' in the eyes of society, before the death of Percy Shelley's first wife allowed them to marry. Perhaps it is ultimately in the very vilification accorded to Lady Caroline Lamb and the social ostracization experienced intermittently by Mary Shelley that we can see the source of their profound attraction to a dramatist whose gift lies so strongly in his sensitive treatment of those cast outside their social groups because of their sexual sins.

Nor were female Romantics the only ones to notice Ford. Academic criticism of Ford's plays began effectively with Langbaine in 1691, and so did the controversy which, until very recently, has raged around him almost every time that his name was mentioned, and which certainly came to the fore in the Romantic period. Langbaine objected that Ford had been too sympathetic to the incest in *'Tis Pity She's A Whore*;[22] and apart from the lone voice of Charles Lamb proclaiming the sublime, Christ-like beauty of Calantha's dance,[23] there was for a long time a general agreement that Ford was an irresponsible, amoral decadent. Condemnation was directed mainly at *'Tis Pity*, partly on the grounds that all the other plays, with the possible exception of *The Broken Heart*, were even worse: it was on *'Tis Pity* that Ford's reputation must rest. Thus Hazlitt declared that 'I do not find much other power in the author (generally speaking) than that of playing with edged tools, and knowing the use of poisoned weapons. And what confirms me in this opinion is the comparative inefficiency of his other plays'.[24]

Even one of Ford's early editors, William Gifford, considered him unduly favourable to incest and frequently immoral, and complained that 'excepting Spinella in "The Lady's Trial", and perhaps Penthea, we do not remember in Ford's plays any example of that meekness and modesty which compose the charm of the female character'.[25] Hartley Coleridge suggested in the dramatist's defence that although Ford's choice of the 'horrible stories of *'Tis Pity*, *The Broken Heart*, and *Love's Sacrifice*' might seem perverse,

> it would be unfair from hence to conclude that he delighted in the contemplation of vice and misery, as vice and misery. He delighted in the sensation of intellectual power, he found himself strong in the imagination of crime and agony; his moral sense was gratified by indignation at the dark possibilities of sin, by compassion for rare extremes of suffering. He abhorred vice – he admired virtue; but ordinary vice or modern virtue were, to him, as light wine to a dram drinker.[26]

This suggestion, however, did not find favour. The claim for Ford's immorality appeared with new force in S. P. Sherman's essay 'Forde's Contribution to the Decadence of the Drama', which appeared as an introduction to Bang's 1908 Louvain edition of *John Fordes Dramatische Werke, Erster Band*, in the series *Materialien Zur Kunde des alteren Englischen Dramas*. Here Ford is said to have 'sinned in his subject matter', to be an apologist for incest, and to have made a significant contribution not only to the decadence but also to the final collapse of English Renaissance drama, since

> the unmistakable savour of decadence in his work delights kindred souls, but sorely offends the Conservative and the Puritan. There can be little doubt that this savour provoked the much-suffering nostril of the militant Prynne, and had its influence in closing the theatres in 1642.[27]

Similarly, Schelling in 1910 referred to 'the most notable trait of Ford, a peculiar and dangerous power of analysis, of poetical casuistry, which stretches art and ethics beyond their legitimate spheres'.[28]

Sherman's essay established an idea of Ford as the final spluttering out of Elizabethan drama, catering to a jaded audience, which was slow to relinquish its hold. It was taken for granted that a bored Cavalier audience needed more robust fare than had the groundlings of Elizabeth's merry England, and that Ford's own amoral temperament had combined with audience pressure to produce the worst plays of a generally bad lot. J.M. Robertson declared that after 1623 'serious people were increasingly indifferent or hostile to the theatre; and plays were written for less critical and thoughtful audiences. Thus the standard of taste declined with the decline in the quality of recruits to the profession of playmaking'. He goes on to argue that 'it is a mistake to say, as some do, that the later playwrights were necessarily driven to violent and unnatural or corrupt effects by a sheer exhaustion of good themes'; and he adds, with a strange disregard for the chronological progression on which his argument depends, that 'Ford and Cyril Tourneur [...] were men of neurotic proclivity, but they were not made so by dearth of good tragic plot material'.[29] In much the same vein, Janet Spens wrote in 1922 that 'Middleton and Ford and Webster may stress a democratic morality, but they are clearly not addressing country-folk or humble artisans, and it seems to be a law that to appeal to these is the condition of immortality'.[30] Even William Archer's 1923 defence of Ford was qualified: he declared that 'Ford's spirit was, indeed, more subtle than that of Webster. He loved the abnormal more than the merely brutal'.[31] Allardyce Nicoll, two years later, referred to 'the Cavalier spirit expressed by Ford and Fletcher and Shirley', and to 'the decadent lubricity of the Fords and others who descended to the most disgusting and nauseating of sexual emotions'. He added that 'the novelties in the torments introduced upon the stage have no dramatic purpose; they are there merely to arouse feelings of curiosity and thrill in the hearts of a jaded public'.[32] A *History of English Literature* published the next year referred to Ford's 'decadence' as an established fact, and remarked that

> his plays move in a heavy, still and thundery atmosphere. Their lack of even the lightest breath of lively and wholesome air is disquieting. Ford's persistence in painting exquisite suffering and the refinements of perversity is a manifest sign of decadence, yet it constitutes his originality which outweighs his reminiscences and his borrowing.[33]

Alongside the criticism in this comment, however, is a real appreciation of the special qualities of Ford, such as had already been displayed by Havelock Ellis in his sensitive introduction to the Mermaid edition of Ford.

Generally, however, Ford was still considered mainly as an apologist for incest. Herbert J. Grierson, in a series of lectures delivered in 1926 and 1927, declared that

> Fletcher's levity and florid rhetoric go ill with his tragic horrors; but only Ford, I think, a more serious spirit, can be charged with decadence, in that he set forth deliberately the thesis that a great passion is its own justification, condones any crime.[34]

In 1932, in *The Cambridge History of English Literature*, W. A. Neilson criticized Ford on the two favourite grounds, immorality and incompetence in the handling of comic material. He felt that in *'Tis Pity* 'no objection lies against the introduction of the fact of incest, but the dramatist's attitude is sympathetic', and adds that

> in his attempts at comedy, Ford sinks to a lower level than any dramatist of his class, and his farce lacks the justification of much of the coarse buffoonery of his predecessors. It is not realistic; it is not the expression of high spirits; it is a perfunctory attempt to season tragedy and romance with an admixture of rubbish, without humour and without joy.[35]

The next year G. B. Harrison, in the introduction to his edition of selected plays of Webster and Ford, slightly modified the by now customary accusation of decadence. He argued that Ford 'suffered that complete lack of moral indignation which often comes from much study of psychology' and that 'Ford can be condemned for the choice of an unholy theme, but his skill and insight are subtle'; but he nevertheless felt that in *'Tis Pity She's A Whore* 'Ford's sympathies are clearly with the defiant, not the repentant sinner', and he remarks of Webster and Ford that 'they had no particular creed except agnosticism, but they were abominably clever'.[36] The next year Hazelton Spencer remarked that 'the poet's doctrinaire sympathy with lovers as such, his worship of beauty, and his contempt for conventional morality, are constantly reflected in his works'.[37] It was also in 1934 that T. S. Eliot's influential essay on Ford appeared in *Elizabethan Essays*, and this, like the comments by Legouis and Cazamian in the 1924 *History of English Literature*, combined a generally censorious view with a sensitive appreciation of the distinguishing features of Ford's talent. Eliot felt that in *'Tis Pity* 'Ford handles the theme with all the seriousness of which he is capable, and he can hardly be accused here of wanton sensationalism'; he spoke of 'that which gives Ford his most certain claim to perpetuity: the distinct personal rhythm in blank verse which could be no one's but his alone'; but ultimately he considered most of Ford's work to be second-rate, and even concluded that *'Tis Pity* – despite its 'seriousness' – 'may be called "meaningless" '.[38] This is a remark to which subsequent critics have more than once taken exception: R. J. Kaufmann, for instance, contending that 'Giovanni is a legitimate tragic figure', takes issue with Eliot's dismissal on the grounds that 'Ford struggles purposively with humanity's genius for self-deprivation, with its puzzling aspiration to be the architect of its own unhappiness'.[39]

The year after the publication of *Elizabethan Essays*, in 1934, the first book-length study of Ford appeared, a valuable, sensitive, and very thorough work by M. Joan Sargeaunt. She gave serious consideration to Ford's non-dramatic work (she had previously been the first to attribute to him *Christ's Bloody Sweat* and *The Golden Mean*, both now universally accepted as his), and she also provided illuminating expositions of several of the themes and ideas which inform his work. This was followed the next year by Una Ellis-Fermor's *The Jacobean Drama*, where the theory of the decadence of the audience is offered to exculpate the dramatist himself from the charge:

> superficially, Ford's plays show all the signs of a late and decadent art in their use of sensational episode and setting. But as one approaches him more closely it becomes clearer that these groupings and situations, are, like the utterly incongruous comic sub-plots of his plays, concessions to the needs

of the theatre rather than a spontaneous expression of his thought.

Here, too, we find considerable understanding of Ford's peculiar genius, as illustrated by the remark that 'side by side with the violence and sensationalism of the theatrical element in his plays, Ford pursues what was indeed the theme to him of major interest, the study of characters whose strongest quality was a reticent dignity in endurance'.[40] Three years after that, however, H. W. Wells could still write that in '*Tis Pity*

> Ford treats the sins of his two chief lovers more gently than might have been expected. Though presumably, like the audience of the play, still believing in God and in the Christian concept of sin and morals, he by no means takes so uncompromising a view of Giovanni's impiety and skepticism as Tourneur takes of the atheism of D'Amville. Although he evidently holds most of Giovanni's arguments of defence of incest to be sophistical, with Cavalier slipperiness as much as with tragic insight he ascribes some nobility to Giovanni's character and even introduces a note of pure tragedy into the speeches addressed to Annabella just before her death.[41]

The next year, though, a counter-tendency became clear. Fredson Bowers pointed out that in the conduct of the revenges in *'Tis Pity* 'Ford is absolutely in accord with the ethics of the period' and issued the timely warning that with both *'Tis Pity* and *The Broken Heart* 'there is a tendency for critics [...] to mistake for the dramatist's own statement of the moral, the arguments of a character in a fevered state of emotion'.[42] Also in 1940 there appeared S. Blaine Ewing's book tracing the influence of Burton on Ford,[43] and in 1944 came the study by G. F. Sensabaugh, who argued that Ford was a passionate supporter of the neoplatonic coterie set up at court by Queen Henrietta Maria, and was consequently an amoral believer in free love of all types[44] – a view also subscribed to by F. S. Boas two years later.[45] In 1947 both sides of the argument were again stated. Karl J. Holzknecht contended that *''Tis Pity She's A Whore* is a serious treatment of the tragic theme of incest, which, far from condoning such a repulsive sin, treats it with rare understanding and restraint, and with not the least trace of lubricity'.[46] Wallace A. Bacon, however, once again accused Ford of having allowed a neoplatonic attitude towards love to draw him into sympathy with the most sinful of his own characters, and, further, of wanting the audience to feel the same. He therefore concluded that 'Ford is a lesser playwright because he never really understood that he was asking the impossible of his audience'.[47] Three years later Hardin Craig echoed much the same view when he declared that Chapman 'was to be followed by other dramatists – Webster, Massinger and Ford – in thus espousing the cause of passion and thus sympathising with the sinner against the moral law'.[48] A further contribution was soon afterward made by H. J. Oliver's book *The Problem of John Ford*. Oliver is perceptive on many points, speaking for instance of 'Ford's particular skill – in suggesting emotion not by words so much as by the absence of them'; but his determination to remove the blame for the 'decadence' of the work from the dramatist by attaching it instead to the jaded Caroline audience leads him to some extraordinary conclusions, such as that it was only because Ford's audience was so hard to please that he was 'content to have Giovanni appear with Annabella's bleeding heart on his dagger'.[49] Oliver thus imagines a Ford who is effectively mugged by his own characters as Giovanni, as the embodiment of the supposed taste of the audience, leaps into quasi-autonomous life, and one is left with the vague idea that, if left to himself, Ford would have had his characters spend all their time at tea-parties. To regard the violence as wholly meretricious in this way, though, is to take no account of the obvious symbolic and emblematic potential with which it is so heavily freighted.

In 1960, three pieces of work appeared. Cyrus Hoy and Robert Ornstein both showed how little Ford's own views can be associated with Giovanni's,[50] and there also appeared one of the finest of all articles on Ford, R. J. Kaufmann's 'Ford's Tragic Perspective'. For Kaufmann, Ford is essentially a proto-existentialist: 'It is the most special quality of the Fordian hero that he "calls" himself to a role that his residual nature (conscience and shaping habits) will not permit him to fulfill'; as for the French existentialists, the only solution is an ultimately nihilistic one – 'A powerful and personally organized death is the resolution of the soul's misalliance in Ford' – and 'The Sartre of *The Flies* would recognize a brother in the Ford of '*Tis Pity*'.[51] This inaugurated an emphasis on Ford's modernity which proved influential: Denis Gauer saw 'Ford as Shopenhauer's [*sic*] predecessor', although he thought in fact that

> Ford may after all be more radical, if possible, than Shopenhauer, since for him Desire, as manifested by woman, is absolute, and without code or landmark: it is Desire before the emergence of the Law. And it is precisely this which turns

woman into a disqueting creature standing out of reach of the Law and its discourse [...] But of course such a thing won't do, if only because woman is at the core of the whole social and economic system: it is she who mainly bears the brunt of perpetuating the species (along with man's name) as well as ensuring the circulation of wealth (money and goods). Therefore her desire must be tamed and her body controlled: Hippolita's adultery and Annabella's incest precisely upset the good functioning of the social machine.

Gauer sees a Ford for whom 'Desire [...] can only lead to Death. Such are the two poles of life according to Ford',[52] while Claudine Defaye follows Kaufmann's lead in seeing Ford as essentially an existentialist *avant la lettre*: 'It is as if, by conforming to the role of sinner assigned by religion, terrible and constraining though it be, Annabella succeeded in escaping from her own innate and immediate torment, from a kind of existential anguish, where all issues seem blocked'.[53] Along similar lines, Jennifer A. Low argues that

> If *'Tis Pity* does offer the audience a role, it is that of the onlooker, the peeping Tom whose desires have been legitimized because commodified [...] Even more than its gore and its subject matter, the position in which it places its audience members may be the element that links *'Tis Pity* with an Artaudian Theatre of Cruelty.[54]

The introduction of new perspectives did not cause the old to vanish overnight, though, and it is notable that Kaufmann too struggles with the vexed question of Ford's attitude to incest:

> Without being baroquely overdrawn, the world of the play is made to act (in its negations of beauty) as a foil to the desperate choices of Giovanni and his sister. This is not, of course, because Ford approves of incest, but it is done to put the unthinkable within access of thought. Not the least of the functions of tragedy is to enlarge our imaginative tolerance.[55]

Three years after Kaufmann's essay the split in opinion was still apparent, with Alan Brissenden writing an article more or less disregarding the question of decadence and attempting to elucidate Ford's themes and concerns,[56] while T. B. Tomlinson, on the other hand, argued that 'the dangers of taking minor Jacobean drama at face value are well illustrated by the case of writers who – like Chapman and Ford – appear to be making a serious point when in fact they are only making a sentimental one'. He then goes on to speak of 'the frank enjoyment of sin that Fletcher and Ford go in for', and to claim that 'Ford is the real villain of the piece in Jacobean tragedy. He is untrustworthy'. [57] It was in 1964, too, that *Le théâtre et son double* was first published, with Artaud's famous discussion of the Maeterlinck version of *'Tis Pity She's A Whore*.

In 1968 came Mark Stavig's book *John Ford and the Traditional Moral Order*, which asserted Ford's moral uprightness if anything rather too vigorously, for it failed to allow for the dramatist's breadth of sympathy and understanding.[58] In the same year, Robert B. Heilmann dismissed Ford as a 'great melodramatist whose work at times feels the pressure of the tragic',[59] and David L. Frost passingly remarked that 'Webster and Ford do not think on moral issues; this is perhaps a necessary corollary of being uninterested in ideas except where they are useful dramatically'.[60] In 1969 came M. C. Bradbrook's *Themes and Conventions of Elizabethan Tragedy*, which although not particularly favourable to Ford contained some very perceptive passages on him.[61] Three years after that came Donald K. Anderson's book *John Ford*, in which he declared that 'although *'Tis Pity She's A Whore*, which presents incest not unfavourably, probably should be called "decadent"', most of Ford's other plays, including *The Broken Heart*, should not'. He adds that 'probably the chief contribution of the present book is in its exposition of Ford's knowledgeable dramaturgy', and also comments that

> Stavig and Sensabaugh mark the two poles of twentieth-century commentary, the former arguing the dramatist's conservatism, the latter his 'unbridled individualism'. Most of the current critics, including myself, place Ford midway between these two extremes, finding him both compassionate and condemnatory towards his characters.[62]

The same year also saw the publication of two remarkably hostile discussions of Ford: Arthur C. Kirsch's comparison of him to the worst of Fletcher,[63] and A. K. McIlwraith's remark that Ford

> does not try to persuade, as Chapman and Webster did, by asking or making terms with public opinion. He aggravates a scandalous defence of sensuality and adultery by wantonly linking it with the sexual love of brother and sister, with

incest. It is an immature reaction to anticipated opposition to go to the farthest extreme and still present his theme as beautiful.[64]

In 1977, Larry S. Champion's *Tragic Patterns in Jacobean and Caroline Drama* contained a perceptive chapter on *'Tis Pity She's A Whore*;[65] A. P. Hogan produced an interesting piece on the same play;[66] and Ronald Huebert's important and thought-provoking book *John Ford: Baroque English Dramatist* also appeared, containing some very valuable observations and offering a perspective on the dramatist's works that was in many ways completely new, comparing the mood of his plays to the aesthetic of baroque art. In 1979 came a discussion of Ford in Nicholas Brooke's *Horrid Laughter in Jacobean Tragedy*, and the publication of Dorothy M. Farr's *John Ford and the Caroline Theatre*, which paid some useful attention to questions of staging, particularly the use of the upper stage, and, albeit tentatively, also registered the fact that 'The sexual significance of the dagger is of some importance in the two last episodes'. (Ironically, Farr goes on to praise the 'superb understatement' of Annabella's 'Brother unkind, unkind'; one might well feel that her own analysis too qualifies as understatement).[67]

One particularly noticeable feature of the critical response to Ford has been the extent to which critics have found themselves wanting to talk about the author's intentions. Dorothy M. Farr, for instance, who is already clearly channelling the spirit of A. C. Bradley when she writes that 'At heart Annabella is a traditionalist, and because she has less imagination than Giovanni, within her limits she is a realist',[68] writes in obvious surprise that

> The uniqueness of *'Tis Pity* is in the sheer audacity of Ford's handling of this difficult and dangerous subject without a touch of prurience and with such care to balancing the ethical standpoints surrounding it that critics are still divided as to the dramatist's intention![69]

The exclamation mark speaks volumes, but the emphasis it insists on is one which Farr's readers may well not share: *she* may be surprised that disagreement might still exist about the author's intention, but *we* are surely surprised that anyone should still consider attempting to clarify the author's intention to be a useful or indeed even a particularly legitimate aim of critical inquiry. Farr is not alone in this, however. Colin Gibson confidently declares that 'When Giovanni appears on stage with Annabella's heart on the dagger Ford intends the effect to be doubly shocking',[70] and for Rowland Wymer

> The principle [*sic*] representative of moral orthodoxy in the play is the Friar and it is important to decide what kind of authority Ford intends him to have [...] The knowledge that some of the details of his hellfire speech to Annabella come from Ford's own religious poem *Christes Bloodie Sweat* merely helps to confirm that the Friar's views, articulating the full weight of traditional religious opposition to incest, whether Catholic or Protestant, are meant to be taken seriously.[71]

For such critics, the play – specifically the incest motif – is clearly so troubling that they find themselves impelled to ask what Ford meant by it, in a way that I think they might well not apply to other dramatists. Indeed, Wymer does apply a very different approach to his discussion of *The Duchess of Malfi* in the same book, declaring that 'Bosola seems less puzzling as soon as one realises that he is inhabitant of what Primo Levi, talking of Auschwtiz, called "The Grey Zone", that space in which the distinction between guard and prisoner, oppressor and victim, starts to break down', and that

> The scene on the road near Ancona – the little family group clutching a few possessions and confronted by armed men – awakens memories of a hundred newsreels and no doubt had a similar emotional impact on seventeenth-century audiences who were not ignorant of the effects of war and tyranny on domestic happiness.[72]

Of course, Webster cannot possibly have intended parallels with either concentration camps or newsreels, but for Wymer that seems not to matter: these things are what the play has come to signify us now. This quasi-presentist approach forms a striking contrast with the persistent attempt to recover Ford's original intention; indeed one might almost be tempted to see a parallel between Giovanni's desperate determination to uncover the truth of what lies hidden in his sister's heart and critics' quest to pluck out the heart of Ford's own mystery and find out what what he was thinking.

Wymer's coupling of Webster and Ford in the same book is one manifestation of the fact that in recent years critics have started to see Ford more firmly in the light of literary tradition. It had long been noted that *'Tis Pity* owed a great deal to *Romeo and Juliet*,[73] but links with other plays also started to be noticed. Dorothy M. Farr, for instance, stresses the play's affiliation with the well-worn genre of revenge tragedy and comments on its debt to *The Duchess of Malfi*, a debt which she sees as casting further light on Ford's intention and craftsmanship:

> Ford is at some pains to show that the play is about a true and honest love, not about a perversion. A weakness in these closing scenes is the obvious difficulty he finds in making the point of view convincing, but it is one to which the evocation of the Duchess of Malfi insensibly impels us.[74]

Michael Neill also comments on the influence of *The Duchess of Malfi* and also traces a debt to Fletcher's *The Mad Lover* and to Wilmot's *Tancred and Gismund*,[75] while Verna Foster observantly suggests that the play has some features in common with city comedy, not least in that 'The events we see in *'Tis Pity* occur in a city modelled in many respects on Stuart London, or at least on the London made familiar by dramatic convention'.[76] Denis Gauer also pays attention to the play's representation of its social milieu when he notes of the first two scenes of the play, 'Thus does Ford systematically (and even according to a strict hierarchy) introduce the three main social orders that traditionally constitute the Community: the priest, the warrior, and the merchant'.[77] Rowland Wymer follows Cyrus Hoy in stressing the debt to *Dr Faustus*, but also notes that *The White Devil* might have been an influence as well as *The Duchess of Malfi* – 'Giovanni, like Webster's Flamineo, seems to be faced with different and incompatible forms of knowledge which reduce him to a state of tragic confusion' – and, taking issue with T. S. Eliot's complaint that *'Tis Pity* is too particular and lacks 'general significance', suggests that 'by provocatively raising the whole question of "the nature of Nature", the question which is at the heart of *King Lear*, *'Tis Pity* aspires to some of the "general significance" of Shakespeare's play'.[78] Finally, Kathleen McLuskie comments on Ford's fondness for scenes in which a foolish wooer practises courting his mistress and compares them to the *lazzi* of the *commedia dell'arte*.[79] Towards the end of the twentieth century, then, and above all in the wake of his quatercentenary in 1986, a flurry of new interest in Ford saw him firmly inserted into the canon of Renaissance drama.

Notes

1   See Lisa Hopkins, '*Close My Eyes*: A Modern Reworking of Ford', *Marlowe Society of America Newsletter* XIV.2 (fall 1994), pp. 2–3.

2   Dorothy L. Sayers, *Busman's Honeymoon* (London: Victor Gollancz, 1937), p. 214.

3   Robert Graves, *Wife to Mr Milton* (1942) (Harmondsworth: Penguin, 1984), pp. 25, 170, 181.

4   See for instance Thomas Otway, *Venice Preserved*, in *Restoration Plays*, ed. Robert G. Lawrence (London: J.M. Dent & Sons, 1976), II.iii, p. 256.

5   See Robert Davril, 'John Ford and La Cerda's *Ines de Castro*', *Modern Language Notes* 66 (1951), pp. 464–66.

6   John Ford, *The Lover's Melancholy*, ed. R.F. Hill (Manchester: Manchester University Press, 1985), Introduction, p. 33.

7   John Ford, *The Broken Heart*, ed. T.J.B. Spencer (Manchester: Manchester University Press, 1980), Introduction, p. 26. Spencer has a full and very interesting account of early responses to Ford.

8   On the Romantics' interest in Ford, see also Rowland Wymer, *Webster and Ford* (Basingstoke: Macmillan, 1995), pp. 4–5.

9   See Lisa Hopkins, *John Ford's Political Theatre* (Manchester: Manchester University Press, 1994), Chs 1 and 2.

10 The poet Robert Southwell, whose similarities to Ford's own work have often been remarked, was related to both the Gages of West Firle and to the Shelleys of Michelgrove and Petersfield, and dedicated to his cousin William Shelley (see Christopher Devlin, *The Life of Robert Southwell* [London, 1956, rpt 1967], p. 11).

11 Patricia D. Brady, 'Mary Shelley's *Perkin Warbeck* and Lord Byron', *The Ricardian* IX.115 (December 1991), pp. 172–3, p. 173.

12 For Ford's influence on Percy Shelley, see Jonathan Bate, *Shakespeare and the English Romantic Imagination* (Oxford: Clarendon Press, 1989), p. 213.

13 See Lisa Hopkins, 'The Self and the Monstrous: *The Fortunes of Perkin Warbeck*', in *Iconoclastic Departures: Mary Shelley's Other Work*, ed. Syndy Conger and Frederick Frank (Associated University Presses, 1997), pp. 260–74.

14 Leonore Fleischer, *Mary Shelley's Frankenstein* (London: Pan, 1994), pp. 275–76.

15 Elizabeth Jenkins, *Lady Caroline Lamb* (London: Gollancz, 1932; revised edn, Sphere, 1972), p. 127.

16 Quoted in Duncan Wu, 'Appropriating Byron: Lady Caroline Lamb's *A New Canto*', *The Wordsworth Circle* XXVI.3 (summer 1995), pp. 140–46, p. 144.

17 Caroline Lamb, *Glenarvon* (1816) (Oxford: Woodstock Books, 1993), vol. I, p. 134. All further quotations from the novel will be from this edition and references will be given in the text.

18 Quoted in Roper's edition, Appendix III, p. 132.

19 Betty T. Bennett, 'Radical Imaginings: Mary Shelley's *The Last Man*', *The Wordsworth Circle* XXVI. 3 (summer 1995), pp. 147–52, p. 149.

20 Jean de Palacio, *Mary Shelley dans son oeuvre* (Paris: Editions Klincksieck, 1969), p. 130. De Palacio also interestingly traces the use of the story of Warbeck from Schiller onwards (pp. 148–49).

21 Mary Shelley, *Mathilda*, in *The Mary Shelley Reader*, ed. Betty T. Bennett and Charles E. Robinson (Oxford: Oxford University Press, 1990), p. 200.

22 Gerard Langbaine, *An Account of the English Dramatic Poets* (London, 1691; reprinted Hildesheim, 1968), p. 222.

23 Charles Lamb, *Specimens of the English Dramatic Poets who Lived About the Time of Shakespeare* (London: Edward Moxon, 1808), p. 228.

24 William Hazlitt, *The Complete Works of William Hazlitt*, ed. P. P. Howe, 21 vols (London: Dent, 1931), VI, p. 269.

25 William Gifford, review of Weber's edition, *The Quarterly Review*, December

1811; reprinted in *Famous Reviews*, edi. R. Brinley Johnson (London: Pitman, 1914), p. 146.

26   Hartley Coleridge, *The Dramatic Works of Massinger and Ford* (London: Edward Moxon, 1840), 2 vols, I, introduction, p. xlviii.

27   W. Bang, ed., *John Fordes Dramatische Werke, Erster Band* (Louvain: A. Uystpruyst, 1908), pp. v ii, xii, and xvii.

28   Felix E. Schelling, *Elizabethan Drama 1558–1642*, 2 vols (Boston, MA: Houghton Mifflin, 1910), II, p. 330.

29   J. M. Robertson, *Elizabethan Literature* (London: Thornton Butterworth, 1914), pp. 244–45.

30   Janet Spens, *Elizabethan Drama* (London: Methuen, 1922), p. 143.

31   William Archer, *The Old Drama and the New: An Essay in Re-Valuation* (London: Small, Maynard, & Co., 1923), p. 63.

32   Allardyce Nicoll, *British Drama: An Historical Survey from the Beginnings to the Present Time* (London: George G. Harrap, 1925), pp. 102, 168, 193.

33   Emile Legouis and Louis Cazamian, *A History of English Literature*, trans. Helen Douglas Irvine (London: Dent, 1964), p. 509.

34   Herbert J. Grierson, *Cross Currents in English Literature of the XVIIth Century* (London: Peter Smith, 1965), p. 73.

35   W. A. Neilson, 'Ford and Shirley', in *The Cambridge History of English Literature*, ed. A. W. Ward and A. R. Waller, 15 vols (Cambridge: Cambridge University Press, 1932), VI, pp. 193, 196.

36   *John Webster and John Ford: Selected Plays*, ed. G. B. Harrison (London: Dent, 1933), Introduction, pp. xii , xiii.

37   *Elizabethan Plays*, ed. Hazelton Spencer (London: Houghton Mifflin, 1934), p. 1094.

38   T. S. Eliot, *Elizabethan Essays* (London: Faber, 1934), pp. 140, 144, 139.

39   R. J. Kaufmann, 'Ford's Tragic Perspective', in *Elizabethan Drama: Modern Essays in Criticism*, ed. Ralph J. Kaufmann (1961) (Oxford: Oxford University Press, 1970), pp. 356–72, pp. 356, 369.

40   M. Joan Sargeaunt, *John Ford* (New York: Russell & Russell, 1966), pp. 227–28.

41   H. W. Wells, *Elizabethan and Jacobean Playwrights* (New York: Columbia University Press, 1939), p. 51.

42   Fredson Bowers, *Elizabethan Revenge Tragedy 1587–1642* (Princeton, NJ: Princeton University Press, 1940), pp. 207, 211.

43   S. Blaine Ewing, *Burtonian Melancholy in the Plays of John Ford* (Princeton, NJ: Princeton University Press, 1940).

44   G. F. Sensabaugh, *The Tragic Muse of John Ford* (Palo Alto, CA: Stanford University Press, 1944).

45   F. S. Boas, *An Introduction to Stuart Drama* (Oxford: Oxford University Press, 1946), p. 341.

46   Karl J. Holzknecht, *Outlines of Tudor and Stuart Plays 1497–1642* (London: Barnes & Noble, 1947), p. 390.

47   Wallace A. Bacon, 'The Literary Reputation of John Ford', *Huntington Library Quarterly* 2 (1947–48), pp. 181–99, p. 183.

48   Hardin Craig, *The Enchanted Glass – The Elizabethan Mind in Literature* (Oxford: Oxford University Press, 1950), p. 137.

49   H. J. Oliver, *The Problem of John Ford* (Melbourne: Melbourne University Press, 1955), pp. 3, 53.

50   Cyrus Hoy, ' "Ignorance in Knowledge": Marlowe's Faustus and Ford's Giovanni', *Modern Philology* 57 (1960), pp. 145–54; Robert Ornstein, *The Moral Vision of Jacobean Tragedy* (Madison, WI: University of Wisconsin Press, 1960).

51   Kaufmann, 'Ford's Tragic Perspective', p. 358.

52   Denis Gauer, 'Heart and Blood: Nature and Culture in *'Tis Pity She's a Whore*', *Cahiers Élisabéthains* 31 (1983), pp. 45–57, pp. 49, 55.

53   Claudine Defaye, 'Annabella's Unborn Baby: The Heart in the Womb in '*Tis Pity She's a Whore*', *Cahiers Élisabéthains* 15 (1979), pp. 35–42, p. 37.

54   Jennifer A. Low, '"Bodied forth": Spectator, Stage, and Actor in the Early Modern Theater', *Comparative Drama* 39.1 (spring 2005), pp. 1–29, p. 15.

55   Kaufmann, 'Ford's Tragic Perspective', p. 366.

56   Alan Brissenden, 'Impediments to Love: A Theme in John Ford', *Renaissance Drama* 7 (1964), pp. 95–102.

57   T. B. Tomlinson, *A Study of Elizabethan and Jacobean Tragedy* (Cambridge: Cambridge University Press, 1964), pp. 256, 265, 268.

58   Mark Stavig, *John Ford and the Traditional Moral Order* (Madison, WI: Wisconsin University Press, 1968).

59   Robert B. Heilman, *Tragedy and Melodrama: Versions of Experience* (Seattle, WA: University of Washington Press, 1968), p. 299.

60   David L. Frost, *The School of Shakespeare: The Influence of Shakespeare on English Drama 1600–42* (Cambridge: Cambridge University Press, 1968), pp. 122–23.

61   M. C. Bradbrook, *Themes and Conventions of Elizabethan Tragedy* (Cambridge: Cambridge University Press, 1969).

62   Donald K. Anderson, Jr, *John Ford* (New York: Twayne, 1972), pp. 14, 139, 137.

63   Arthur C. Kirsch, *Jacobean Dramatic Perspectives* (Charlottesville, VA: University Press of Virginia, 1972), pp.113–21.

64   A.K. Mcllwraith, ed., *Five Stuart Tragedies* (Oxford: Oxford University Press, 1972), Introduction, p. xviii.

65   Larry S. Champion, *Tragic Patterns in Jacobean and Caroline Drama* (Knoxville, TN: University of Tennessee Press, 1977).

66   A. P. Hogan, '*Tis Pity She's A Whore*: The Overall Design', *Studies in English Literature 1300–1900* 17 (1977), pp. 303–16.

67   Dorothy M. Farr, *John Ford and the Caroline Theatre* (Basingstoke: Macmillan, 1979), pp. 56, 51.

68   Farr, *John Ford and the Caroline Theatre*, p. 47.

69   Farr, *John Ford and the Caroline Theatre*, pp. 38–39.

70   Colin Gibson, '"The stage of my mortality": Ford's Poetry of Death', in *John Ford: Critical Re-Visions*, ed. Michael Neill (Cambridge: Cambridge University Press, 1988), pp. 55–80, p. 64.

71   Rowland Wymer, *Webster and Ford* (Basingstoke: Macmillan, 1995), p. 123.

72   Wymer, *Webster and Ford*, pp. 58, 61.

73   See for instance Oliver, *The Problem of John Ford*, p. 86, and Clifford Leech, *John Ford and the Drama of his Time* (London: Chatto, 1957).

74   Farr, *John Ford and the Caroline Theatre*, pp. 36 and 50-1.

75   Michael Neill, '"What strange riddle's this?": Deciphering '*Tis Pity She's a Whore*', in *John Ford: Critical Re-Visions*, ed. Michael Neill (Cambridge: Cambridge University Press, 1988), pp. 153–79, pp. 169, 158–59.

76   Verna Foster, '*Tis Pity She's a Whore* as City Tragedy', in *John Ford: Critical Re-Visions*, ed. Michael Neill (Cambridge: Cambridge University Press, 1988), pp. 181–200, p. 185.

77   Gauer, 'Heart and Blood: Nature and Culture in '*Tis Pity She's a Whore*', p. 46.

78   Wymer, *Webster and Ford*, pp. 124–27.

79   Kathleen McLuskie, '"Language and matter with a fit of mirth": Dramatic Construction in the Plays of John Ford', in *John Ford: Critical Re-Visions*, ed. Michael Neill (Cambridge: Cambridge University Press, 1988), pp. 97–127, pp. 10.

CHAPTER TWO

The Performance History

Kate Wilkinson

We do not know when *'Tis Pity She's a Whore* was first performed. However, Gerald Eades Bentley states that the play had its first performance in 1633, when it was recorded as being 'Acted by the Queenes Maiesties Seruants at the Phoenix in Drury Lane',[1] although J. L. Styan writes that while the play was published in 1633 it may have been produced a few years earlier.[2] In 1639 *'Tis Pity* was included in a list of plays belonging to the Cockpit Theatre, the play's appearance in this list suggesting that it remained commercially profitable.[3] Bentley notes that the play appeared in a list of plays seen by Edward Browne in 1662 at Norwich,[4] although it was most famously seen on Monday 9 September 1661 by Samuel Pepys. Pepys wrote in his diary that he visited 'Salisbury Court play house, where was acted the first time ' "Tis pity Shee's a Whore," a simple play and ill acted'.[5] Pepys made no other comment on the production, preferring to note that 'it was my fortune to sit by a most pretty and most ingenious lady, which pleased me much'.[6] The play seems then to have been largely neglected until the twentieth century, perhaps as a consequence of being, in Pepys's words, 'simple', but more likely as a result of its taboo subject matter: William Gifford wrote that a play dealing with incest 'carries with it insuperable obstacles to its appearance upon a modern stage'.[7] A consequence of these 'obstacles' was that when the play did re-emerge on a Parisian stage in 1894 it was in Maeterlinck's 'watered-down adaptation',[8] *Annabella*. Indeed, *'Tis Pity She's a Whore* did not return to the British stage until 1923, relatively late for revivals of Renaissance plays, when it was performed by the Phoenix Society, and even then the text was cut to reduce its impact.

Over the course of the twentieth century, however, the play has become more frequently performed, having its first full public performance since the seventeenth century in 1941 at the Strand Theatre, London. Audrey Williamson referred to this production as a 'most courageous and interesting experiment' although she also writes that it was staged 'for two performances [. . .] after which the inevitable Public Informer stepped in and nipped this Jacobean blossom in the bud'.[9] It was the 1960s which acted as a watershed for the play, the liberalization of sexual and moral attitudes opening the stage for numerous productions[10] and, indeed, the screen for a couple of filmed interpretations. This was particularly so through the last three decades of the twentieth century which saw productions by the Actors' Company (1972), the Young Vic (1999), a production in New York (Akalaitis, 1991 and 1992) and two productions each from the National Theatre (1972 and 1988), Royal Shakespeare Company (1977 and 1991) and Glasgow Citizens' Theatre (1988 and 2001). *'Tis Pity She's a Whore* has become the most frequently performed of Ford's plays, with many productions updating the action to the twentieth century and focusing on the threat which Giovanni and Annabella's relationship poses to society. This trend has continued into the opening of the twenty-first century. In this chapter, I will discuss eight of these theatrical events, covering the major productions of the play in the twentieth and twenty-first centuries to date, and three celluloid adaptations of the play.

Theatrical Productions

Roland Joffé's touring production for the National Theatre in 1972 juxtaposed Elizabethan costumes with a simple, modern, clinical set composed of five interlocking screens 'like those that are used to curtain off beds in hospital wards'.[11] Using white cloths to create 'walls', these screens 'were manipulated to unfold 'the full width of the stage, providing half a dozen entrances' or to refold 'in depth to suggest antechambers or corridors'.[12] The performing of the action of the play against this style of backdrop 'intensified' the horror of some moments, as Roger Warren argues.[13] Warren states that the set in fact influenced the reading of the play, writing that the production was 'also clinical in its approach to the characters',[14] refusing to offer a verdict for or against any party. Despite this seemingly non-judgemental approach, the production did offer an interrogatory reading that 'stressed the corruption of a society concerned only with money, authority and status'.[15] In this interpretation, the lovers, played by Nicholas Clay and Anna Carteret, were shown to be 'extremely young',[16] a comment which would suggest their innocence in contrast to the corruption of the society they exist in. The performance of the comic sub-plot, featuring David Bradley as Bergetto, also added relief from the wider interpretation and the production was notably praised for its 'genuinely funny comic scenes',[17] highlighting in one of the earliest modern performances of the play how 'the obligatory comic distraction'[18] could add depth with fully realized characters. The rounded presentation of the lesser characters was also evident in this production in the performances of the servants: Putana was notably performed by James Hayes (who doubled the role with that of the Cardinal) as a male eunuch. Warren has written that, rather than literary criticism of the play, it is performances of *'Tis Pity She's a Whore* that show the 'servants emerge at least as strongly as the masters',[19] their roles proving to be pivotal and aiding in the presentation of other characters.

Staged a number of months before Roland Joffé's National Theatre production, the Actors' Company performed *'Tis Pity* in 1972 at the Edinburgh Festival before also taking the production on tour. Interestingly, in a review of the National Theatre's 1988 production, theatre reviewer Irving Wardle stated that it was the Actors' Company's production rather than the National's own 1972 production which was the 'last major revival'[20] of the play. The director, David Giles, gave the play a twentieth-century setting, a 'fiction', as Robert Cushman wrote, 'whose maintenance seemed [...] to take up a disproportionate amount of time and energy'.[21] The set, designed by Kenneth Mellor, was 'of Parmesan colonnades [*sic*]',[22] which Cushman states was 'evocative, but a bit stodgy';[23] however, Cushman goes on to state that it 'established a definite ambience for the play'.[24] In keeping with the updated time period, the costumes consisted of 'black suits, white carnations and oiled hair'.[25] This design created the impression of a society in which dangerous things happened under the veneer of respectability.[26] The lovers were performed by a young Ian McKellen and Felicity Kendal.[27] While Annabella has simply been described as displaying 'stinging unconcern',[28] McKellen's Giovanni has been written of both with praise and criticism: Irving Wardle wrote that he 'showed Giovanni changing from a passionate boy into an unassailable angel of death, stalking into the banqueting room with Annabella's heart'.[29] In support of this interpretation, Michael Scott also perceived the development of the character, writing that McKellen presented Giovanni 'as an intense scholar who [...] became increasingly and nervously more narcissistic and bestially sensual'.[30]

It is worth bearing in mind that although these two support each other, Wardle's review was written of the 1988 National Theatre production and therefore relies on memories some 16 years old. In contrast, Cushman suggests that McKellen did a little less 'changing' and developing as a character than Wardle states as he writes that Giovanni remained 'a cocksure schoolboy to the last',[31] the schoolboy element seeming to allude to the impression created by McKellen's first appearance wearing bicycle clips.[32] Further to this, Cushman writes that McKellen 'somehow failed to bring it off', 'it' in this context being a 'full realisation of Giovanni's damnation'.[33]

The difficulty of creating and developing a convincing Giovanni is a theme that has informed criticism of most of the productions of *'Tis Pity* since the 1970s. So too has been the difficulty of convincingly creating the final images of the play; as Alan Dessen has noted, 'a director [...] must contend with the danger of losing this climactic scene to one or other spectator reaction',[34] these reactions being either shock or laughter, both serving to alienate the audience from the characters. The sense of McKellen 'stalking' onto the stage with Annabella's heart on his dagger conjures rather comical images despite the apparent sincerity of the impression of the 'unassailable angel of death'.[35] Perhaps alluding to this irreverence, Cushman stated that this production was the 'best Jacobean bloodbath I've seen in years'.[36] However, he elaborates on this, describing David Giles's approach, noting that Giles 'had the courage to take it slowly, allowing each death to register instead of hurrying them through before the audience had time to laugh'. Making this nod to the effect that the deaths can have, Cushman highlights the directorial bravery that is evident in persisting with the action rather than being embarrassed by it. However, despite acknowledging this, Cushman does not say if indeed the audience did laugh at this production, and we can only assume from this that they did. Even so, the description of the violence of the play suggests the absence of comedy: although Cushman describes Soranzo in terms of 'icy rage',[37] Scott's account would suggest much more hot-headedness as he says that Soranzo 'dragged Annabella across the floor by her hair'.[38] Many productions of *'Tis Pity* have made Soranzo very violent in Act IV scene iii, after his discovery of Annabella's pregnancy. This level of violence towards the pregnant young woman in the Actors' Company production highlighted Giles's interpretation of the hypocrisy of the characters; the external 'calm' threw the horror of the internal violence into sharp relief and created uncertainty of what kind of danger the characters were actually in.[39]

The Royal Shakespeare Company's first production of *'Tis Pity She's a Whore* in 1977 was staged in The Other Place, the smallest and most intimate of the RSC's three auditoria at the time.[40] The audience were seated on three sides with the stage in the centre. A pale, paved space, the stage contrasted with the dark backdrop which consisted of a black wall against which were a large crucifix and a statue of the Virgin Mary which were completely fenced in by railings in front. The effect of the railings was to make religion inaccessible, closed and unattainable. Many critics have noted that the first half of the production ended with Poggio returning to the stage after the death of Bergetto and rattling the railings 'in an agony of grief and frustration'.[41] Wymer interpreted the railings as the gates to the Cardinal's house. There was an iron spiral staircase which led up to a balcony above the railings and the set also used large, ornate wooden chairs which, together with the religious backdrop, helped to create an imposing atmosphere, completed by the use of candles and church music. The director, Ron Daniels, updated the setting of the play to the early twentieth century and this, together with the costumes, helped to suggest a Mafia atmosphere: Soranzo and Vasques in particular were styled as gangsters with dark suits and spats. However, although modernized, the set itself evoked both the 1920s and the 1970s for Warren,[42] and the religiosity of the backdrop also provided a link to Ford's seventeenth century. Warren writes that bringing the play into the 1970s '[gave] the events a certain plausibility by creating a society whose values are at once closer to yet still distinct from our own'.[43]

Alan Dessen thought that Daniels focused his attention on the lovers,[44] although Irving Wardle wrote that the master-servant relationships were shown as 'more passionately loyal than the sexual bond'.[45] This emergence of the lower characters over the central pair may have been the result of the failure of Simon Rouse's Giovanni and Barbara Kellerman's Annabella to engage with the audience; indeed Michael Scott writes that 'neither [Giovanni nor Annabella] were greatly sympathetic', although he found this to be a positive aspect.[46] Rouse's Giovanni was presented as a 'pasty acned', 'anaemic' youth who was uncomfortable with and consequently in conflict about his desire for his sister.[47] Dressed in 'innocent' white, Kellerman's Annabella also exhibited reluctance and uncertainty.[48] However, the conflict between the desire and the discomfort suggested an inevitability about the relationship and their yielding to that desire. All of this seems to have fed the tension, culminating in the murder of Annabella which was, according to Scott, 'achieved through the perversion of their sexual act' with Giovanni stabbing

Annabella in the womb.[49] This staging of the murder reflects Marion Lomax's ideas relating to the gendered approach to sexuality within the play as she argues that 'In *'Tis Pity* women associated with dangerous sexual passions are controlled though the mutilation of their bodies'.[50] In this instance, Giovanni not only mutilated Annabella but also her unborn baby, further drawing attention to the full extent of their situation. Giovanni's treatment of Annabella here feeds into the more general portrayal of the wider society within the production: Daniels staged a dark society which was populated by the stereotypical gangsters, Soranzo and Vasques (played by Geoffrey Hutchings who garnered particular praise in the role as the 'hatchetman') and which was described as 'repugnantly amoral'.[51] The comic scenes were also widely praised. Farcically staged (e.g. Bergetto wore comedy teeth) the scenes were performed against the backdrop of fairground organ music[52] which also presumably added a sinister twist in fitting with Poggio's more serious response to Bergetto's death as noted above. Michael Billington noted that the treatment of these pushed the play 'in the direction of black comedy rather than moral melodrama', consequently avoiding the creation of sympathy for the moral taboos with which the play deals.[53] The fairground music was also used during the sex scenes, again suggesting both the childishness of the lovers but also highlighting the sinister aspect of the incestuous relationship.

Of the three productions performed during the 1970s, two updated Ford's play to the twentieth century, placing it within the context of a gangster-run society. This setting allowed the directors to explore the idea of the incestuous relationship that results from the corruption of wider society. The 1970s also saw the release of two of the *Godfather* films (*The Godfather* was released in 1972, and *Godfather II* in 1974) which famously deal with gangster families and themes. The influence of these films on productions of *'Tis Pity* is far reaching, but particularly obvious in the David Giles and Ron Daniels productions. The popularity and influence of these films on productions gives the audience a cultural touch-point by which to interrogate and find meaning in Ford.

In 1988 Michael Coveney wrote that most theatres 'would hesitate to put [the title, *'Tis Pity She's a Whore*] on their posters in these newly timid and censorious times',[54] but in 1988 as in 1972, two theatre companies put on different productions of *'Tis Pity*. Although they ran almost concurrently, the first was performed by the Glasgow Citizens' Company at the Glasgow Citizens' Theatre, opening on 19 February (the National's production directed by Alan

Ayckbourn opened later in the month on the 25th). In contrast to the productions of the 1970s which either fully updated the play or at least clothed it in the Elizabethan costume and staged it in a modern, abstract set, Philip Prowse, who both directed and designed the production at the Citizens, did not update the play at all but set it 'emphatically' in counter-Reformation Catholic Europe.[55] This allowed for the themes of the play to be shifted off permissiveness and the corruption of society in light of the sympathetic but incestuous relationship, and on to the 'portrayal of a society at odds with heaven's laws'; indeed the context of the setting made the 'notion of sin and the fall from grace' more 'credible'.[56] Prowse's set created the impression of 'a busy, fully operational cathedral'.[57] The stage was white and lit by candles with a number of altars across the rear. Bells tolled throughout the production creating a 'grim underscore' and hooded characters were seen throughout carrying crosses, coffins and catafalques.[58] Significantly, a catafalque, which is a platform in a church used to hold a coffin or effigy of the deceased, also doubled as a bed,[59] foreshadowing and prophesying the conclusion of the play. Perhaps echoing the National Theatre's 1972 production, white screens were used to create the more intimate moments of this production.

Prowse adapted and edited Ford's text: there were no sub-plots as such. Richardetto and Philotis were completely absent; Bergetto, while still in the play, was reduced to a wordless 'retarded idiot',[60] a 'penitent in the train of the Cardinal';[61] and, as sometimes happens in theatrical productions as a consequence of there being more actresses than actors, Florio was changed to a woman, becoming the mother, Floria. Coveney called Prowse's adaptation a 'visionary and masterful distillation'[62] and a consequence of this editing was that, contrary to the earlier nineteenth-century adaptations, the focus was placed entirely on the incestuous relationship, the Church and the moral implications.

The characters also seem to have fitted into this religious theme: Vasques was described by Dawson Scott as 'Italian-hating [...] full of menace, a thin-lipped piece of incarnate evil'.[63] Less emphatic although still highlighting the potential for violence, Vasques's master was described as 'a hooligan' although it was also noted that he '[showed] astonishing subtlety in his pleading with Annabella'.[64] In contrast, the lovers failed to impress: Rowland Wymer described them as 'charmless and cool'.[65] Tristram Wymark's performance of Giovanni was particularly criticized as being 'very poor',[66] presenting a rather selfish young boy.

Nevertheless, despite the apparent failings of the lead actors, the final scenes of the production highlighted the horror of the plot; indeed they were 'more horrific for being chillingly underplayed', the horror finally being hammered home in the closing image of Putana's corpse burning on a bonfire next to the dead Annabella.[67] That this was singled out in the production and reviews suggests a certain victimization of the female players in the story.

At the same time as Prowse's production was playing in Scotland, Alan Ayckbourn was staging Ford's play for the National Theatre in London. This almost concurrent playing encouraged reviewers to make comparisons between the two as one was playing and before the other began, hoping that what was missing in Glasgow might be found in the Ayckbourn or vice versa. Ayckbourn's production used the revolving stage of the Olivier theatre, a space which Simon Barker refers to as 'enormous'.[68] Designed by Roger Glossop, the set, the most intricate for any of these productions of *'Tis Pity*, was reminiscent of an Escher drawing: circular and on three levels, it consisted of columns and archways with numerous stairways curving around the outside. The set was dark on stage level with Mike Hughes's lighting used to '[uncover] unexpected locales' in, as Irving Wardle described it, Glossop's 'macabre carousel'.[69] Wardle was very admiring; in his review for *The Times*, he praised Rupert Graves's Giovanni, detailing a performance which 'begins as [it] continues, a fresh-faced juvenile'.[70] According to Wardle's account, Graves's Giovanni was rather naive, remaining 'blissfully unaware of the gathering villainy until the last moment'.[71] In contrast, Suzan Sylvester portrayed an Annabella who developed throughout the play, her emotions ranging from 'joy to bewilderment and marital anguish'.[72] Wardle writes of Sylvester's Annabella as a victim who 'has had to suffer the social consequences' and indeed her treatment at the hands of Michael Simpkins's 'venomous' Soranzo enforced this as she '[sang] to herself as the enraged Soranzo [knocked] her around the bedroom'.[73] As is common in productions, a strong and violent Soranzo was accompanied by an equally evil Vasques, played in Ayckbourn's production by Clive Francis whose performance, according to Wardle, 'gradually dominat[ed]'.[74]

Wardle's account of the Ayckbourn production was thus full of praise, however, this was not the case across the board of reviewers, and indeed some found the production distinctly lacking. John Peter reviewed it in the context of the text of Ford's play, praising the writing as a way to critique the acting: when writing of lines that speak of 'black, sinful excitement',[75] Peter states that the performance of the lovers 'never grows up to match it'. Further to this, Peter wrote that the 'company lacks the technical panache', that the acting was old-fashioned, and that 'some of the laughs are clearly unintended'. [76] This last point is interesting to compare with Wardle who states that the comic side of the play is important, saying that Ayckbourn left 'the comic-tragic option open'.[77] Indeed, Wardle stated that the lovers in Ford's text 'do not initially see themselves as tragic' as justification for this approach. However, the reviewer for the *Financial Times* regarded the production values 'laughably old-fashioned', finding, as Peter did, that the production failed to explore Ford's text and language sufficiently, suggesting that Ayckbourn was 'overwhelmed' by the 'shocking simplicity of Ford's language and his plot'.[78]

In contrast to the small space of The Other Place which was used for the RSC's 1977 production, David Leveaux's production for the RSC in 1991 was performed on the thrust stage of the Swan Theatre. Though the play was given an Edwardian setting, the stage was nevertheless bare at the opening and remained empty for much of the production. The rear of the stage was curtained off, hiding a discovery space in which the lovers first consummated their relationship. This was hidden by the curtain which Giovanni pulled across as he led Annabella in. Above this space was a balcony area which was very open with only a simple wooden railing. The aesthetic of this balcony describes that of the set more generally, functional rather than ostentatious, focusing attention on the characters. The opening scenes of the play were dark and shady, giving way in later scenes to brightness at both the wedding and final feast as events got out of hand. Wayne Dowdeswell's lighting design thus emphasized the hidden nature of Giovanni and Annabella's relationship, the brightness symbolizing the bringing of the relationship, and Hippolita's secret, into the public domain.

There were echoes of Shakespeare in Leveaux's production, but where theatre reviewers have found other Giovannis, such as Jude Law's 1999 performance,[79] Hamlet-like, this production teased out the parallels with *Romeo and Juliet*. Giovanni's desperate manner with Bonaventura, crying at the priest's feet, coupled with his verbal emphasis on being lost and ruined, was suggestive of a melancholy Romeo. Annabella's youth was emphasized in her simple, pale dress in the opening scenes and Putana was very much a nurse figure here; older but bawdy and encouraging, her speeches drew a lot of laughter. Despite her youth, Annabella's distress seemed very much to match that of her brother and she carried the knife which he handed to her, throwing it angrily across the stage to him as she commanded him to 'love me or kill me'.[80] What happens to the dagger at this point in the play is a moment to which Wymer attaches importance, remarking that in a 1981 production for the Oregon Shakespeare Festival Giovanni 'continues to hold it erect between them as they kneel, suggesting a more violent form of eroticism and anticipating the eventual murder'.[81] In Leveaux's production the throwing of the knife suggested a dangerous playfulness while foreshadowing the later actions of the play. The innocence and immaturity of the two characters was presented, the seriousness of this scene giving way to childish embarrassed giggling as the two confessed their love although this, in turn, quickly gave way to a more adult understanding. After Act I scene ii the curtain was opened to reveal a dishevelled bed, the characters dressing downstage to underline what had taken place. The Bergetto scene between these scenes mutually emphasized his own innocence while further representing the growing complications of Giovanni's and Annabella's innocence and relationship.

Wymer's account of Bergetto in this production highlights the importance of the comic scenes to the rest of the play: although he only writes that 'Richard Bonneville was both funny and touching as Bergetto'[82] this gives us the information that Ford's humour is funny but also that the character continues to have the power to move the audience, as was shown in earlier productions. Wymer goes on to write that 'modern productions [...] [provide] repeated and irrefutable evidence of the theatrical effectiveness of the minor characters'.[83] In Leveaux's production Bergetto and Poggio were used to provide an example of loyalty that by mutual comparison presented other relationships in the play; Wymer found this particularly as Poggio returned to the stage for Bergetto's hat after Bergetto had been murdered,[84] a directorial addition similar to that of Ron Daniels in 1977.

As has become usual in productions, Leveaux used the scenes involving Soranzo to underscore the general sense of dangerous sexuality. Leveaux used Celia Gregory's Hippolita as a parallel to Annabella, something presented through similarities in their youth and clothing. These similarities foreshadowed the marriage between Annabella and Soranzo by highlighting the violence that lay beneath the surface of his character: Hippolita's anger was shown to be impotent, apparently failing to arouse a response from Soranzo who spoke kindly and sensibly and in fact returned her embrace as she ran to him and held him. However, this front quickly turned violent and threatening: Soranzo pulled Hippolita's hair, forcing her head back, and threw her to the floor. While this created an uneasy sense of the violent undercurrent to his character, it also created a greater sympathy for the incestuous relationship.

The presentation of Soranzo's negative sexuality to represent Giovanni and Annabella's relationship as good and true was used throughout the production: the first half ended as Putana told Giovanni of the pregnancy. Although Giovanni fell to the floor in a move that seemed to mirror his desperation at the beginning of the production, in fact, as Marion Lomax notes, 'Giovanni [...] did not recoil in horror [...] but delivered "With child? How dost thou know't?" (3.3.9) as excited questions which showed his delight and immediately identified him as a proud, would-be father'.[85] Soranzo's response was in marked contrast to this: he shouted at Annabella, threw her around the stage, held her roughly by the jaw to address her and pushed her down onto the bed before raising his sword to behead her.

Giovanni returned to the stage in the final scene carrying the heart, although perhaps more significant was the extent to which his own upper body, chest, arms and shirt were covered in blood. Not only signalling the horror of his action, this also suggested that he had in some sense had his own heart ripped out, a suggestion underlining his love and grief for his sister.

Lithuanian-American director JoAnne Akalaitis staged 'Tis Pity twice in the early 1990s, first in 1990 at the Goodman Theater in Chicago and again in 1992 at the New York Shakespeare Festival's Public Theater when she was artistic director of the Festival. These productions were, to all intents and purposes, the same: Akalaitis retained the same design team and production manager and many of the original cast members, although important roles including Giovanni, Annabella and Soranzo were played by different actors.[86]

Because the design and theme of the productions were the same I will be treating them together as a single production. Akalaitis is a feminist director who is interested in political themes; she had previously directed plays by Jean Genet and Franz Xaver Kroetz, plays, in the words of *New York Times* reviewer Frank Rich, 'about dehumanized women'.[87] Akalaitis's production of 'Tis Pity also drew on this idea, being essentially about the oppression of women, less about 'thwarted love'[88] and more 'an indictment of a world in which most men treat women as whores'.[89] The production had very strong visual influences. Although Akalaitis retained Parma as the geographical setting she updated the time to the 1930s in fascist Italy. Consequently she used strong fascist iconography: in an article which discusses the use of art in the production, Cheryl Black writes of 'Banners bearing the fascist slogan *Dio, patria, famiglia*'[90] and 'A troupe [who] bring on the fascist eagle banner and then perform an Olympian routine reminiscent of those immortalized by Leni Riefenstahl'[91] at Annabella's wedding, a scene devoid of happiness but interspersed with 'stylized spasms' and 'malevolent whisperings',[92] 'ghastly hisses, shrieks, and groans'.[93] Although the wedding was particularly notable for the use of fascist iconography, Black notes that before this 'the only obvious fascist imagery [was] Grimaldi's black shirt uniform and an occasional *Il Duce* salute between men';[94] however, it was such moments which Rich highlighted, saying that the 1930s setting was more than such superficial nods to fascism. Indeed, Mimi Kramer stated that the effect of the use of fascist iconography was to 'create the sense of an ossified, decadent, and repressive moral order'.[95] Another important visual influence that pervaded the production was surrealist art, which worked hand-in-hand with the 1930s: Rich wrote that Akalaitis 'situates "'*Tis Pity*" in the hallucinatory 1930s of Surrealistic art, a state of mind as much as a Fascist state'.[96] Images by Giorgio de Chirico, Yves Tanguy, Salvador Dali and Man Ray were used, particularly showing female body parts or referring to the victimization, entrapment, oppression and reproductive function of women.[97] John Conklin's design showed 'art-through-the-ages' and created 'a system of de Chirico archways in which characters can eavesdrop or take shelter from the rain'.[98] However, it also included odd 'sculpture fragments – a foot, an armless statue – that prefigure some of the violence'[99] and also reminded women of their role within the world of the play: baby images from Rungé were used in particular to literally prod Putana as a reminder of her reproductive role and making ' "nature" and "innocence" grostesque'.[100]

This production was violent; indeed, the violence of Soranzo seemed to overshadow that of Giovanni and appears to have been stronger than the violence of all other productions of the play to this point. This was helped by the setting and the atmosphere which 'established a sense of scarcely contained or impending violence'.[101] Performed by Jared Harris in 1992, Soranzo was played with 'bluster and mannerisms and [a] speech impediment'[102] which does not seem to present a violent man; however in both productions Soranzo beat Annabella with 'unrelenting violence, kicking her in the stomach, dragging her by the hair, throwing her against a blood red wall, punching her in the face'.[103] Kent and Nellhaus wrote this of the 1990 production which saw Don Cheadle play Soranzo; however, Rich also noted Harris's 1992 performance of Soranzo's 'terrifying mixture of aristocratic gentility and uncontrollable rage [. . .] repeatedly slamming [Annabella] against a blood-red wall'.[104] The red wall clearly made an impression here against the brutality of the violence, especially so it seems because the pregnant Annabella was beaten in the same room in which the audience had seen her making love to Giovanni, the contrast heightening the horror. The fact that, as Jennifer A. Low states, Ford 'does not stage [this scene] in Annabella's bedchamber' which emphazises 'that Soranzo fails to penetrate Annabella's defenses'[105] is, to a large extent, of little relevance to the play in performance, highlighting the differences between textual and performance studies. Directors have frequently staged the events of this scene and Soranzo's anger in the bedroom (in 1991 Leveaux would have Soranzo attack Annabella on the bed, and Giuseppe Patroni Griffi would show Annabella and Soranzo consummating their relationship in his 1973 film). Indeed, although Ford does not stage the bedroom, modern productions' interest in it intensifies the sense of danger. This was also the effect in Akalaitis's production of an unsympathetic Giovanni later coming to Annabella and demanding 'to know whether [she] refused him because Soranzo is a better lover, while the abrasions on her face remained fully visible to the audience'[106] and presumably to Giovanni also. The violence may also have been so striking in this production because there were apparently no light-hearted moments: although the sub-plots were retained Rich wrote of them as being 'leaden burlesque shtick that prompts winces not laughs'.[107]

Mimi Kramer titled her review of the production 'Victims' and wrote that although Jeanne Tripplehorn, who played Annabella, '[had] trouble with the poetry [...] she makes intelligible a particular brand of female naïveté, which the play proves to be about'.[108] Prior to this comment Kramer stated that to make Annabella interesting it is in part useful to 'cast an actress who knows how to play a victim without playing a sap',[109] detailing through such comments that she clearly sees the women in the play as victims. However, Rich wrote of Akalaitis's women that 'the abused women [...] are too self-possessed to devolve into abject victims' and that Tripplehorn played Annabella with 'a fiery will rather than [as] a trampled, helpless flower'.[110]

The final production of *'Tis Pity She's a Whore* of the twentieth century was staged by David Lan at the Young Vic in London. Richard Hudson's set consisted of 'two tilted wooden blocks that look like a bridge built from either side of a river but have failed to meet in the middle'.[111] The effect of this set was to challenge perspectives; the audience was made to look but could not see clearly all of the time. The production was staged in modern dress: Lyn Gardner described it as 'vaguely 30s'[112] but she also noted that the time setting was not fixed: 'you know that you are watching a 1651 [*sic*] play about 17th-century Parma but you think of it in the here and now'. For Gardner this 'here and now' aspect of Lan's production made it 'electric'; she states that Lan made Ford's play 'seem it could have been written yesterday [*sic*]'.[113] Smoke was used to create atmosphere and a heartbeat-like pulsing drum was heard at climactic moments.[114] Masked figures '[glided] around the stage'[115] and '[leapt] onto it when anything morally dire [occurred]'.[116] Indeed, one of the production images released to the press showed Jude Law's Giovanni being overawed by a number of these figures, suggesting something powerful and supernatural oppressing the players in the story. Reviewers tended to focus their attention on the performance of the lead roles, Lan's production garnering a lot of attention through the casting of a popular young film star in the main male role. However, it was not Law's performance which most impressed but rather that of Eve Best who, fresh from drama school, played Annabella. Best played a 'centred complex Annabella' who '[shivered] with palpable bliss [. . .] but [could] rage with spine-tingling power'; [117] she was 'contained, potentially explosive, hesitant'.[118] Indeed, Best's performance was considered so good that she won both the *Evening Standard*'s first outstanding newcomer and the Critics' Circle's most promising newcomer awards for it.[119] The performance of the lovers in Lan's production emphasized the innocence and perhaps the naivety of the relationship; 'pure and tender' at the beginning they were 'like children playing'.[120] This progressed through the play to corrupted innocence, from love to lust: Gardner wrote that the pair 'peck at each other like shy sparrows and then fall on each other like starving vultures'.[121] However, despite Annabella's apparent strength she was portrayed by the production as a victim while her brother was 'beyond redemption'.[122] Reviewers drew alignments between Giovanni and Hamlet, seeing Law's presentation as 'a very mad'[123] version of Shakespeare's character who was 'inclined to drop to his knees, to give speeches flat on his back, or to execute a backwards somersault'.[124] Law's Giovanni 'projects adolescent despair, but leaves himself no chance of development',[125] a flaw that has been found in many performances of the character in the twentieth century. Govanni's madness seems finally to have created a sense of horror being 'twisted with pain and retribution'[126] in the second half and, at the murder, he showed the 'sweet smile of the slaughterhouse executioner'.

Films and Other Adaptations

'Freely adapted from John Ford's tragedy', Giuseppe Patroni Griffi's 1973 film of *'Tis Pity She's a Whore* is one of only a relative handful of non-Shakespearean Renaissance plays to have been made into films. However, this opening statement should give us fair warning of the treatment of Ford's text within Griffi's film: the sub-plots have disappeared, there is no Bergetto, Poggio, Hippolita, Richardetto, Philotis, Grimaldi, Donado or Cardinal and the text has also been radically cut for the characters that remain in the film. Many of Ford's words are also either no longer there or are changed beyond recognition. This is apparently a result of the original intention to film the play in Italian, so the text was therefore translated from Ford's English, but when it was decided to film the play in English, rather than return to the original pre-translation text, the Italian translation was further translated back into English.[127] This story, although its veracity is unclear, may account for the modern sound of some of the language that is used.

In contrast to the theatrical productions of this play discussed above, Griffi's film does not use the incestuous relationship to discuss the corruption of wider society. Rather, the characters are divorced from the wider world, the film focusing attention instead on the relationship between its four main players: Giovanni, Annabella, Soranzo and Bonaventura, who is here not the older, wiser mentor, but a young monk, a contemporary of Giovanni and Soranzo, the three young men seeming to have been friends together as boys. There is a claustrophobic atmosphere to the film, created in part by the juxtaposition of the wintry setting, which is often shrouded in mist, and the interiors which frequently focus on huge roaring fires. The claustrophobia is heightened by the inertia experienced by Giovanni as he decides what course of action to take with his sister: the viewer simply sees Giovanni silently sitting on his bed looking into the fire in a darkened room. When he has made his decision, he throws open the window shutters, filling the room with daylight, suggesting a positive step and a sense of freedom, if only briefly, from the claustrophobia which will return as 'fate' takes its course.

Claustrophobia is also created by the frequent visual references to imprisonment or entrapment: early in the film Giovanni approaches Bonaventura while the monk is weaving some kind of enclosure with rope; the lovers chase each other into a bird cage which consists of three levels of depth, one cage inside another, in a kind of maze; Annabella is told of Soranzo's proposal by her father while standing next to a grated window behind which Giovanni watches and listens; and at the end of the film Soranzo is constrained in a weird wooden frame, perhaps intended to stretch his wounded body. Indeed, Lisa Hopkins writes of this last example that it 'certainly suggests that, although he may be alive, he is hardly free'.[128] In her discussion Hopkins focuses on the factor of imprisonment, stating that it is 'the film's most sustained and striking visual patterning', and going on to argue that the characters are imprisoned as a result of psychological barriers imposed by the particular society in which they live.[129] However, these visual creations of prisons also serve to highlight the separation of the characters – even when the lovers are getting together, their ultimate separation is constantly being underlined. For example, after the relationship has begun the viewer sees Giovanni and Annabella riding in the countryside to a strange war memorial-like place consisting of a large number of huge flagpoles bearing white flags. The lovers sit together in a large wooden 'baroquely artificial seating structure'[130] which, while framing them in, shows them entirely separated, a feature further shown by their increasingly sombre and apparently introspective mood at this point. This is also true in the bird cage scene: although the room is filled with light and Annabella is laughing while Giovanni chases her to discover who has sent her a ring, the two are mostly separated as Annabella moves into the cage first and continues to separate herself from Giovanni by moving into the next layer and then the next layer. Rather than imprisonment then, it seems that these visual references seek to suggest the isolation of the characters from each other despite their growing and changing relationships.

The foreshadowing of the separation to come between Giovanni and Annabella is also underscored as having already happened in a manner which shows their relationship in a sympathetic light: when Annabella first sees Giovanni she clearly does not recognize him, nor does Giovanni recognize his sister. Griffi's adaptation emphasizes this, highlighting the claims that Giovanni is 'not my brother' and Annabella is 'not my sister'. It is clearly suggested that the separation of the siblings while Giovanni has been studying has been long and has interrupted the bond between the brother and sister. As Hopkins writes, the 'stage is set for what has come to be known to modern science as genetic sexual attraction'[131] and consequently 'the affair of Giovanni and Annabella in this light is [. . .] a tragic fluke rather than any kind of systematic exploration of incest in general'.[132] Rather than simply an exploration of incest and forbidden love, I would suggest the film also explores the idea of childhood and loss of innocence, and the relation of humanity to the animal world.

The isolation of Giovanni is never clearer than when he throws himself into the well after talking with Bonaventura. Hopkins has written that 'Giovanni, for no apparent reason, throws himself down a well'[133] and while this moment is rather comical as Giovanni suddenly runs away from Bonaventura to the well and leaps into it as the monk watches on, there is in fact an apparent reason for this: Giovanni is angered by Bonaventura's refusal to condone his feelings for Annabella and in the speech immediately preceding this action he uses animalistic imagery, with words such as 'beast', 'contaminated' and referring to himself as 'a monster'. Giovanni's action in throwing himself down the well is an attempt to bridge this chasm between his human reality and his desires which are presented in negative animalistic language. Lying at the bottom of the well in the sludge and mud, Giovanni is at once closer to the animal earth and separate from his peers, whom he can no longer contaminate. The action of taking off his clothes further underlines his distance from civilized society and also creates an image of a Christ figure (further suggested by his long dark wavy hair and beard) who is apparently sacrificing himself to save his sister. Giovanni's outstretched arms as he lies looking up toward the sky further this impression, the rain falling on him from heaven, cleansing him. In the light of this religious imagery, compounded by lying in the monastery's well, it is surprising that Giovanni's revelation enabling him to rejoin his society is that it is 'not my desire that drives me but my fate' and this idea is expressed again later as Annabella tells Soranzo that what has happened to him is his 'fate'. The insistence on fate pushes the responsibility for the troubles that ensue away from the characters and emphasizes the tragic quality of the play.

However, Giovanni's relation to the animalistic is not resolved and indeed, Griffi uses animal imagery throughout the film as a metaphor for the lovers and for human relationships in general. This may be a consequence of Griffi's desire to express in the film his own feelings regarding his homosexuality: Wymer writes that

> Griffi [...] found in Ford [...] the narrative structure and 'classic' support for intense explorations of [his] own sexuality. There is still an element of indirection in Griffi, since the incest is a displaced representation of another 'love that dare not speak its name'.[134]

There would seem to be some kind of link explored between this 'love that dare not speak its name' and bestiality as Giovanni is frequently linked to animals and ultimately returns to the animals as his corpse is carried to a catafalque in the stables with the horses watching on. It is horses which Griffi uses throughout the film as a metaphor for relationships: when the lovers are constricted by their seating frame in the countryside the viewer sees their two horses running freely across the screen; Putana describes Soranzo to Annabella as being 'randy as a stallion'; two horses are delivered by water to an excited Soranzo who runs through the streets to greet and embrace them before carrying Annabella away on his horse with him; and Soranzo, in an attempt to encourage Annabella to consummate their relationship, takes her to watch copulating horses in a field. At this point, the viewer is shown two close-up images of the horse's engorged penis before being shown the horse mounting the mare. This is the first actual visual image of sex in the film and it is significant that it is animal sex that is shown, the action paralleling the language and relationships throughout the film. This moment also allows Griffi to extend his animal imagery to include Soranzo as he apologizes to Annabella for the methods he has used, suggesting that he is a 'rough' man who doesn't know nice manners. That Soranzo says to Annabella that he has taken her to watch this to show her that 'natural acts' are nothing to be 'ashamed of' and that she should start behaving 'like a woman not a child' also shows an understanding of human sexuality as related to that of animals and ironically seems to offer support to the relationship between Giovanni and Annabella.

The copulation of the horses acts as a pivotal moment in the film which reflects and foreshadows Annabella's two relationships, creating a sense of symmetry: the consummation of the relationship with Giovanni comes before, that with Soranzo comes after. Significantly the viewer does not see the consummation with Giovanni explicitly, rather we see the two lovers playing in the bedroom, chasing each other and laughing. In contrast, Annabella's consummation of her relationship with Soranzo is shown explicitly in a serious, quiet, slow manner; indeed, as Hopkins points out, the filming of this moment is somewhat strange.[135] That this sex is shown and that the, one might suggest, more important relationship with Giovanni is not, suggests the loss of innocence, that Annabella's relationship with Giovanni was childish and now she has become a woman and is resigned, willing even, to be active in this future with Soranzo.

Charlotte Rampling's portrayal of Annabella is interesting in this film as she does not present the character as the victim we might expect. At the siblings' first meeting it is Giovanni who wears the white clothing while Annabella dresses in red, suggesting that it is she who corrupts him. Indeed, the audience do not see Annabella in conflict with her desire as they do Giovanni, and when the love is confessed Annabella says that she 'hardly dared even think I was [in love] [...] Come'. This command to Giovanni is in fact asking him to accompany her to their mother's grave where they pledge their love more formally, but the suggestion is also sexual and intended to be so: Annabella's manner of speech at this point, and the way in which she looks at Giovanni by dropping her head and looking out from under her brows is very much in the 'come hither' vein. This Annabella is not a victim but a femme fatale, and one who seems to revel in the fact that it is her brother she is sleeping with: Giovanni has to tell her twice, with some agitation, 'don't call me brother, call me love' as Annabella persists in using the familial term. Annabella also plays an active part in the pledging of the love with the knife: at the mother's grave her hand is clasped over both Giovanni's hand and the knife while they say 'love me or kill me' and in a moment mirroring this early scene, both characters' hands are clasped over the knife as Giovanni stabs Annabella at the conclusion. Griffi's film, then, does not take the view so frequently seen in theatrical stagings that Ford's play is about the lovers in terms of their society or about the women as victims – rather, his focus is on growing up.

In contrast to Griffi's film which actively embraced the sexuality of the play and presented the characters sympathetically, the 1980 BBC television drama directed by Roland Joffé seemed to run a bit scared. The programme has, to date, not been released on video or DVD and so knowledge of the production has to rely on second-hand accounts. The text of the play was radically cut and altered: Hippolita was not the wife of Richardetto (who was actually a local doctor) and did not die at the wedding feast but was 'disposed of in a bedroom closet';[136] Soranzo also did not die but was 'triumphant arranging with the Justice a complete cover up';[137] nor did Bergetto die but eloped with Philotis. The absence and editing of these deaths from what has previously been described as a 'Jacobean blood-bath'[138] is marked and can be speculated upon, perhaps suggesting that the BBC was afraid of producing such sights on television. This does seem to be possible: Scott has written that the BBC 'clearly did not trust the appropriateness of the text for the twentieth century'.[139] Despite Wymer's contention that 'liberalisation of moral attitudes in the 1960s has resulted in a steady stream of [...] productions',[140] there seems to have still been a resistance to producing such taboos on television at the opening of the 1980s. The production was set in the nineteenth-century in a country manor house in the North of England. Editing was made to allow for this context so that, for example, the Cardinal became the Lord

Lieutenant.[141] It seems that a balance was sought between the more corrupt aspects of society, with Soranzo and Vasques embodying the 'darker aspect of Victorian society' and Florio presenting the more positive side of this society.[142] However, despite Warren's account, Scott writes that Florio was 'implicated in [Soranzo's trick]',[143] suggesting a more grey than black-and-white division of society than Warren implies. The lovers were shown as they usually are: Kenneth Cranham's Giovanni was neurotic while Cherie Lunghi's Annabella was young and joyful.[144] Warren found that their relationship was 'distinctly preferable to the secret lives of Soranzo and Vasques';[145] however, that these darker characters were allowed by the adaptation to live and cover things up also suggests a condemnation of the relationship.

Tom Stoppard is famous for his adaptations of Renaissance texts, having penned the adaptation of *Hamlet*, *Rosencrantz and Guildenstern Are Dead*, and co-written the 1998 film, *Shakespeare in Love*. In 1982 Stoppard wrote the play *The Real Thing*. While not a straightforward adaptation of *'Tis Pity She's a Whore* the play includes sections of text from Ford's play and is used as a means by which to develop Stoppard's ideas about the 'real thing' which is the theme of the play. *The Real Thing* tells the story of Henry, a playwright, and his relationships: at the beginning of the play Henry is married to Charlotte who stars in his play, *House of Cards*, about adultery. Stoppard's audience is led to believe that the opening scene of the play, in which the character Max confronts his 'wife' Charlotte about her infidelity, is the 'real' world of the play, an illusion which is shown to be untrue in the second scene which shows Charlotte with her real husband Henry and her onstage husband Max with his real wife Annie. Henry and Annie, it transpires, are the couple actually having an affair. *'Tis Pity*, perhaps chosen by Stoppard because it too is a play 'about sexual betrayal and jealousy',[146] is brought into the play in the later scenes when Annie, also an actress and now married to Henry, is cast in the role of Annabella in a production of the play in Glasgow and begins a new affair with Billy, who is playing Giovanni. Stoppard uses Ford's love scenes to highlight the artificiality of love language and the difficulties for modern playwrights writing such language. Annie's relationship with Billy is effectively conducted through Ford's language from *'Tis Pity*,[147] although even here Ford's text is interspersed with the characters' own words, blurring the lines between fiction and reality, between playing and living, as an example from scene vi shows:

ANNIE: O, you are a trim youth!
BILLY: Here! (*His 'reading' has been getting less and less discreet. Now he stands up and opens his shirt.*)
ANNIE: (*giggling*) Oh, leave off. (*She looks around nervously.*)
BILLY: (*starting to shout*)
And here's my breast; strike home!
Rip up my bosom; there thou shalt behold
A heart in which is writ the truth I speak.
ANNIE: You daft idiot.[148]

Stoppard shows the seductiveness of such language; Ford creates both the effect of distancing and consequently a safe place in which to flirt. *'Tis Pity* is not shown as it is performed but on a train in the first instance and in a rehearsal room in the second. Thus, it is even easier for the line between reality and play-world within Stoppard's play to be blurred for the real audience of *The Real Thing*: these characters are not yet in character as Giovanni and Annabella so the real audience is not being asked to further suspend their disbelief and imagine them only as Ford's characters. It is possible for the audience to see both Billy and Annie and Giovanni and Annabella simultaneously within the same actors. However, Stoppard does not allow the audience to believe that Ford's love language is representative of real emotion. Henry longs to be able to write real love but finds it impossible:

> I try to write it properly, and it just comes out embarrassing. It's either childish or it's rude [...] Perhaps I should write it completely artificial. Blank verse. Poetic imagery [...] 'By my troth, thy beauty, makest the moon hide her radiance'.[149]

Real emotion, the theme of the play, the 'real thing', is thus hard to capture as it cannot be written in the actual words which we use and the words of the Renaissance are 'artificial'. Indeed, the affair built between Annie and Billy using *'Tis Pity* is explicitly shown to be artificial in itself, not the beginning of a real relationship such as Annie shares with Henry, as Annie states in scene x in her explanation to Henry:

> it's like love or something: no – love, absolutely [...] You weren't replaced, or even replaceable [...] But I meant it. It meant something. And now that it means less than I thought and I feel silly, I won't drop him as if it was nothing, a pick-up, it wasn't that [...] This is me behaving well. I have to choose who I hurt and I choose you because I'm yours.[150]

Although the affair built through Ford's language meant something when the Ford was being performed it ceases to mean anything later and Annie returns to her 'real' love. Thus Stoppard uses the language and events of *'Tis Pity She's a Whore* to explore the themes of his own play.

Seventeen years after the BBC's radically adapted television series, an ITV detective drama produced a version of Ford's play. In the *Midsomer Murders* pilot episode, 'The Killings at Badgers Drift', *'Tis Pity* provides a basic plotline to a traditional English detective story: an old spinster is murdered in her home after having observed something in the woods which frightened and disturbed her. Inspector Barnaby, the series' hero, is called in to investigate and finds that her last known words were 'Poor Annabella' and that a book of Jacobean plays sits on her table. These pointers though serve to baffle the police, providing, as Barnaby is enlightened at the very end of the episode as the viewer has been throughout the programme, a nice little twist. What the old lady witnessed was a couple making love; not only were the two known to her but they were also brother and sister, a sister who was engaged to a local wealthy, disabled landowner with the intention, it transpires, to use his money to fund the siblings' relationship and future. *Midsomer Murders* is set in the heart of the Home Counties in a number of fictitious villages. Invariably the programmes feature wealthy, well-to-do characters with some underlying, dark secrets. It is usual that a number of characters will meet their deaths in a gory manner through the course of an episode. In 'The Killings at Badger's Drift' the incestuous relationship was very slowly discovered, the truth kept just out of reach of the viewer until the denouement. However, the siblings were never presented as fully sympathetic; as is true for many classic detective stories, they were among a number of characters who could have 'done it', in a way intended to keep the audience guessing. The revelation of the incest, the deception in the marriage, the murders committed in order to keep the secret, the suicide of the lovers on discovery and the good character of the first victim all conspired to present the Annabella and Giovanni storyline as something rotten at the heart of chocolate box England rather than a sympathetic relationship at the heart of a rotten society.

As the world experienced dramatic changes over the course of the twentieth century so *'Tis Pity She's a Whore* was used to reflect and explore sexual issues in relation to corrupt societies. Where the twenty-first century will take Ford's play remains to be seen but it continues to be one of the most performed non-Shakespearean Renaissance plays.

Reviews of Productions

Clapp, Susannah. *The Observer*. 10 October 1999. (Lan)

Coveney, Michael. *Financial Times*. 22 February 1988. (Prowse)

Dawson Scott, Robert. *The Times*. 23 February 1988. (Prowse)

Gardner, Lyn. *The Guardian*. 12 October 1999. (Lan)

Kent, Assunta and Nellhaus, Tobin. *''Tis Pity She's a Whore* by John Ford'. *Theatre Journal* 42.3 (October, 1990): 373-375. (Akalaitis)

Kramer, Mimi. *The New Yorker*. 20 April 1992. 78-79. (Akalaitis)

Peter, John. *The Times*. 6 March 1988. (Ayckbourn)

Rich, Frank. *The New York Times*. 6 April 1992. (Akalaitis)

Taylor, Paul. *The Independent*. 29 April 1992. (Akalaitis)

Walsh, Maeve. *The Independent*. 17 October 1999. (Lan)

Wardle, Irving. *The Times*. 4 March 1988. (Ayckbourn)

Notes

1   Gerald Eades Bentley, *The Jacobean and Caroline Stage*, 5 vols (Oxford: Oxford University Press, 1941), III, p. 462.

2   J. L. Styan, *The English Stage: A History of Drama and Performance* (Cambridge: Cambridge University Press, 1996), pp. 232–33.

3   Rowland Wymer, *Webster and Ford* (Basingstoke: Macmillan, 1995), p. 121.

4   Bentley, *The Jacobean and Caroline Stage*, p. 462.

5   Samuel Pepys, diary entry for 9 September 1661, online: www.pepysdiary.com/archive/1661/09/09/.

6   Pepys, diary entry for 9 September 1661.

7   William Gifford, quoted in the programme notes to the 1991 Royal Shakespeare Company production. Gifford (1756–1826) was the editor of John Ford's *Dramatic Works* (2 vols, 1827).

8   RSC programme note, 1991.

9   Audrey Williamson, *Theatre of Two Decades* (London: Rockliff, 1951), p. 281. Williamson also notes that the lovers, played by Wolfitt and Rosalind Iden, were well performed, although she found that the minor characters, despite being 'good parts [. . .] were not well-acted', stressing 'the melodrama at times to the point of laughter' (p. 282).

10 Wymer, *Webster and Ford*, p. 121.

11 Roger Warren, 'Ford in Performance', p. 12.

12 Irving Wardle, quoted in Michael Scott, *Renaissance Drama and a Modern Audience* (Basingstoke: Macmillan, 1982), p. 102.

13 Warren, 'Ford in Performance', p. 12.

14 Warren, 'Ford in Performance', p. 12.

15 Scott, *Renaissance Drama and a Modern Audience*, p. 102.

16 Scott, *Renaissance Drama and a Modern Audience*, p. 102.

17 Wardle, quoted in Wymer, *Webster and Ford*, p. 130.

18 Styan, *The English Stage*, p. 234.

19 Warren, 'Ford in Performance', p. 13.

20 Wardle, theatre review, *The Times*, 4 March 1988.

21 Cushman, 'The Actors' Revenge', *Plays and Players* (December 1972), pp. 44–46, p. 44.

22 Scott, *Renaissance Drama and a Modern Audience*, p. 102.

23 Cushman, 'The Actors' Revenge', p. 44.
24 Cushman, 'The Actors' Revenge', p. 45.
25 Scott, *Renaissance Drama and a Modern Audience*, p. 102.
26 Scott, *Renaissance Drama and a Modern Audience*, p. 102.
27 Although Scott writes that Annabella was performed by Paola Dionisotti.
28 Cushman, 'The Actors' Revenge', p. 45.
29 Wardle review, 1988.
30 Scott, *Renaissance Drama and a Modern Audience*, p. 102.
31 Cushman, 'The Actors' Revenge', p. 45.
32 Scott, *Renaissance Drama and a Modern Audience*, p. 102.
33 Cushman, 'The Actors' Revenge', p. 45.
34 Dessen, *''Tis Pity She's a Whore*: Modern Productions and the Scholar', p. 89.
35 Wardle review, 1988.
36 Cushman, 'The Actors' Revenge', p. 45.
37 Cushman, 'The Actors' Revenge', p. 45.
38 Scott, *Renaissance Drama and a Modern Audience*, p. 102.
39 Scott, *Renaissance Drama and a Modern Audience*, p. 102.
40 The Other Place was closed in 2001 as part of then artistic director Adrian
    Noble's now defunct 'Project Fleet'. An academy was held there for a year
    producing a run of *King Lear* in 2002 and the theatre now forms the foyer to the
    temporary Courtyard Theatre while the Royal Shakespeare Theatre undergoes
    dramatic rebuilding and refurbishment. What will happen to The Other Place
    after the Courtyard is dismantled is currently unclear.
41 Wymer, *Webster and Ford*, p. 131.
42 Warren, 'Ford in Performance', p. 15.
43 Warren, 'Ford in Performance', p. 15.
44 Dessen, *''Tis Pity She's a Whore*: Modern Productions and the Scholar', p. 91.
45 Wardle, quoted in Warren, 'Ford in Performance', p. 16.
46 Scott, *Renaissance Drama and a Modern Audience*, p. 103.
47 Scott, *Renaissance Drama and a Modern Audience*, p. 103.
48 Scott, *Renaissance Drama and a Modern Audience*, p. 103.
49 Scott, *Renaissance Drama and a Modern Audience*, p. 103.
50 Marion Lomax, ed., *'Tis Pity She's a Whore and Other Plays* (Oxford: Oxford
    University Press, 1995), Introduction, p. xviii.
51 Scott, *Renaissance Drama and a Modern Audience*, p. 103.
52 Scott, *Renaissance Drama and a Modern Audience*, p. 103.
53 Billington, quoted in Scott, *Renaissance Drama and a Modern Audience*, p. 103.
54 Michael Coveney, *Financial Times*, 22 February 1988, online: http://member-
    s.aol.com/citzsite/citz/gctispty.htm.
55 Joseph Farrell, review, *The Scotsman*, 22 February 1988, online: http://
    members.aol.com/citzsite/citz/gctispty.htm.
56 Farrell review.
57 Coveney review.
58 Farrell and Coveney reviews.
59 Robert Dawson Scott theatre review, *The Times*, 23 February 1988.
60 Farrell review.
61 Coveney review.
62 Coveney review.
63 Dawson Scott review.
64 Farrell review.
65 Wymer, *Webster and Ford*, p. 132.
66 Dawson Scott review.
67 Coveney review.
68 John Ford, *'Tis Pity She's a Whore*, ed. Simon Barker (London: Routledge,
    1997), Introduction, p. 15.
69 Wardle review, 1988.
70 Wardle review, 1988.

71   Wardle review, 1988.
72   Wardle review, 1988.
73   Wardle review, 1988.
74   Wardle review, 1988.
75   John Peter theatre review, *The Times*, 6 March 1988.
76   Peter review.
77   Wardle review.
78   *Financial Times* review.
79   Susannah Clapp theatre review, *Observer Review*, 10 October 1999.
80   John Ford, *'Tis Pity She's a Whore*, I.ii.257.
81   Wymer, *Webster and Ford*, p. 133.
82   Wymer, *Webster and Ford*, p. 130.
83   Wymer, *Webster and Ford*, p. 131.
84   Wymer, *Webster and Ford*.
85   Lomax, *'Tis Pity*, Introduction, p. xix.
86   Cheryl Black, 'A Visible Oppression: JoAnne Akalaitis's Staging of John Ford's *'Tis Pity She's a Whore'*, *Theatre Studies* 40 (1995), pp. 5–16, p. 5, note.
87   Frank Rich, "*'Tis Pity She's a Whore*; Jacobean Tale of Lust and Revenge Updated to the Fascist 1930's', *New York Times*, 6 April 1992, online: http://query.nytimes.com/gst/fullpage.html?res = 9E0CEEDD153CF935A35757-C0A964958260.
88   Assunta Kent and Tobin Nellhaus, "*'Tis Pity She's a Whore* by John Ford', *Theatre Journal* 42.3 (October 1990), p. 373.
89   Rich review.
90   The Italian fascist motto *Dio, patria, famiglia* translates as 'God, country and family'.
91   Black, 'A Visible Oppression', p. 13.
92   Rich review.
93   Black, 'A Visible Oppression', p. 13.
94   Black, 'A Visible Oppression', p. 13, note.
95   Mimi Kramer, 'Victims', *The New Yorker*, 20 April 1992, p. 79.
96   Rich review.
97   Cheryl Black's article is excellent on the use and meaning of surrealist art in Akalaitis's production.
98   Kramer, 'Victims'.
99   Kramer, 'Victims'.
100 Black, 'A Visible Oppression', p. 12.
101 Kent and Nellhaus, "*'Tis Pity She's a Whore* by John Ford', p. 373.
102 Kramer, 'Victims', p. 79.
103 Kent and Nellhaus, "*'Tis Pity She's a Whore* by John Ford', p. 374.
104 Rich review.
105 Jennifer A. Low, ' "Bodied forth": Spectator, Stage, and Actor in the Early Modern Theater', *Comparative Drama* 39.1 (spring 2005), pp. 1–29, p. 15.
106 Kent and Nellhaus, "*'Tis Pity She's a Whore* by John Ford', p. 374.
107 Rich review.
108 Kramer, 'Victims', p. 78.
109 Kramer, 'Victims', p. 78.
110 Rich review.
111 Lyn Gardner theatre review, *The Guardian*, 12 October 1999.
112 Gardner review.
113 Gardner review.
114 Susannah Clapp, *Observer Review*, 10 October 1999.
115 Gardner review.
116 Clapp review.
117 Maeve Walsh theatre review, *The Independent*, 17 October 1999.
118 Clapp review.
119 Although reviewers did not consider Jude Law's performance to be as strong as

that of Eve Best he too was nominated for an award for his performance. The Ian Charleson award is awarded to actors and actresses under 30 playing classical roles and is considered a great achievement. Law was nominated in 1999 for his Giovanni in Lan's production but missed out to Rupert Penry-Jones.

120   Gardner review.
121   Gardner review.
122   Gardner review.
123   Clapp review.
124   Clapp review.
125   Clapp review.
126   Walsh review.
127   Wymer, ' "The Audience is Only Interested in Sex and Violence": Teaching the Renaissance on Film', *Working Papers on the Web*, online: http://extra.shu.ac.uk/wpw/renaissance/wymer.htm.
128   Lisa Hopkins, *Screening the Gothic* (Austin, TX: University of Texas Press, 2005), p. 68.
129   Hopkins, *Screening the Gothic*, pp. 67–68.
130   Hopkins, *Screening the Gothic*, p. 67.
131   Hopkins, *Screening the Gothic*, p. 61.
132   Hopkins, *Screening the Gothic*, p. 62.
133   Hopkins, *Screening the Gothic*, p. 59.
134   Wymer, 'The Audience is Only Interested in Sex and Violence'.
135   Hopkins, *Screening the Gothic*, p. 67.
136   Scott, *Renaissance Drama and a Modern Audience*, p. 101.
137   Scott, *Renaissance Drama and a Modern Audience*, p. 101.
138   Cushman, 'The Actors' Revenge', p. 45.
139   Scott, *Renaissance Drama and a Modern Audience*, p. 89.
140   Wymer, *Webster and Ford*, p. 121.
141   Warren, 'Ford in Performance', p. 16.
142   Warren, 'Ford in Performance', p. 17.
143   Scott, *Renaissance Drama and a Modern Audience*, p. 101.
144   Warren, 'Ford in Performance', p. 18.
145   Warren, 'Ford in Performance', p. 18.
146   Hersh Zeifman, quoted in Zinman, '*Travesties, Night and Day, The Real Thing*', in Kelly, *The Cambridge Companion to Tom Stoppard*, p. 130.
147   Stoppard uses lines from '*Tis Pity She's a Whore* I.ii.181–216 and II.i.1–15.
148   Stoppard, *The Real Thing*, scene vi, pp. 213–14.
149   Stoppard, *The Real Thing*, scene iv, p. 188.
150   Stoppard, *The Real Thing*, scene x, pp. 237–38.

CHAPTER THREE

The State of the Art

Sandra Clark

A twenty-first century assessment of Ford by Mario DiGangi notes that 'Ford scholarship has not kept place with the upsurge in Renaissance dramatic scholarship since the 1980s',[1] adding that no complete modern edition of his dramatic works currently exists (although one is in preparation from Oxford University Press). However, the general critical trend in this scholarship away from moral, psychological and aesthetic approaches in favour of the social and political is clearly reflected in work on Ford, and especially in discussions of 'Tis Pity She's a Whore, even if there can hardly be said to be much consensus about the stances Ford takes. Scrutinies of the play's moral framework have given way to examinations of the social pressures that come to bear on (and complicate) the central relationships. In the last 15 years (the period with which this chapter is mainly concerned) the interest in Renaissance studies in new understandings of post-Reformation religious culture in England, and especially in the place of Catholicism in the earlier seventeenth century, has made a significant impact on Ford scholarship. A leader in this direction has been Lisa Hopkins, who makes a strong case for Ford's Catholic sympathies in John Ford's Political Theatre,[2] arguing from a close study of his extensive network of dedicatees, their families and their connections that he was a crypto-Catholic 'whose words contained a hidden agenda, accessible only to his own coterie of associates and dedicatees, which unites support for the aristocratic opposition to Charles I with an argument for the preferability of Catholic practices in worship'.[3] She argues in relation to 'Tis Pity She's a Whore for the influence of Catholic practice on such aspects of the play as its handling of food and fasting, and especially on its language, suggesting, for instance, that the signs of linguistic breakdown in the play emanate from a sense of language as lacking in substance, 'attributable to the absence of the healing fullness conferrable by Catholic ritual'.[4] In his treatment of body parts such as the heart and blood in the play she suggests that, in showing them capable of independent communication and 'exposing what happens when Protestant literalism is applied to Catholic metaphor', Ford harks back to such Catholic poets as Southwell and Crashaw.[5]

Following Hopkins's view of Ford's religious position, Laurel Amtower, in ' "This idol thou ador'st": The Iconography of *'Tis Pity She's a Whore'*,[6] extends Hopkins's view of Ford as implicitly sympathetic to certain aspects of Catholic belief and practice to an exploration of the play's iconography. Thus, Giovanni's creation of a personal value system to justify his own desires becomes analogous to 'the appropriation and subversion of Catholicism in the advancement of the Church of England'.[7] Building also on studies by Denis Gauer, 'Heart and Blood: Nature and Culture in *'Tis Pity She's a Whore'*[8] and Bruce Boehrer, *Monarchy and Incest in Renaissance England*,[9] Amtower traces in Giovanni's misuse of language and his conflation of religious and corporeal signifiers an indication of 'Ford's concern for what he may see as a cultural tendency to adulterate "pure" language so that it misleads its users',[10] as in the Church of England's use and adaptation of traditional Catholic symbology. Ford's relation to established religion is seen in different terms by Huston Diehl in 'Bewhored Images and Imagined Whores: Iconophobia and Gynophobia in Stuart Love Tragedies';[11] for her, Stuart love tragedy (including *Othello, The Duchess of Malfi, Women Beware Women* and *'Tis Pity She's a Whore*) is an ambivalent genre: '[These plays] express Reformist culture's deep antipathy for images and theatricality even as they self-consciously explore their own idolatrous potential'.[12] Such plays are informed by Puritan anti-theatricalism, but at the same time irresistibly drawn to the representation of the objects of their censorship. It is evident, then, that there is no consensus on the position taken by Ford to the state religion; Hopkins's exploration of his network of possible Catholic connections has not generally led to the sort of claims for coded Catholic readings of his plays that critics such as Richard Wilson have made for Shakespeare. Hopkins's belief in Ford's 'hidden agenda' for pro-Catholic support has not been widely taken up, though her view of his oppositional stance to the domestic politics of Charles has proved more attractive. Some critics who take a broad overview of his work such as Ira Clark, Rowland Wymer and Julie Sanders[13] allow that he was, in many ways, conservative; Clark uses phrases such as 'almost no questioning of authority' and 'little notice of politics', and asserts that 'his plays assume royal absolutism', contrasting him here with Massinger.[14] Wymer takes a similar, and now perhaps rather unfashionable, line: while regarding Ford as a moderate Protestant on the basis of *Christ's Bloody Sweat*, he does not see him as in any way engaged with the politics of the early Stuart era. It is easier to make claims for Ford's overt concern with contemporary politics in relation to *Perkin Warbeck* rather than *'Tis Pity She's a Whore*, but, even so, Clark and Wymer are in the minority here. And if, as DiGangi says, the theatrical situation of Ford's times and the production of his work in both public and private theatres precludes the expression of narrow political allegiances, there are many reasons why '[his] role in shaping the aesthetic, social, and political parameters of Caroline drama can no longer be ignored'.[15]

A strong emphasis in recent Ford criticism has been on his place in Caroline culture. Terri Clerico, in a much-cited article, 'The Politics of Blood: John Ford's *'Tis Pity She's a Whore*',[16] examines the intricate relationship between the literal uses of blood in the play and its metaphorical uses as an indicator of social standing: 'the flow of blood negotiates the subtle circulation and intersection of social, political, and sexual values in Parmesan society'.[17] She was critical of what seemed to her then (in 1992) 'an almost universal refusal to allow theatrical "play" to interact with the body politic', and her aim was to bring criticism of the play 'into the mainstream of cultural materialist thought'.[18] She provided a paradigm for this by exploring the meanings of blood in terms of class and of social structures, drawing on medical and anthropological discourses of the period to do so. For her, the incest is a defensive act, reflecting current social anxieties about alliances between different social classes; it is a defensive reaction to the exogamous relationships preferred by a corrupt society. In fact, Clerico had been partly superseded by Richard Marienstras in *New Perspectives on the Shakespearean World*[19] in this kind of reading; he also utilized concepts from anthropology such as relations between the king, the kingdom and outsiders, and between family and community, to explore how the play reflects the social fragmentation that ensued when Charles I came to power. New works on the reign of Charles, such as Kevin Sharpe's *Criticism and Complaint: The Politics of Literature in the England of Charles I*, as well as Martin Butler's ground-breaking book, *Theatre and Crisis: 1632–1642*, have drawn attention to the social complexities of this period and created new interest in it.[20] *'Tis Pity She's a Whore* as a political critique of its period has become almost (but not entirely) the new orthodoxy. Boehrer, in his influential book *Monarchy and Incest in Renaissance England*, also sees the play as critical of royalist absolutism in the Caroline period. For him, it is about what happens when the absence of a just temporal ruler forces individuals such as Annabella and Giovanni to create their own space of privacy and spiritual seclusion, 'and within that space they reconstruct justice, mercy, and even God out of the most readily available materials: each other'.[21] He argues that Ford's depiction of incest functions to warn against the Caroline consolidation of power within the private sphere. Molly Smith, following Boehrer in her book *Breaking Boundaries: Politics and Play in the Drama of Shakespeare and his Contemporaries*, claims that *'Tis Pity She's a Whore* stages an assault on Caroline patriarchy 'even as it enacts a more horrifying transgressive act in the form of incest'.[22] She also situates the incest in relation to the marital practices of royal and aristocratic families of the period, where endogamy was used to protect wealth and estates, as described by the historian Lawrence Stone. Richard McCabe in his wide-ranging exploration, *Incest, Drama and Nature's Law 1550–1700*,[23] sees the play, along with *The Broken Heart*, in reaction to the domestic politics of Charles and Henrietta Maria, a royal couple glorified for their very marital status in a way that produced a state 'unhealthily introverted, politically and spiritually endogamous, doomed to turn inwards upon itself'. [24]

Such readings of the play owe much to the kinds of theoretical appropriations whose absence Clerico had desiderated. Verna Foster, in her account of the play as 'city tragedy',[25] had already drawn attention to its 'social tone'[26] and focused on its portrayal of class relations. Since then, class and status have become primary terms in many historicizing readings, and Julie Sanders in her brief discussion takes it as read that Giovanni and Annabella 'suffer not because of their sins but because of their lower social position'.[27] Hopkins in 'Incest and Class: *"Tis Pity She's a Whore* and the Borgias' [28] couples 'incest and class' in her title, developing an intricate argument about Ford's use of the Parmesan setting to reflect on the connections of the Farnese family (the princes of Parma) with the Roman Borgias, notorious in the period for incestuous practices and political corruption. She makes the case that while incest was a dynastic strategy in royal families, for example the Spanish Hapsburgs, Ford's construction of Parma emphasizes that Giovanni and Annabella are emphatically not of the ruling classes, and therefore their relationship cannot in any way be condoned. Class issues are differently handled by Valerie Jephson and Bruce Boehrer in a provocative article, 'Mythologizing the Middle Class:'*Tis Pity She's a Whore* and the Urban Bourgeoisie';[29] they argue for the play as socially ultra-conservative, identifying with the royalist interests of the later part of Charles I's reign. They claim that nearly all of the characters, including Florio, Putana and Bergetto, are guilty of the sins of the bourgeoisie, particularly greed, social aspiration and aping the manners of the upper classes. Thus *'Tis Pity She's a Whore* 'makes aristocratic modes of behaviour conspicuous by their absence' in such a way as to 'affirm the health and integrity of the social body through the symbolic punishment of a demonised, bourgeois, incestuous other'. [30] They are particularly hard on Bergetto, an upstart whose death is comic retribution for his 'two-fold crime against the ranks'[31] – being a rich bourgeois and trying to play the part of an aristocrat. (There is an interesting contrast with some of the productions of the play discussed by Wymer,[32] where the Poggio/Bergetto relationship is sympathetically handled, and the servant genuinely grieved at his master's death.) Jephson and Boehrer stress their social point with reference to the play's theatrical context, as performed by the Queen's Men, at the Phoenix Theatre, for the delectation of a 'restricted upscale market'.[33]

Feminist criticism of the play has taken several paths. Denis Gauer's structuralist reading (1987), which opposed nature and culture, women and men, and asserted that it was men who 'produced and controlled' all the discourses of the play, and especially the 'trafficking in feeling [and] desire',[34] initiated much discussion, and some challenges to his 'too rigid essentialist reading of the split between nature and culture'.[35] Although not disagreeing with Gauer's stress on female passivity, Alison Findlay in *A Feminist Perspective on Renaissance Drama* [36] makes the point, seemingly obvious but not often highlighted, that a focus on Annabella is indicated by the play's title. She shows how Annabella is constructed as a figure of desire and sacrifice by the men around her[37] and how all the women's lives are confined by the narrow choice of roles available to them, roles all dictated by men. However, in the last act Annabella chooses a role for herself, that of tragic sacrifice, in her forlorn attempt to redeem her brother. Pompa Banerjee, in 'The Gift: Economies of Kinship and Sacrificial Desire in *'Tis Pity She's a Whore*',[38] an interdisciplinary reading informed by anthropology and in particular the gift theory of Marcel Mauss, argues more strongly for Annabella's roles as active and self-chosen. At the heart of the play she locates the treatment of kinship ties, in the perversion of which Giovanni rules himself out from any talionic or reciprocal structure of exchange by laying claim to his sister: 'Annabella is a gift that he cannot bear to give away'.[39] But through this relationship she claims agency for herself, refusing 'to remain an object of passive masculine exchange between her father, her brother Giovanni, and her husband Soranzo', thus complicating 'the masculine gendering of gift exchanges in the play'.[40] In this, she is aided by Putana, who acts as her surrogate mother and sanctions the incest. Placing her own life outside 'the economies of desire and revenge',[41] she gives herself away, first to Soranzo, and then to God, her heavenly as opposed to her earthly father. This reading throws new light on the role of market economies and the meaning of social exchange in the play.

Susannah B. Mintz in 'The Power of "Parity" in Ford's *'Tis Pity She's a Whore'*[42] also focuses on Annabella, not so much as an agent, but as a figure whose fulfilled incestuous desire places her outside the 'conventionally patriarchal acts'[43] in which Giovanni is fixed. Annabella's love for Giovanni 'symbolizes [. . .] "parity of condition", a way of relating to self and other that protests both paternal authority and a patriarchal sexual economy in which women are exchanged between men'.[44] Male behaviour in the play is validated both socially and linguistically, 'always informed by an underlying structure of patriarchal law and language whereby that behaviour *makes* sense'.[45] Annabella exists outside these structures; when her lovers Giovanni and Soranzo believe themselves in control over her, she is in terms of neoplatonic discourse a goddess and a divine being; when they can control her no more, there is no word for her but 'whore'. Mintz here follows the influential analysis of the play's handling of the confused meanings of incest by Susan Wiseman.[46] Wiseman argues that both secular and sacred languages in the play are inadequate to interpret incest, and therefore at the end of the play 'Annabella is returned from incest to the dangerous (but less dangerous) general category for the desirous female' as a whore.[47]

Jennifer A. Low's article ' "Bodied Forth": Spectator, Stage, and Actor in Early Modern Theater'[48] draws on feminist approaches to the play to discuss relations between theoretical conceptions of the (female) body and the experienced self in the physical space of the theatre. She says that Ford's 'representation of the female habitus, or experience of being in the body, manifests a significant confusion about the nature of female selfhood'; although he is concerned with the relation between Annabella's body and her inner self, he offers 'no entrance into the focal character's experience' in part because of the staging, which creates for the audience no other role than that of an onlooker, 'the peeping Tom whose desires have been legitimized because commodified'.[49] In fact, this is not entirely true, for Ford does allow Annabella a soliloquy at the beginning of Act V, only partially overheard by the Friar, in which she tries to articulate her awareness of sinful selfhood. Low, like many critics preoccupied with formulating a complex theoretical argument, does not notice this, nor, although she is interested in proxemics in the early modern stage, does she engage with the spatial elements of the sort of hall theatre in which the play was originally staged.

Recent theoretical approaches to the play, along with various forms of cultural materialism and feminism, include the anthropological (Marienstras, Banerjee) and those who try to combine different modes of reading it. Zenón Luís-Martínez, in his book *In Words and Deeds: The Spectacle of Incest in English Renaissance Tragedy*,[50] which includes a very useful introductory chapter on recent trends in scholarship dealing with incest in Renaissance drama, is eager to escape from one approach he rightly sees as prevalent, the exploration of the family/state analogy, aiming to disengage 'private desire from the tyranny of political readings'.[51] Instead he attempts 'to find a meeting point between psychoanalytically oriented and performance criticism and the more traditional methods of philology, literary commentary, and literary history',[52] although philology does not play much of a part in his discussion. As he well observes, incest is significant dramatically not only for its uses as social/political metaphor (as in the work of Clerico, McCabe, Boehrer or Smith, for example) or for the design of plotting and dramatic structure (as in the work of Lois Bueler[53] or Charles Forker[54]) but because of its 'close relation to the problem of subjectivity'.[55] He devotes a chapter to domestic tragedies (including *The Revenger's Tragedy, Women Beware Women* and *'Tis Pity She's a Whore*) which give spectators access to private spaces – the house and the body – but with *'Tis Pity She's a Whore* his real interest is in poststructuralist analysis of the relation between Giovanni's language and actions. As Luís-Martínez sees it, he can find no language in which to express his desire, since the available codes, neoplatonism and Petrarchanism, leave unexpressed that which exists on the margins. He quotes with approval Lisa Hopkins's discussion of the banquet scene in 'Speaking Sweat':[56]

> Ironically, however, his action serves only to reveal the extent to which it is impossible to escape from language: by attempting to substitute the literal signifier for the distrusted

signifier, he merely exposes his own imbrication in the slippery discourses of Petrarchan love, much as his dramatic role model, Romeo, has his rhetoric exposed as shallow by the greater practicality of Juliet'.[57]

Like Low, and despite his wish to utilize performance criticism, he does little with it in relation to *'Tis Pity She's a Whore*.

Performance criticism, however, does not entirely lose out to theory in recent work on Ford. While many historically-minded critics, such as Jephson and Boehrer, and Hopkins, have discussed the implications for his plays of their status as coterie theatre in the Caroline era, this has usually been in political terms. Others have taken a very different line, strongly influenced by the recent and still developing interest in cultures of anatomy and dissection in the period, exploring the similarities between the performance space in theatres like the Cockpit and the anatomy theatre. The seminal work of Jonathan Sawday in *The Body Emblazoned: Dissection and the Human Body in Renaissance Culture*,[58] although relatively little concerned with the drama of the period, drew attention not only to the significance of the culture of dissection (which he defines as the 'network of practices, social structures, and ritual surrounding this production of fragmented bodies')[59] in the understanding of the body, of interiority and of self-knowledge, but also in terms of the physical structure of the anatomy theatre itself. Following on from this, Christian Billing, in 'Modelling the Anatomy Theatre and the Indoor Hall Theatre: Dissection on the Stage of the Early Modern Theatre', [60] compares, with the aid of computer-generated models, the design of three performance spaces: the indoor hall playhouse, the anatomy theatre and the cockfighting ring. He suggests that the shape of the playhouse for which Ford was writing may have exerted an influence on his dramatic imagination and in particular his handling of violence in which 'aggression is enacted almost uniquely as a function of anatomical imperatives'. Like Sawday, he characterizes Ford's formative years, especially the early 1600s, as 'the greatest period of somatic change [...] to take place in early modern Europe', and even suggests that Beeston's Phoenix Theatre 'cashed in' on the public desire to witness anatomical demonstration and to hear variant views about the meaning of the dissected body.[61] The illustrations he provides are fascinating and suggestive, but the comparisons between the various performance spaces are far-fetched and speculative in terms of what they can tell us about Ford's dramaturgy.

Hilary M. Nunn, in her book *Staging Anatomies: Dissection and*

Spectacle in Early Stuart Tragedy,[62] does not refer to Billing's article, which presumably came out too late for her to draw on, but develops his perspective with discussion of theatrical texts, comparing *'Tis Pity She's a Whore* with *The Second Maiden's Tragedy*, both of them plays performed in the Phoenix Theatre, the plan of which was strikingly similar to that of the Barber-Surgeons' Hall in Inigo Jones's architectural designs. She draws various conclusions from these similarities: that there might have been visual similarities between the onstage murder of Annabella and a real-life anatomy, and that for the audience, 'these images of mutilation may blur together, allowing them to call upon lessons generated in different contexts to interpret the dramatic spectacle unfolding before them'.[63] Nunn, like Clerico in her exploration of the meanings attached to blood, also brings William Harvey and his lectures on the circulation of the blood and the function of the heart to bear on the play. While assessing such views and the impact of these new ideas, an undeniably exciting prospect, it is as well to bear in mind certain constraints. While Harvey did give public lectures on his discoveries in Physicians' Hall, his book *De Cordis Motu* was not published until 1628, and then only in Latin; the actual Barber-Surgeons' Hall was not built until 1636; and in the play Giovanni does not dismember Annabella's body onstage, and the audience does not witness the opened body. Ford was interested in psychological theory,[64] but this is another matter. William Slights, in 'The Narrative Heart of the Renaissance',[65] also considers what he calls the 'adjusted conceptions' of the body produced by new studies of anatomy and their effects on literature, though he steers well clear of performance issues. In fact, his concern is rather to contrast poetry with drama in their dealings with the increase of knowledge in the period about the interior of the body. While allowing that the new anatomy made a 'traumatic impact' on the traditional Christian understanding of the heart as the main metaphor for human spirituality, he claims that in Protestant poetry, for example, Spenser's *The Faerie Queene*, the sense of the inner self may be enlarged by such new knowledge; but on the Jacobean and Caroline stage 'the display of the bleeding heart [. . .] reaches orgiastic levels'.[66] In *'Tis Pity She's a Whore* the evisceration of Annabella's body is not a show of power but 'a spectacle of futility'[67] which affords no new moral discovery. Slights accepts that the new anatomy was highly influential on poetry and plays that centred on questions of personal integrity, but his assessment of that influence is largely negative.

Iconographical approaches to the play, such as those of Amtower and Diehl, lead to a focus on the last two scenes, the murder of Annabella and the banquet scene, where Giovanni displays on the end of his dagger the heart he has cut from her body. In an older article, Diehl relates the grotesque image of the heart on the dagger to existing iconographical traditions in the visual arts of the period, showing how, in a broad sense, violence can be used 'to advance ethical themes'.[68] More recently, she relates the violence against a beautiful woman here to violence against beautiful religious images in Reform culture.[69] Amtower also interprets the visual symbolism of these scenes from a religious perspective. For her, the banquet scene modifies and distorts Catholic ritual; it illustrates 'the "parodying" of Catholic values in the Anglican political/religious system'. As DiGangi rightly says, a multiplicity of meanings for both heart and dagger can be discovered. Michael Neill's article, 'What Strange Riddle's This?: Deciphering'*Tis Pity She's a Whore*',[70] traced the stage picture of the heart-on-dagger through various emblematic traditions as well as dramatic realizations to suggest some of these meanings – the search for truth contained in the heart, the cruelty of love, male power asserted over the submissive female. In his later book, *Issues of Death: Mortality and Identity in English Renaissance Tragedy,* he saw (as Nunn does) Giovanni's spectacular entrance as 'making visible [...] a whole set of submerged associations between tragic and anatomical performance'.[71] Many scholars find moral meanings for the heart-on-dagger moment. Richard Madelaine, in ' "The dark and vicious place": The Location of Sexual Transgression and its Punishment on the Early Modern Stage', compares various locations of violence and eroticism in the drama, relating the heart-on-dagger scene to the closet scene in *The Changeling*. Giovanni emerges from Annabella's bedchamber with the heart, as De Flores emerges from Beatrice-Joanna's closet with his dagger and her wounded body. Like De Flores, Giovanni presents himself as an executioner, facing his witnesses; Annabella's bed is the site both of sin and of its punishment. Marienstras and Banerjee, drawing on anthropological perspectives, interpret the action in terms of sacrifice; simply put, 'the sacrifice of the heart on the dagger [...] partially cleanses Giovanni's incredibly corrupt society by destroying most of the agents of that corruption'.[72] It is also an atavistic ritual in which 'Giovanni enacts a kind of private sacrifice when he presents the bleeding heart of his sister Annabella at the banquet of the notables. Here again, the sacred can be perceived in the horror of sacrilege whose very excess touches upon the absolute'.[73] This kind of tragic excess is exactly what attracted Antonin Artaud to the play in his essay, 'Theatre and the Plague', which is discussed by some of

Ford's recent critics. Artaud's vision of the banquet scene (which of course he had never seen staged) looks forward to those readings of the play in terms of Catholic ritual: '[Giovanni] kills his beloved and rips out her heart as if to eat his fill of it in the midst of that feast where the guests had hoped to devour him themselves'.[74] Mark Houlahan, in 'Postmodern Tragedy? Returning to John Ford',[75] regards Artaud as a significant figure in the reassessment of Ford as a serious and self-conscious artist, in that he (along with Georg Lukacs in *The Historical Novel*) valued Ford's talent for portraying extreme passions.[76] Peter Womack too, in his provocative snapshot of the play in *English Renaissance Drama*,[77] wants to rescue it from a commonplace context inside the generic conventions of revenge/ love tragedy and rediscover 'the dangerous play that Artaud read'.[78] He sees Giovanni's 'final atrocity' as the performance of 'an actor in an indescribable theatre':[79] 'Shrink not, courageous hand, stand up, my heart, | And boldly act my last, and greater part' (V.v.105–6). Interpreted in Lacanian terms by Luís-Martínez, Giovanni's act serves to undo a distance otherwise unbridgeable: 'it is the distance between the symbolic order (kinship, prohibition, conscience, pleasure, torment, tragedy) and the Real (heart and blood, together with the audience's dumb horror at the display of violence)'.[80]

While it is clear that the twin sensational features of the play, its central theme – incest – and the heart-on-dagger moment in the final scene, have proved particularly fruitful to recent critical approaches, there are more general aspects of the play which have been opened up to new modes of critical thinking. Ford's 'belatedness', in the sense of coming chronologically at the end of a long dramatic tradition and looking backward rather than forward, has been recognized for some time. Richard Ide's article, 'Ford's *'Tis Pity She's a Whore* and the Benefits of Belatedness',[81] challenged the once prevalent view of Ford's works as the decadent conclusion of a dramatic tradition that had run its course, and since then critics have come to regard his re-use of his predecessors as a creative impulse rather than an expression of exhaustion. Poststructuralist criticism which values the sort of techniques that work against dramatic subjectivity, such as metatheatricality and intertextuality, has been influential here. DiGangi observes that Ford's handling of his main characters is determined by his 'manipulation of generic expecta- tions and stock character types'; Annabella's characterization demonstrates the 'dispersed subjectivity produced by [. . .] metathea- trical forms',[82] drawing on a range of models of stage femininity such as the sexually assertive woman, the wily woman, the wealthy merchant's daughter, the physically abused wife and the 'beautiful (but ultimately destroyed) idol of Stuart love tragedy'.[83] Ford's regular use of situations and motifs from earlier plays – *The Spanish Tragedy, Dr Faustus, Romeo and Juliet, Othello* – as well as more recent ones – Fletcher's *The Mad Lover*, Middleton's *The Second Maiden's Tragedy* – creates a 'metatheatrical dimension'[84] which, in preventing the characters from achieving any coherent identity, exposes the fragmented and incoherent world in which they live. The re-evaluation of Ford's referential style of dramaturgy is also closely linked with the re-evaluation of Caroline theatre, initiated by Martin Butler.[85] Critics now prepared to take Caroline theatre seriously have found much of interest in Ford's relationship with his cultural milieu and with the kind of coterie theatre like the Phoenix for which *'Tis Pity She's a Whore* was written. Kate McLuskie in 'Dramatic Construction in the Plays of John Ford',[86] reviewing ways of responding to Ford other than interpretation, suggests reading his stylistic features as collusion with an informed audience who would be alert to his play with generic conventions and would read his metatheatricality as a conscious device.

The involvement of the play with new kinds of knowledges has been a fruitful approach, not just in terms of the new anatomy, as discussed above. In fact, Lisa Hopkins, noting that the word 'know' and its derivatives are more common in the play than 'blood', calls it 'a tragedy of knowledge'[87] in which, through Ford's exploration of the different and often contradictory epistemological assumptions made in different kinds of knowledge, carnal knowledge, knowledge of God, and worldly knowledge, epistemology becomes part of the play's 'thematic structure'.[88] 'What strange riddle's this?' (V.vi.29) asks Vasques, when Giovanni identifies the bloody object on the end of his dagger as a heart containing another heart. The recognition that the play, and especially the incest, requires decoding through the context of its time, and through the various discourses that endow it with meaning, has led to new explorations of early modern culture and its symbolic forms. Source study in the traditional sense continues to unearth new findings, as Lisa Hopkins's many articles demonstrate. To discover the meanings that the incestuous body might have held for an early modern audience in the theatre, Susan J. Wiseman suggests comparing the play with other texts in similar fields, such as legal texts or conduct books, and considering how punishments for sexual deviance were theorized in the ecclesiastical courts and in the world of neighbourhood policing.[89] Although there have been book-length studies of incest in the period by Boehrer, McCabe and Luís-Martinez written since Wiseman's article, none of them takes on the kind of broad cultural perspective that she evokes.

McCabe in a recent article, "'*Tis Pity She's a Whore* and Incest',[90] begins the process by separating 'incest per se' from 'the social, moral and political issues associated with it'[91] to discuss texts such as sermons and essays of the period which indicate a range of social attitudes to the practice.

While no recent critic has focused on Ford's language as such, there have been several indications of new approaches to it. Luís-Martínez analyses Giovanni's problem in terms of his lack of a language in which to articulate his desire; his attempts to express it through the codes of neoplatonism and Petrarchanism are failures. He can find no way to make the audience understand his desire, and, for this critic, 'in the impossibility to reconcile audience and hero – the ego and the Other – lies the dramatic singularity of the play'.[92] Lisa Hopkins, in *John Ford's Political Theatre,* also locates a failure of language in Giovanni in that his language is divorced from experience; and in the play more broadly language is often inaccurate and unreliable, key terms such as justice, honour and revenge all being detached from their accepted meanings. She also explores how the language of the body in this play and in Ford's work more generally is expressed through the use of terms particularly associated with Jesuitical confessional discourse, such as blood, eyes, tears, sweat and flames. For Molly Smith the problem of the play's language lies in the uncomfortable affinities of the speech of Giovanni and the Friar with the vocabulary of spiritual love. Her view is that Ford's appropriation of the language of traditional devotional literature has the effect of sacralizing sibling incest. Smith draws suggestive parallels with devotional texts of the period, such as the writings of Elizabeth I, the translations of Marguerite of Navarre, and *The Glass of the Sinful Soul* (1548) to demonstrate the use of familial expressions of devotion in a religious context, showing how readily the vocabulary of kinship ties can transfer between the sacred and the profane. Robyn Bolam, in 'Ford, Mary Wroth, and the Final Scene of '*Tis Pity She's a Whore*',[93] also touches on the ambiguity of kinship vocabulary in a comparison of the language in 'the heart's riddle' of the final scene with that of a sonnet by Mary Wroth from her sequence *Pamphilia to Amphilanthus* (number 42), probably addressed to her cousin William Herbert, who was also her lover. These different ways of attending to the language of the play indicate that there may be more avenues of inquiry to be explored, through approaches that range from the historicist to the poststructuralist.

'The strange extremities of [Ford's] theater compel us still', remarks Mark Houlahan, in a summary of 'creative adaptations' of this play by writers such as Angela Carter and Sarah Kane.[94] He likens the cultural climate of Ford's time to that of Tarantino, in that both, like Kane, address themselves to an audience 'which seemed jaded and all-knowing'. Decadence, once to be lamented in the liberal humanist tradition of Una Ellis-Fermor, is newly fascinating and audiences are no longer puzzled and dissatisfied when they find themselves 'caught between opposed emotional responses to the play's engagement with "disease" and "decadence" '.[95] Recent criticism has shown *'Tis Pity She's a Whore* to be a play with 'multiple registers of meaning',[96] which open it up excitingly to further study.

Notes

1 Mario DiGangi, 'John Ford' in *A Companion to Renaissance Drama*, ed. Arthur F. Kinney (Oxford: Blackwell, 2004), p. 370. DiGangi gives a useful brief account of recent trends in Ford scholarship, and also indicates fruitful directions for further study of his work generally.
2 Lisa Hopkins, *John Ford's Political Theatre* (Manchester: Manchester University Press, 1994).
3 This summary is actually taken from Hopkins's article, 'Speaking Sweat: Emblems in the Plays of John Ford', *Comparative Drama* 29.1 (1995). In a review of her book in *Medieval and Renaissance Drama* 10 (1998) Rowland Wymer challenges Hopkins's view of Ford as a Catholic sympathizer and particularly her use of evidence for it from the dedicatees of his works.
4 Hopkins, *John Ford's Political Theatre*, p. 100.
5 Hopkins, *John Ford's Political Theatre*, p. 125.
6 Laurel Amtower, ' "This idol thou ador'st": The Iconography of *'Tis Pity She's a Whore*', *Papers on Language and Literature* 34.2 (1998), pp. 179–206.
7 Amtower, ' "This idol thou ador'st" ', p. 180.
8 Denis Gauer, 'Heart and Blood: Nature and Culture in *'Tis Pity She's a Whore*', *Cahiers Elisabéthains* 31 (1987), pp. 45–57.
9 Bruce Boehrer, *Monarchy and Incest in Renaissance England* (Philadelphia, PA: University of Pennsylvania Press, 1992).
10 Amtower, ' "This idol thou ador'st" ', p. 184.
11 Huston Diehl, 'Bewhored Images and Imagined Whores: Iconophobia and Gynophobia in Stuart Love Tragedies', *English Literary Renaissance* 26 (1996), pp. 111–37.
12 Diehl, 'Bewhored Images and Imagined Whores', p. 133.
13 Ira Clark, *Professional Playwrights: Massinger, Ford, Shirley and Brome* (Lexington, KY: University Press of Kentucky, 1992), Rowland Wymer, *Webster and Ford* (Basingstoke: Macmillan, 1995), Julie Sanders, *Caroline Drama: The Plays of Massinger, Ford, Shirley and Brome* (Northcote House: Plymouth, 1999).
14 Clark, *Professional Playwrights*, pp. 78 and 80.
15 DiGangi, 'John Ford', p. 569.
16 Terri Clerico, 'The Politics of Blood: John Ford's *'Tis Pity She's a Whore*', *English Literary Renaissance* 22 (1992), pp. 405–34.
17 Clerico, 'The Politics of Blood', p. 405.
18 Clerico, 'The Politics of Blood', pp. 408, 413.
19 Richard Marienstras, *New Perspectives on the Shakespearean World* (Cambridge: Cambridge University Press, 1985).

20   Kevin Sharpe, *Criticism and Compliment: The Politics of Literature in the England of Charles I* (Cambridge: Cambridge University Press, 1987), and Martin Butler, *Theatre and Crisis: 1632–1642* (Cambridge: Cambridge University Press, 1984).

21   Boehrer, *Monarchy and Incest in Renaissance England*, p. 123.

22   Molly Smith, *Breaking Boundaries: Politics and Play in the Drama of Shakespeare and His Contemporaries* (Aldershot: Ashgate, 1998), p. 162.

23   Richard McCabe, *Incest, Drama and Nature's Law 1550–1700* (Cambridge: Cambridge University Press, 1993).

24   McCabe, *Incest, Drama and Nature's Law 1550–1700*, p. 236.

25   Verna Foster, "'Tis Pity She's a Whore as City Tragedy', in *John Ford: Critical Revisions,* ed. Michael Neill (Cambridge: Cambridge University Press, 1988).

26   Foster, "'Tis Pity She's a Whore as City Tragedy', p. 187.

27   Sanders, *Caroline Drama*, p. 28.

28   Lisa Hopkins, 'Incest and Class: 'Tis Pity She's a Whore and the Borgias', in *Incest and the Literary Imagination,* ed. Elizabeth Barnes (Gainesville, FL: University Press of Florida, 2002), pp. 94–116.

29   Valerie Jephson and Bruce Boehrer, 'Mythologizing the Middle Class: 'Tis Pity She's a Whore and the Urban Bourgeoisie', *Renaissance and Reformation* 18.3 (1994), pp. 5–28.

30   Jephson and Boehrer, 'Mythologizing the Middle Class', pp. 8, 20.

31   Jephson and Boehrer, 'Mythologizing the Middle Class', p. 10.

32   Wymer, *Webster and Ford*, p. 131.

33   Jephson and Boehrer, 'Mythologizing the Middle Class', p. 22.

34   Gauer, 'Heart and Blood', pp. 50, 49.

35   Clerico, 'The Politics of Blood', p. 432.

36   Alison Findlay, *A Feminist Perspective on Renaissance Drama* (Oxford: Blackwell, 1999).

37   Findlay, *A Feminist Perspective on Renaissance Drama*, p. 25.

38   Pompa Banerjee, 'The Gift: Economies of Kinship and Sacrificial desire in 'Tis Pity She's a Whore', *Studies in the Humanities* 29.2 (2002), pp. 137–49.

39   Banerjee, 'The Gift', p. 140.

40   Banerjee, 'The Gift', pp. 140, 141.

41   Banerjee, 'The Gift', p. 142.

42   Susannah B. Mintz, 'The Power of Parity in 'Tis Pity She's a Whore', *Journal of English and Germanic Philology* 102 (2003), pp. 269–91.

43   Mintz, 'The Power of Parity', p. 275.

44   Mintz, 'The Power of Parity', p. 274.

45   Mintz, 'The Power of Parity', p. 277. The italics are hers.

46   Susan J. Wiseman, "'Tis Pity She's a Whore: Representing the Incestuous Body', in *Renaissance Bodies: The Human Figure in English Culture c. 1540–1660,* ed. Lucy Gent and Nigel Llewellyn (London: Reaktion, 1990).

47   Wiseman, "'Tis Pity She's a Whore', p. 195.

48   Jennifer A. Low, ' "Bodied Forth": Spectator, Stage, and Actor in Early Modern Theater', *Comparative Drama* 39.1 (spring 2005), pp. 1–29.

49   Low, ' "Bodied Forth" ', pp. 10, 11, 15.

50   Zenón Luís-Martínez, *In Words and Deeds: The Spectacle of Incest in English Renaissance Tragedy* (Amsterdam: Rodopi, 2002).

51   Luís-Martínez, *In Words and Deeds*, p. 17.

52   Luís-Martínez, *In Words and Deeds*, p. 22.

53   Lois Bueler, 'The Structural Uses of Incest in English Renaissance Drama', *Renaissance Drama*, 15 (1984), pp. 115–45.

54   Charles Forker, *Fancy's Images: Contexts, Settings, and Perspectives in Shakespeare and his Contemporaries* (Carbondale, IL: Southern Illinois University Press, 1990).

55   Luís-Martínez, *In Words and Deeds*, p. 24.

56   Lisa Hopkins, 'Speaking Sweat: Emblems in the Plays of John Ford',

Comparative Drama 29.1 (1995), pp. 133–46.

57   Hopkins, 'Speaking Sweat', p. 141, fn 45.

58   Jonathan Sawday, *The Body Emblazoned: Dissection and the Human* Body in Renaissance Culture (London: Routledge, 1995).

59   Sawday, *The Body Emblazoned*, p. 2.

60   Christian Billing, 'Modelling the Anatomy Theatre and the Indoor Hall Theatre: Dissection on the Stages of Early Modern London', *Early Modern Literary Studies* special edition 13 (2004) online: http://extra.shu.ac.uk/emls/si-13/billing/index.htm.

61   Billing, 'Modelling the Anatomy Theatre and the Indoor Hall Theatre'.

62   Hilary M. Nunn, *Staging Anatomies: Dissection and Spectacle in Early Stuart Tragedy* (Aldershot: Ashgate, 2005).

63   Nunn, *Staging Anatomies*, p. 147.

64   See Lisa Hopkins, 'John Ford's *'Tis Pity She's a Whore* and Early Diagnoses of Folie à Deux', *Notes and Queries* 41.1 (1994), pp. 71–74.

65   William Slights, 'The Narrative Heart of the Renaissance', *Renaissance and Reformation* 26.1 (2002), pp. 5–23.

66   Slights, 'The Narrative Heart of the Renaissance', p. 7.

67   Slights, 'The Narrative Heart of the Renaissance', p. 11.

68   Diehl, 'The Iconography of Violence in English Renaissance Tragedy', *Renaissance Drama* 11 (1980), pp. 27–44.

69   Diehl, 'Bewhored Images'.

70   Michael Neill, ' "What strange riddle's this?: Deciphering *'Tis Pity She's a Whore'*, in *John Ford: Critical Revisions*, ed. Michael Neill (Cambridge: Cambridge University Press, 1988).

71   Michael Neill, Issues of Death *Mortality and Identity in English Renaissance Tragedy* (Oxford: Oxford University Press, 1997), p. 136.

72   Banerjee, 'The Gift', p. 145.

73   Marienstras, *New Perspectives on the Shakespearean World*, p. 6.

74   Antonin Artaud, *The Theatre and its Double*, trans. Victor Corti (London: Calder & Boyars, 1970), p. 20.

75   Mark Houlahan, 'Postmodern Tragedy? Returning to John Ford' in *Tragedy in Transition*, ed. Sarah Annes Brown and Catherine Silverstone (Oxford: Blackwell, 2007), pp. 249–59.

76   Houlahan, 'Postmodern Tragedy?', p. 253.

77   Peter Womack, *English Renaissance Drama* (Oxford: Blackwell, 2006).

78   Womack, *English Renaissance Drama*, p. 251.

79   Womack, *English Renaissance Drama*, p. 253.

80   Luís-Martínez, *In Words and Deeds*, p. 209.

81   Richard S. Ide, 'Ford's *'Tis Pity She's a Whore* and the Benefits of Belatedness', in ' "*Concord in Discord": The Plays of John Ford, 1586–1986*, ed. Donald K. Anderson, Jr (New York: AMS Press, 1986), pp. 61–86.

82   DiGangi, 'John Ford', pp. 575–76.

83   DiGangi, 'John Ford', p. 576.

84   Martin Butler, '*Love's Sacrifice*: Ford's Metatheatrical Tragedy', in *John Ford: Critical Revisions*, pp. 201–3, p. 228. Ford's metatheatricality is also discussed by Clark, *Professional Playwrights*, pp. 86–87 and Richard Ide, *"Tis Pity She's a Whore* and the Benefits of Belatedness'.

85   In *Theatre and Crisis: 1632–1642*.

86   Kate McLuskie, 'Dramatic Construction in the Plays of John Ford', in *John Ford: Critical Revisions*, pp. 97–127.

87   Lisa Hopkins, 'Knowing their Loves: Knowledge, Ignorance, and Blindness in *'Tis Pity She's a Whore'*, *Renaissance Forum* 3.1 (1998), online: www.hull.a-c.uk/renforum/v3no1/index.html.

88   Hopkins, 'Knowing their Loves'.

89   Wiseman, *"Tis Pity She's a Whore*: Representing the Incestuous Body', pp. 196–97.

90   Richard McCabe, "*Tis Pity She's a Whore* and Incest', in *Early Modern English Drama: A Companion*, ed. Garrett A. Sullivan, Jr., Patrick Cheney and Andrew Hadfield (Oxford: Oxford University Press, 2006), pp. 309–20.

91   McCabe, "*Tis Pity*', p. 309.

92   Luís-Martínez, *In Words and Deeds*, p. 211.

93   Robyn Bolam, 'Ford, Mary Wroth, and the Final Scene of '*Tis Pity She's a Whore*', in *A Companion to English Renaissance Literature and Culture*, ed. Michael Hattaway (Oxford: Blackwell Publishing, 2000), pp. 276–83.

94   Houlahan, 'Postmodern Tragedy? Returning to John Ford', p. 253.

95   Carla Dente, 'Reading Symptoms of Decadence in Ford's '*Tis Pity She's a Whore*', in *Romancing Decay: Ideas of Decadence in European Culture*, ed. Michael St John (Aldershot: Ashgate, 1999), pp. 27–38.

96   DiGangi, 'John Ford', p. 570.

CHAPTER FOUR

New Directions: Fatal Attraction: Desire, Anatomy and Death in *'Tis Pity She's a Whore*

Catherine Silverstone

In *A Lover's Discourse* Roland Barthes offers a series of lyrical meditations which identify the dominant tropes that articulate desire. With acute economy of language, Barthes draws his reader through a series of fragments with claims that border on the aphoristic, from his designation of the heart as 'the organ of desire' to his identification of the '[d]ream of total union' with the loved one, which 'is impossible, and yet it persists'.[1] Collectively these short fragments, which focus on topics such as objects, alone, suicide, will-to-possess, flayed, annulment, absence, identification, I-love-you, fulfilment and the heart, to name but a few, might have been offered as a theoretical gloss to John Ford's searing text of desire, *'Tis Pity She's a Whore* (1633).[2] For in *A Lover's Discourse* Barthes elegantly distils a series of tropes about desire that can be tracked through Ford's play and the poetry, drama and taxonomies of his contemporaries. Indeed, as even a cursory glance at a concordance of Shakespeare reveals, these tropes of desire recur repeatedly, from Orsino's sense in *Twelfth Night* that his 'desires, like fell and cruel hounds, | E'er since pursue' him (I.i.21–22), a claim that is echoed in Antonio's contention that his 'desire, | More sharp than filèd steel, did spur [him] forth' (III.iii.4–5), to Troilus's assertion in *Troilus and Cressida* that 'desire is boundless' (III.ii.77) and, in *Antony and Cleopatra*, Cleopatra's anticipation of her death in which the 'stroke of death is as a lover's pinch, | Which hurts and is desired' (V.ii.286–87).[3] In the dramatic and poetic texts of Shakespeare and his contemporaries and the vast tracts which seek to offer taxonomies of human behaviour, such as Timothy Bright's

A Treatise of Melancholy (1586) and Robert Burton's *The Anatomy of Melancholy* (1621), desire is repeatedly defined in terms of its relentless driving nature and its relationship to the heart and death, the last of which is expressed as a violent metaphorical substitution in Shakespeare's Sonnet 147 as 'Desire is death' (147.8).

The conjunction I have proposed between Barthes and Ford and his contemporaries raises interesting questions for how critics might historicize and analyse desire in early modern culture. The resonances between these texts of desire are echoed, not without difference, in the psychoanalytic and poststructural projects of theorists such as Sigmund Freud, Jacques Lacan, Luce Irigaray, Jacques Derrida, Judith Butler, Catherine Belsey and Jonathan Dollimore, among others.[4] They recur again in texts as generically diverse as Plato's *Symposium* (*c.* 385 BC) which elucidates the myth of the split creatures who have a 'desperate yearning for the other', Wagnerian opera, novels such as Jeanette Winterson's *The Passion* (1987), Michael Ondaatje's *The English Patient* (1992) and Haruki Murakami's *South of the Border, West of the Sun* (1992), the plays of Sarah Kane, especially the excoriating desire-scape of *Crave* (1998), the sculptural installations and collages of Tracey Emin and the contemporary love song, exemplified by Nick Cave and his prolific output with The Bad Seeds.[5] What, then, is the critic to make of these verbal and epistemological affinities between early modern culture and the plethora of critical and cultural texts of desire produced in the intervening 400 years?

Given these similarities – which though manifold are beyond the scope of this chapter to catalogue – it is tempting to argue that desire might stand as a transhistorical, transcultural, or, even transcendental category with its narratives of absence, longing, the heart, excess and death repetitiously playing out in a multitude of cultures throughout history. Indeed, Barthes's text stands as a kind of historical palimpsest of desire, with the marginal references noting his debt to Balzac, Diderot, Freud, Lacan, Nietzsche, Plato, Proust and Sartre, to name but several, suggesting a cultural and historical concurrence of desire. As Barthes notes '[i]n order to compose this amorous subject, pieces of various origin have been "put together"', some from various types of reading, some 'from conversations with friends' and some from his 'own life'.[6] This narrative simultaneity in the figuration of desire across time and culture is certainly evident, even as its expression takes different forms. However, given the careful work instigated by new historicist and cultural materialist criticism in the 1980s, and its legacy in the work of more recent historicist criticism, contemporary categories of critical analysis do not necessarily map easily onto early modern texts and their deployment can run the risk of anachronism, especially as the subject constituted by these theoretical positions is a comparatively (post)modern phenomenon. As Stephen Greenblatt argues,

> psychoanalytic interpretation is causally belated, even as it is causally linked: hence the curious effect of a discourse that functions *as if* the psychological categories it invokes were not only simultaneous with but even prior to and themselves causes of the very phenomena of which in actual fact they were the results.[7]

Here psychoanalysis is figured as a kind of self-referential, self-fulfilling mode of inquiry: its central conditions are not only figured as transcendent, but also the cause of the phenomena of which they are, in fact, the results. Just as this circularity can, potentially, lead to the flattening of historical difference, claims of transhistoricism, transculturalism or transcendentalism often fail to identify desire's particular local forms. Given these difficulties, in what follows I am less interested in 'applying' contemporary theories of desire to Ford's *'Tis Pity She's a Whore* than I am in seeing how the resonances between these texts and periods with respect to tropes of desire might enable a reading of the play that is attentive both to its local cultural contexts and to contemporary critical contexts. This analysis is, then, embedded in the powerful theoretical frameworks and desire-saturated products of my own cultural moment, which of course, in part, determine the historical and cultural framework through which I read the constituent parts of desire in early modern culture. In this work my analysis also seeks to be attentive to the particular forms desire takes in Ford's text and early modern culture more generally. In particular, this chapter seeks to offer an archaeology of desire in *'Tis Pity She's a Whore* with specific reference to anatomization and death.

The Anatomy of Desire

A fascination with the text of the (anatomized) body and its relationship to truth, desire and power is pervasive in early modern culture. As Jonathan Sawday succinctly notes, the 'image of the body as a book, a text there to be opened, read, interpreted, and, indeed, rewritten, was a persuasive one to the early explorers of the human frame'.[8] In the early modern period dissections moved away from the recitation of a text over an opened corpse, where the corpse was used to affirm the authority of the written text, to a process whereby the corpse became the subject of inquiry and generative of new anatomical texts and forms of knowledge. The work of the Belgian anatomist Andreas Vesalius, who advocated dissecting the body in order to investigate it rather than employing dissection to reinforce an existing body of knowledge, was central to what Sawday describes as the early modern 'culture of dissection', even as Vesalius's work reaffirmed some prevailing inaccuracies about the body.[9] Vesalius's *De Humani Corporis Fabrica* (*On the Fabric of the Human Body*) (1543) contains images of corpses depicted as objects of inquiry and, perhaps most memorably, actively presenting themselves as such objects, posing for the inspection of their musculature and skeletal frames. Thomas Laqueur summarizes this shift in inquiry, noting that 'the new science [...] proclaimed so vigorously that Truth and progress lay not in texts, but in the opened and properly displayed body'.[10] Early modern cultural interest in anatomy was not, of course, limited to dissecting human bodies and there was a fad for the production and consumption of anatomies of various bodies of knowledge in early modern culture, such as John Lyly's *Euphues: The Anatomy of Wit* (1578), Thomas Nashe's *The Anatomie of Absurditie* (1589), Francis Bacon's *The Proficience and Advancement of Learning* (1605) and Philip Stubbes's *Anatomy of Abuses* (1583). These texts, of which Burton's *The Anatomy of Melancholy* is exemplary, sought to impose a sense of order on a particular body of knowledge by dissecting it into sections and subsections. Through this process of literary dissection, these writers attempted, in Devon L. Hodges's words, 'to strip away false appearances and expose the truth. With violent determination, writers of anatomies used their pens as scalpels to cut through appearances and reveal the mute truth of objects'.[11]

The culture of dissection also pervaded particular modes of literary and artistic expression. As Patricia Fumerton has shown in her careful analysis of the courtly fascination with miniatures and love poetry, the process of attempting to expose or penetrate inner secrets was also bound up with the operation of Elizabethan courtly life. In the case of miniatures, these jewels must be opened to reveal the pictures inside them. But these pictures, as with sonnets, never simply reveal the truth of the heart; rather they ' "represent" their private loves through conventional artifice that keeps them hidden'.[12] Fumerton's analysis neatly identifies the paradox at the heart of the anatomization of desire: despite attempts to locate the core or truth of desire, it remains hidden and elusive. Not only was the human body physically dissected but it was also metaphorically anatomized in literary texts. One of the central literary modes for anatomizing the body in this way is the blazon. Thus the speaker, as in Shakespeare's Sonnet 130, catalogues the various parts of his mistress, separating out and displaying her constituent elements – her eyes, lips, breasts, hair, cheeks, breath and voice. By a process of negative associations such as 'My mistress' eyes are nothing like the sun' (130.1), the sonnet plays with the convention of the blazon and works to make the speaker's point that his love is 'as rare | As any she belied with false compare' (130.13–14). While the blazon is ostensibly used as a mode of praise, Valerie Traub suggests that 'the poet-lover masters his lady by inscribing her in a text, constructing and dismembering her, part by body part'.[13] Similarly, writing about *The Rape of Lucrece* (1594), Nancy Vickers contends that the praise of Lucrece before her rape by Tarquin illustrates the way in which the form of a blazon enabled men to play out their rivalry on the body of a woman.[14] It is also worth noting that male bodies are, on occasions, also subject to similar scrutiny and displayed as objects of desire, such as the narrator's lengthy tribute to Leander's excellent body (his hair, straight body, smooth breast, white belly, cheeks, eyes and lips) in Christopher Marlowe's poem *Hero and Leander* (1598).[15] In cataloguing Leander's beauty, the narrator comments 'but my rude pen | Can hardly blazon forth the loves of men, | Much less of powerful gods' (ll. 69–71). Here the narrator identifies both the blazon as a form of praise and its limits in elucidating adequately Leander's virtues. As well as displaying the body as an object of desire, the project of anatomization was also used both literally and figuratively as a method of obtaining knowledge of a particular body. Thus Lear asks for Regan's body to be anatomized so that he might 'see what breeds about her heart' (III.vi.70–71). Here metaphorical language collapses into a grisly physical instruction, predicated on the notion that anatomization will reveal the motivation for Regan's behaviour but which, literally, will result in her death. Cumulatively, these examples suggest that the body's surfaces, both interior and exterior, were available to be read and consumed as texts. Marked by hierarchies of power, anatomization offers the promise of knowing the 'truth' of a particular body, even as that 'truth' may, ultimately, remain resistant to excavation as in the case of *'Tis Pity She's a Whore*.

This preoccupation with anatomization in *'Tis Pity She's a Whore* is played out on the human body with respect to desire. Like Ford's other two tragedies, *Love's Sacrifice* (1633) and *The Broken Heart* (1633), *'Tis Pity She's a Whore*, with its images of burning, anatomized and broken hearts, is a play obsessed with the iconography of the heart linked, with crystalline precision, to desire. Akin to the way in which Barthes figures the heart as a token of exchange within an economy of desire, where it is 'constituted into a gift-object – whether ignored or rejected',[16] the play sets up an economy of hearts. In these exchanges the heart is given or offered as a token of desire in much the same way that jewels (II.vi.31–33) and rings (II.vi.35–41) are used as tokens of desire in the play. Indeed Giovanni often refers to his heart as an object of exchange. He tells Annabella to 'keep well my heart' (II.i.32) and asserts that his heart is 'entombed' in Annabella's physical heart (V.vi.27). He returns to this metaphor of exchange after Annabella's death, claiming that he 'killed a love, for whose each drop of blood | I would have pawned my heart' (V.v.101–2). Whereas the heart is often treated as a metaphorical token of exchange, these metaphorical exchanges are redesignated as physical exchanges when Giovanni brandishes Annabella's heart on his dagger, instructing Soranzo to 'see this heart which was thy wife's: | Thus I exchange it royally for thine' (V.vi.72–73). The way in which Giovanni uses Annabella's heart as a unit of exchange graphically illustrates the lack of autonomy that Annabella has come to have over her own desires: she literally has no heart to give as a token of her desire. It is as though when Annabella says that she forgives Giovanni 'With my heart' (V.v.78) he takes her comment as a cue literally to take possession of that heart. Like the poetic technique of the blazon, which can be seen as an attempt to control subjects by metaphorically 'carving' up their bodies, Giovanni's literal anatomization can be read as an extreme manifestation of this attempt to control and order the body and desires of the lover.

In *'Tis Pity She's a Whore*, as with Ford's other tragedies, the heart is also treated as a register of truth concerning an individual's desires. Indeed, Denis Gauer observes that the heart is 'supreme as the seat of truth, thus becoming a tell tale heart [...] which may be read as easily as a book'.[17] When Giovanni declares his love to Annabella he bares his breast, offering her his dagger so that she might 'Rip up' his bosom and 'there thou shalt behold | A heart in which is writ the truth I speak' (I.II.210–11). As well as acting as a precursor to what subsequently happens to Annabella's heart, Giovanni's comment presents his heart as a text of truth concerning his feelings. Similarly, Soranzo threatens to rip up Annabella's heart, thinking that he will find the name of her lover written there (IV.iii.53–54). Here Ford offers an image of the heart being not merely extracted from the body, but ripped apart. It is as though the truth of Annabella's desire is contained within the heart of her heart.

The concept of the heart as a text of desire is given further treatment when Soranzo confides to Vasques that in the 'faithless face' of Annabella he 'laid up | The treasure of my heart' (IV.iii.107–8). Here Soranzo's heart, or the organ of his desire, is mapped onto Annabella's face. This suggests that in looking at her face he sees the image of his heart's desire reflected back to him. While he might be able to see his own desire in the body of Annabella, Soranzo is unable to read Annabella's desires from her body. The surface of her body will not reveal the identity of the father of her child – a man who is synonymous with the object of her desires – and as Susan Wiseman observes, '[e]ven a pregnant body does not tell all its own secrets, and incest is undiscoverable from external evidence'.[18] Giovanni later asserts that Annabella's 'fruitful womb' (V.vi.48), which he has 'ploughed up' (V.vi.31), contains the results of their desire in the form of 'a child unborn' (V.vi.50). Thus the most the pregnant body can disclose is the result or fruit of desire, not the desire itself.

Although these characters assert that physical anatomization will reveal the essential truth of the heart and its desire, the reality of an anatomized heart achieves a quite different result. Mid-way through the play, Soranzo attempts to woo Annabella. In an effort to convince her of the sincerity of his desire he appeals to his heart, saying 'Did you but see my heart, then you would swear—' (III.ii.23). Soranzo is unable to finish his sentence because Annabella interjects, concluding that if she were to see his heart, she would swear that Soranzo 'were dead' (III.ii.24). The reality of the anatomized heart, then, is not so much that it indicates the truth of desire, but that to see such a heart entails the death of the physical body. While Annabella and Soranzo's exchange explores the physical reality of the anatomized heart in theory, in the last scene of the play Giovanni literalizes this proposition by theatrically displaying the anatomized heart of Annabella on his dagger. Thus the body is literally anatomized in an extreme manifestation of the metaphorical attempts to anatomize, discover and control desire that recur in all three of Ford's tragedies. However, the heart, disassociated from the body, no longer seems to have any meaning as an organ of desire, or even as an organ of Annabella's. Giovanni talks of 'the rape of life and beauty' (V.vi.19) that he has acted on Annabella, but Florio's 'Ha! what of her?' (V.vi.21) suggests that he has not connected the organ on the dagger to Annabella. Even when Giovanni says that the organ is 'A heart my lords, in which is mine entombed' (V.vi.27), the other characters still do not relate the heart to Annabella: Vasques uncomprehendingly asks 'What strange riddle's this?' (V.vi.29). To counter the confusion Giovanni then explicitly names the heart as Annabella's, saying ''Tis Annabella's heart, 'tis; why d'ee startle? | I vow 'tis hers' (V.vi.30–31). Lest any doubt remain, he elucidates further 'These hands have from her bosom ripped this heart' (V.vi.59).

Giovanni, whose desire has relentlessly driven him to commit an act of excessive violence in his effort to control and possess Annabella's desire, has literalized the metaphor of exposing the heart to reveal desire. As Lisa Hopkins suggests, 'in ripping out the heart' Giovanni 'attempts to force an equation between signifier and signified'.[19] But what we see is that there is no one-to-one correspondence. Despite the continual references to anatomizing the heart in order to see the 'true' text of desire, the concept of the heart as an organ of desire functions successfully only in metaphorical terms. Further, as Michael Neill observes, the heart in its literal form 'threatens to become nothing more than itself, a grisly tautology – a piece of offal *en brochette*, brutally stripped of all vestiges of metaphor'.[20] Outside its metaphorical context the biological heart has no fixed meaning: the body is cut open and the heart is extracted only to reveal that the heart, in purely physical terms, is unable to be interpreted or read as an organ of desire. This is made strikingly clear in the theatre where the proffered object, be it animal or synthetic, cannot help but draw attention to itself as a representational object rather than as an index of desire. On one level this is because the heart is not the 'real thing' but even if the 'real thing' were on view in a snuff *'Tis Pity*, the organ would, no doubt, signify primarily as a marker of death and murder, not as a marker of desire. The display of the 'heart' succeeds only in demonstrating the way in which the metaphorical equivalence of the heart and desire collapses into a bloody physicality: once again, desire exceeds anatomical signification.

In this play, the heart is obsessively referred to and both metaphorically and literally anatomized as the receptacle of desire. The heart, though, refuses to give up its secrets. Even when Giovanni is pushed to the extreme action of physically anatomizing Annabella's heart in order to control her desires, the heart resists attempts to codify it and the searched-for truth or core of desire seems to be missing. As such the process of anatomizing to find the truth of desire can be seen as analogous to the operation of desire itself. That is, the longed-for truth of desire, like the longing to satisfy desire, gives the illusion of being accessible, here through the anatomized body. However, when the body is cut open this promise of fulfilment is again deferred. Effectively the subject of desire attempts to control and order desire through anatomization, but desire refuses to be contained in this way. Instead, in its most extreme manifestations, desire exceeds these anatomical structures, destroying both its subjects and objects. There is also a grim irony implicit in anatomizing the body in order to discover the truth of the lover's desire. That is, if the anatomy is physical, not only are the signs of desire impossible to read, but the lover is, in Michael Ondaatje's words, 'disassembled' and so dies.[21] And it is to the deathly nature of desire that this discussion will now turn.

The Death of Desire

' "[D]eath" ', writes Michael Neill,

> is not something that can be imagined once and for all, but an idea that has to be constantly reimagined across cultures and through time; which is to say that, like most human experiences we think of as "natural", it is culturally defined.[22]

Neill suggests that in the early modern period, death was not only 'invented' by those involved in the practices of burial and associated rituals such as the production of *memento mori* (objects through which to remember the dead) and *Danse Macabre* (Dance of Death), but also through art and literature, especially tragedy, which for Neill 'was among the principal instruments by which the culture of early modern England reinvented death'.[23] Indeed, early modern tragedy exhibits a compulsive turn toward death and it is not uncommon for this deathly turn to be implicated in narratives of desire; notable examples include *Romeo and Juliet* (1594–95), *Othello* (1604), *The Revenger's Tragedy* (1607) and *The Duchess of Malfi* (1614), the first of which serves as material for adaptation in *'Tis Pity* with the adolescent lovers from opposing houses recast as brother and sister, with a different, and arguably more extreme, set of familial oppositions and restrictions to contend with. *'Tis Pity She's a Whore* is certainly enmeshed in the conventions of early modern tragedy, looking back to the Elizabethan vogue for the revenge tragedy as much to the tragedies of love that punctuate the canon of early modern tragedy more widely. These narratives of deadly desire often work through the way in which desire is underpinned by the fantasy of its own extinction, a trope which recurs repeatedly in contemporary theories of desire. For Barthes, the desiring subject is shattered most completely in death; he contends that '[i]n the amorous realm, the desire for suicide is frequent' and that this impulse is directed outward 'aggressively against the loved object (a familiar blackmail) or in fantasy uniting myself with the loved object in death'.[24] An instantiation of the fantasy of being united with the loved one in death effectively destroys the desiring subject; in the evaporation of the subject's desires in death through an imagined union with the lover, the subject, constituted by desire, is annihilated in both cerebral and physical terms. Similarly, in his analysis of relationships between death, desire and loss in western culture, Jonathan Dollimore suggests that 'the absolute object of desire is, experientially, a fantasy of the *absolute release from desire*, i.e., death of desire/death of the self'.[25] These ideas find their sharpest articulation, however, in Freud's bald contention that '*the aim of all life is death*'.[26] For Freud, the basic drive of life is toward death, even as this is repressed by the workings of the drives toward pleasure. As Dollimore explains: 'socialized desire is a lack, impossible to appease because it is the lack of death itself, and life merely an enforced substitute for death'.[27]

In the remainder of this section I want to explore what might be described as the death/desire dynamic in *'Tis Pity She's a Whore*, attentive to the narrative arcs of early modern tragedy and informed by theoretical conceptions of desire as death-driven. In this play the relationship between death and desire takes two main forms: union with the other and death (which might entail a fantasy of a union with the other in death), both of which entail the possibility of the annihilation of the subject. This is a text that is obsessed with the relentless, driving movement of desire toward death, evident from the first scene that sets in motion a series of images that link desire and death. As the play opens, Giovanni, in council with the Friar, has 'unclasped' his 'burdened soul' (I.i.13) to reveal his love for his sister Annabella. Less than overjoyed with Giovanni's choice, the Friar warns him that 'death waits on thy lust' (I.i.59) and he later gives Annabella a similar warning, telling her that when she is in hell, she will wish that 'each kiss your brother gave | Had been a dagger's point' (III.vi.27–28). At Soranzo and Annabella's wedding banquet, the Friar again reiterates a conjunction between death and desire, saying 'that marriage seldom's good, | When the bride-banquet so begins in blood' (IV.i.110–11).

The most explicit verbal connections between death and desire are, however, articulated by Giovanni and Annabella. In offering Annabella his dagger so that she might rip up his bosom to behold 'the truth' of his desire (I.ii.211), Giovanni links his dead body with his desiring body, his words resonating with those of Fernando and

Bianca in *Love's Sacrifice* who tell each other to read their hearts when they are dead as this act will reveal the name of the other carved there in '*bloody lines*'.[28] That is, by inviting Annabella to rip open his bosom in order to see his desire, Giovanni is, by implication, inviting her to see him dead. When Annabella asserts "twere fitter I were dead' (I.ii.220) in response to Giovanni's elucidation of his desire, desire and death are again conjoined, this time foreshadowing the fate of Annabella at the end of the play. As their conversation continues, the couplings between death and desire become more explicit. Giovanni tells Annabella "tis my destiny | That you must either love, or I must die' (I.ii.228–29), and they subsequently make symmetrical vows which bind death and desire to one another in the economical and deadly injunction 'Love me, or kill me' (I.ii.256, 259). While their vows set up desire and death as mutually exclusive, antithetical possibilities, as the play progresses we see that these terms are inextricably bound together and admit the possibility that to love is also to kill, at least on the part of Giovanni. They are propelled, then, to borrow a phrase from Barthes, towards an 'amorous catastrophe'; these are 'panic situations: situations without remainder, without return',[29] where the lover no longer enables the constitution of the subject but instead voids it. In this respect, the narrative of '*Tis Pity She's a Whore* offers what Cynthia Marshall might designate as an experience 'of psychic fracture or undoing'; these are experiences which, as Marshall argues in relation to a range of early modern texts, including *The Broken Heart*, stand as a 'counter force to the nascent ethos of individualism', proposed by new historicist and cultural materialist critics of which Greenblatt's *Renaissance Self-Fashioning* stands as exemplary.[30]

In '*Tis Pity She's a Whore*, one of the key ways in which death and desire are yoked is through the narrative arcs of revenge that the play explores. As the play develops, Ford details several meticulously planned revenge plots, precipitated by a failure to obtain the other, that frequently spiral beyond the control of the writer-directors of these plots. For example, in one of the play's sub-plots, Hippolita, rejected by Soranzo, plans to revenge her wronged desires by poisoning him at his wedding banquet. However, Soranzo's loyal servant Vasques intervenes and Hippolita ends up drinking the poison and dies. After she drinks from the poisoned cup Vasques proffers to her, he tells Hippolita that she is 'like a firebrand, that hath kindled others and burnt thyself' (IV.i.72–73). In his observation Vasques imagines a force that is both directed outward while at the same time consuming the self. Thus Hippolita's desire both to have and destroy Soranzo is directed back upon the self, resulting in her death. The circular, all-consuming nature of desire and revenge is also evident in the fate of Soranzo. Unable to ascertain the name of Annabella's lover, he wants to direct his violent impulse outward, threatening to 'rip up' Annabella's heart (IV.iii.53) and with his teeth 'tear the prodigious lecher [her lover] joint by joint' (IV.iii.54–55). However, Soranzo's comment that his 'soul | Runs circular in sorrow for revenge' (V.iii.260–61) suggests that the impulse he directs outward is in fact circulating within himself. In his comment that Giovanni can go to Annabella and 'glut himself in his own destruction' (V.iv.45) Soranzo clearly recognizes the deathliness that inheres within desire. But, when Giovanni kills him, it is Soranzo who becomes the next victim of the deathly, revenge-driven operation of desire. Annabella's anatomized body can also be seen as a casualty of this conjunction between desire, death and revenge. Thus Giovanni kills Annabella saying, 'Revenge is mine' (V.v.86) and announces her heart by saying that he is 'proud in the spoil | Of love and vengeance!' (V.vi.11–12). Finally, when he is stabbed by the banditti, Giovanni becomes the last victim of the deathly combination of desire and revenge. Thus, the revenge plots in *'Tis Pity She's a Whore* seem to spiral away from the control of the writer-directors, pushing the subjects and objects of desire toward deathly consequences.

Giovanni's murder of Annabella can certainly be read as a desire to revenge himself upon Soranzo. However, both his and Annabella's deaths can at the same time be read as a desire to become one, or be united with the other, tracing at a distance Barthes's desire 'to be the other, I want the other to be me, as if we were united, enclosed within the same sack of skin'.[31] The play emphasizes the solipsistic oneness of their relationship from Giovanni's initial discussion with the Friar, when he talks of himself and Annabella being 'ever one | One soul, one flesh, one love, one heart, one *all*' (I.i.33–34, emphasis in text). Thus even following her marriage to Soranzo, Giovanni asserts the 'glory | Of two united hearts like hers and mine!' (V.iii.11–12), claiming that Annabella is 'still one to me' (V.iii.8). Not only does Giovanni project their relationship into a solipsistic fantasy world of oneness, but for him this world far surpasses any other existence. So when Giovanni says that he 'would not change this minute for Elysium' (I.ii.264), and that 'My world, and all of happiness, is here, | And I'd not change it for the best to come: | A life of pleasure in Elysium' (V.iii.14–16), he suggests that their world is a self-contained paradise that exceeds the conventional pleasure zone of Elysium.

Giovanni's conception of his relationship with his sister as one of pleasure, of naturalness, contrasts sharply with attempts to regulate incest in a range of religious and secular discourses in the period, even as Wiseman notes that 'such discourses differ in the ways in which they consider incest, and therefore, the meanings assigned to incest differ between legal documents and dramatic or theatrical texts'.[32] In *'Tis Pity She's a Whore* incest is figured as the dominant obstacle to Giovanni and Annabella's relationship and they are unable to maintain feasibly their solipsistic love-world within the confines of Parma's society. Despite Florio's eagerness to domesticate and control his daughter's desire by marrying her to Soranzo (III.iv.9–23), Annabella's desire refuses to be contained by the conventional structure of a marriage alliance. Instead desire exceeds society's containing structures and ultimately manifests itself in death, killing those that uphold the law as well as those that transgress it. Indeed, upon the revelation of Giovanni and Annabella's relationship and of Annabella's death, Florio dies. In response, the Cardinal reproves Giovanni with, 'Monster of children, see what thou hast done, | Broke thy old father's heart!' (V.vi.62–63). Florio's last words 'have I lived to—' (V.vi.61) are left incomplete suggesting his unspeakable (literally) horror at what he has seen and heard. Coupled with the Cardinal's comments, Florio's dying words suggest that the articulation of incestuous desire contravenes social convention to such an extent that he is unable to continue living in the face of such a transgression: the question he commences with 'Have I lived to—' is left unformed and the act of attempting to comprehend desire is truncated by death.

Whereas Florio's death is a byproduct of Annabella and Giovanni's desires, as the narrative moves toward its climax the lovers appear inexorably driven toward death. Thus Annabella sings to Soranzo in Italian *'Che morte più dolce che morire per amore?'* (What death is sweeter than to die for love? IV.iii.59) and *'Morendo in gratia a lui, morirei senza dolore'* (Dying in favour with him I would die without pain, IV.iii.63), phrases which might stand as a brief precursor to a Wagnerian *liebestod* (love-death). In a series of comments toward the end of the play, Annabella appears to desire death; she dares Soranzo to 'strike, and strike home' (IV.iii.70), claims that she welcomes death after her meeting with the Friar (V.i.59) and encourages Giovanni to welcome the banquet which she describes as a 'harbinger of death | To you and me' (V.v.27–28). However, unlike several characters from Ford's other tragedies, including Fernando and the Duke in *Love's Sacrifice* and Penthea in *The Broken Heart*, Annabella does not commit suicide. Rather,

Giovanni, who earlier promised 'no harm' (I.ii.180), becomes her murderer. Having talked about the possibility of an afterlife where they may 'kiss one another, prate or laugh, | Or do as [they] do here' (V.v.40–41) Giovanni kisses Annabella and stabs her so as 'To save thy fame, and kill thee in a kiss' (V.v.84). In this claim he echoes Othello's 'I kissed thee ere I killed thee. No way but this: | Killing myself, to die upon a kiss' (V.ii.368–69) and Romeo's 'Thus with a kiss I die' (V.iii.120), reinforcing a strand of early modern tragic production in which death and desire are intimately conjoined. Further, when Giovanni says that he has 'killed a love' (V.v.101), the earlier imperative 'love me or kill me' is transformed into 'love me and I'll kill you'. In this moment death and desire are fused together in the stage picture of Giovanni's murder of Annabella.

In killing Annabella, Giovanni activates his own death wish. Thus, when he is stabbed he thanks Vasques, telling him that 'thou hast done for me | But what I would have else done on myself' (V.vi.97–98). As Giovanni dies he embraces death (V.vi.104–5) and once again his words offer echoes of earlier tragedies, referring the spectator to Antony's 'I will be | A bridegroom in my death, and run into't | As to a lover's bed' (V.xv.99–101) and Juliet's 'O happy dagger, | This is thy sheath! There rust and let me die' (V.iii.168–69). In Giovanni's final words, 'Where'er I go, let me enjoy this grace, | Freely to view my Annabella's face' (V.vi.106–7), he expresses a wish to be reunited with Annabella. While Giovanni's last comment can be read as an anticipated reunion, Gilles D. Monsarrat reads these lines as meaning that Giovanni can view her face, which is in heaven, from his position in hell. Thus, like 'the story of Lazarus and the rich man: one of them went to heaven and the other to hell [...] [so] they could see each other', Giovanni and Annabella will suffer 'an eternal separation'.[33] Thus Giovanni's life ends, literally embodying, among other things, the deathly desire to be at one with his sister/other/lover, a desire that may, in the theology of the play and culture, be denied him still. In Giovanni's utterance, the death of the subject here also offers the possibility of the death of desire itself through the imagined plenitude of satisfaction in the union with the other. In more starkly post-Nietzschean terms, it also offers a fantasy of the extinction of the desiring subject through the extinction of the self.

Desire's Excess

I suggested at the outset of this chapter that the conceptualization of desire in early modern culture bears striking similarities to contemporary critical and artistic production. Informed by this rich seam of production, and attentive to early modern cultural contexts, this chapter has sought to flesh out and account for the operation of desire in *'Tis Pity She's a Whore* through a consideration of anatomization and death. In the various attempts to control Annabella and Giovanni's desires, the play participates in what Catherine Belsey describes as attempts in the early modern period to make desire 'more thoroughly contained and confined within the institution of marriage, and thus brought under the control of the Law'.[34] However, Belsey's readings show that desire refuses to be contained by domestic institutions; instead it exceeds them and in the process annihilates subjects that submit to its absolute imperative. Similarly, as this chapter has shown, in *'Tis Pity She's a Whore*, as with a multitude of early modern tragedies, desire operates by exceeding structures intended to contain it and frequently destroys both the subject and object of desire. Indeed Belsey argues that '[d]esire, which is an absence, takes possession of the subject, tantalizes with an imagined omnipotence, and ultimately delivers nothing more nor less than annihilation'.[35] To desire in *'Tis Pity She's a Whore*, along with a raft of other early modern tragedies, is almost inevitably to have a fatal attraction, a conjunction that continues to be worked though, albeit in different forms, in contemporary culture. *'Tis Pity She's a Whore* stands, then, as an exemplar text of desire as a supremely 'death-driven, death-dealing and death-desiring' phenomenon, elucidating aspects of its early modern cultural moment of production and imbricated in a rhetoric of desire that seems not yet to be exhausted.[36]

Acknowledgements

My thanks are due to Julie Scanlon, Lisa Hopkins and especially to Mark Houlahan.

Notes

1   Roland Barthes, *A Lover's Discourse: Fragments*, trans. Richard Howard (New York: Hill and Wang, 1978), p. 228.
2   All references to *'Tis Pity She's a Whore* will be given in parentheses and are to the Revels edition ed. Derek Roper (Manchester: Manchester University Press, 1975).
3   All references to Shakespeare will be given in parentheses and are to William Shakespeare, *The Norton Shakespeare*, ed. by Stephen Greenblatt *et al.* (New York: Norton, 1997).
4   See, for example: Sigmund Freud, 'On the Universal Tendency to Debasement in the Sphere of Love (Contributions to the Psychology of Love II)', 1912, in *The*

Standard Edition of the Complete Works, vol. 11, ed. James Strachey (London: Hogarth, 1957), pp. 177–90; Jacques Lacan, *Écrits: A Selection*, trans. Alan Sheridan (New York: Norton, 1977); Luce Irigaray, *This Sex Which is Not One*, trans. Catherine Porter (1977; Ithaca, NY: Cornell University Press, 1985); Judith P. Butler, *Subjects of Desire: Hegelian Reflections in Twentieth-Century France* (New York: Columbia University Press, 1987); Jacques Derrida, *The Post Card: From Socrates to Freud and Beyond*, trans. Alan Bass (Chicago: University of Chicago Press, 1987); Catherine Belsey, *Desire: Love Stories in Western Culture* (Oxford: Blackwell, 1994); Jonathan Dollimore, *Death, Desire and Loss in Western Culture* (New York: Routledge, 1998).

5   Plato, *Symposium*, trans. by Walter Hamilton (London: Penguin, 1951), p. 61.

6   Barthes, *A Lover's Discourse*, p. 8.

7   Stephen Greenblatt, *Learning to Curse: Essays in Early Modern Culture* (New York: Routledge, 1990), p. 142. Greenblatt's emphasis.

8   Jonathan Sawday, *The Body Emblazoned: Dissection and the Human Body in Renaissance Culture* (London: Routledge, 1995), p. 129.

9   Sawday, *The Body Emblazoned*, p. ix.

10   Thomas Laqueur, *Making Sex: Body and Gender from the Greeks to Freud* (Cambridge, MA: Harvard University Press, 1990), p. 70.

11   Devon L. Hodges, *Renaissance Fictions of Anatomy* (Amherst, MA: University of Massachusetts Press, 1985), pp. 1–2.

12   Patricia Fumerton, ' "Secret" Arts: Elizabethan Miniatures and Sonnets', in *Representing the English Renaissance*, ed. Stephen Greenblatt (Berkeley, CA: University of California Press, 1988), pp. 93–133, p. 125.

13   Valerie Traub, *Desire and Anxiety: Circulations of Sexuality in Shakespearean Drama* (London: Routledge, 1992), p. 40.

14   Nancy Vickers, ' "The blazon of sweet beauty's best": Shakespeare's *Lucrece*', in *Shakespeare and the Question of Theory*, ed. Patricia Parker and Geoffrey Hartman (New York: Methuen, 1985), pp. 95–115, p. 96.

15   Christopher Marlowe, *Hero and Leander*, in *The Complete Poems and Translations*, ed. Stephen Orgel (London: Penguin, 1971), pp. 13–41, ll. 51–90.

16   Barthes, *A Lover's Discourse*, p. 52.

17   Denis Gauer, 'Heart and Blood: Nature and Culture in *'Tis Pity She's a Whore*', *Cahiers Elisabéthains: Late Medieval and Renaissance Studies* 31 (1987), pp. 45–57, p. 51.

18   Susan J. Wiseman, *''Tis Pity She's a Whore*: Representing the Incestuous Body', in *Renaissance Bodies: The Human Figure in English Culture c.1540–1640*, ed. Lucy Gent and Nigel Llewellyn (London: Reaktion, 1990), pp. 180–97, p. 184.

19   Lisa Hopkins, *John Ford's Political Theatre* (Manchester: Manchester University Press, 1994), p. 116.

20   Michael Neill, ' "What strange riddle's this?": Deciphering *'Tis Pity She's a Whore*', in *John Ford: Critical Re-Visions*, ed. Michael Neill (Cambridge: Cambridge University Press, 1988), pp. 153–79, p. 165.

21   Michael Ondaatje, *The English Patient* (London: Picador-Macmillan, 1993), p. 158.

22   Michael Neill, *Issues of Death: Mortality and Identity in English Renaissance Tragedy* (Oxford: Clarendon, 1997), p. 2.

23   Neill, *Issues of Death*, p. 3.

24   Barthes, *A Lover's Discourse*, pp. 218–19.

25   Jonathan Dollimore, 'Desire is Death', in *Subject and Object in Renaissance Culture*, ed. Margreta De Grazia *et al.*, Cambridge Studies in Renaissance Literature and Culture, 8 (Cambridge: Cambridge University Press, 1996), pp. 369–86, p. 375. Dollimore's emphasis.

26   Freud, *Beyond the Pleasure Principle*, 1920, in *The Standard Edition: The Complete Psychological Works of Sigmund Freud*, vol. 23, trans. James Strachey (London: Hogarth Press, 1955), pp. 1–64, p. 38. Freud's emphasis.

27   Dollimore, 'Desire is Death', p. 382.

28 Ford, *Loves Sacrifice*, in *John Fordes Dramatische Werke*, ed. W. Bang, Materialen zur Kunde des älteren Englischen Dramas, ser. 1, vol. 23 (Louvain: Uystpruyst, 1908; Vaduz: Kraus reprint, 1963) ll.1237, 1383.

29 Barthes, *A Lover's Discourse*, pp. 48–49.

30 Cynthia Marshall, *The Shattering of the Self: Violence, Subjectivity and Early Modern Texts* (Baltimore, MD: Johns Hopkins University Press, 2002), pp. 1, 2; see also pp. 138–58 for a discussion of *The Broken Heart*. See also Stephen Greenblatt, *Renaissance Self-fashioning: From More to Shakespeare* (Chicago: Chicago University Press, 1980).

31 Barthes, *A Lover's Discourse*, pp. 127–28.

32 See Wiseman, *''Tis Pity She's a Whore'* for a discussion of incest in relation to the play. For a discussion of incest in early modern culture with particular reference to drama see Richard A. McCabe, *Incest, Drama and Nature's Law 1550–1700* (Cambridge: Cambridge University Press, 1993).

33 Gilles D. Monsarrat, 'The Unity of John Ford: *'Tis Pity She's a Whore* and *Christ's Bloody Sweat'*, Studies in Philology 77 (1980), pp. 247–70, p. 269.

34 Catherine Belsey, 'Desire's Excess and the English Renaissance Theatre: *Edward II, Troilus and Cressida, Othello*', in *Erotic Politics: Desire on the Renaissance Stage*, ed. Susan Zimmerman (London: Routledge: 1992), pp. 84–102, p. 95.

35 Belsey, 'Desire's Excess', p. 88.

36 Dollimore, 'Sex and Death', *Textual Practice*, 9 (1995), 27–53, p. 27.

CHAPTER FIVE

New Directions: Identifying the Real Whore of Parma

Corinne S. Abate

Few critics can disagree with Martin Wiggins's assertion that *'Tis Pity She's a Whore* 'has been making some readers squirm for centuries'.[1] John Ford's enduring tragedy presents in conventional terms of love incestuous desire that is successfully consummated by the end of Act I. Add to that scandalous premise several vivid action sequences – including, but not limited to, an unexpected poisoning, an incorrect murder victim, an unholy pregnancy terminated, a mandate of immolation and a human heart displayed – and it is no wonder that *'Tis Pity* stands as one of the most controversial English dramas since it was first published in 1633.[2] Yet despite hundreds of years of detailed explications and scholarly examinations, rarely has anyone undertaken a sustained study of the play's title. It is clear that the 'whore' alluded to in the title refers to Annabella, the sister in the incestuous relationship, yet the play provides several other candidates who could claim this denunciation and our pity. As I shall argue, one such figure amid the unfettered, revengeful townspeople of Parma qualifies as the whore of the play more than a sister who sleeps with a brother, a wife who takes a lover while dispatching her husband on a dangerous journey, or a tutress whose very name resonates with whorishness: the dissolute town of Parma herself.

The phrase ''tis pity she's a whore' appears with no forewarning at the end of the Cardinal's speech which closes the play. It also appears inexplicably italicized. As the highest ranking male character remaining on stage, the Cardinal is attempting to wrest order and logic from the chaos that began, as the stage direction informs, with Giovanni entering, 'a heart upon his dagger',[3] and closes with numerous deaths and disturbing orders about who will be punished and who will not. The two men who have died are Soranzo and Florio. The former is killed by Giovanni in a jealous rage; the latter, due to a broken heart: in quick succession, Florio learns that his beloved children Giovanni and Annabella had a sexual relationship, that Annabella is dead, that she has been killed by her brother and that he has done this because he loved her carnally, the result of which was that she was pregnant with his child. It is no surprise that the news kills him, and he dies with a curse for Giovanni on his lips. Giovanni himself will soon be killed by Soranzo's loyal servant Vasques, who has hit-men on retainer for just such an occasion. Soon after Putana, Annabella's governess, is ordered by the Cardinal to be dragged outside the city limits and burned alive; she has already been bound and blinded at Vasques's behest because she condoned the incestuous relationship and tried to hide the resulting pregnancy from Soranzo, Vasques's master and Annabella's husband. Another husband, Richardetto, finally reveals his true identity (he has been posing as a physician throughout the play), and although eager to speak with his friend Donado about all that has passed between them and their kin, is silenced by the Cardinal who then closes the action with the following speech:

> We shall have time
> To talk at large of all; but never yet
> Incest and murder have so strangely met.
> Of one so young, so rich in Nature's store,
> Who could not say, *'Tis pity she's a whore?*
>
> (V.vi.155–159)

It is interesting that the phrase appears italicized, as if it were a title, self-referencing the very play that has just been performed. As an aphoristic assessment of the play's plot, it is inaccurate. Nor does it fully encapsulate all of the revelations that occur at Soranzo's birthday banquet. Two recent authoritative editions in which the line appears italicized are Marion Lomax's for Oxford's *World's Classics* series and Derek Roper's for The Revels. Roper attempts to explain the anomaly:

> I suspect Ford's title was a catch-phrase: it occurs in *Jackson's Recantation* (1674), p. 20, where it is applied to the beautiful mistress of a highwayman and italicized as though a quotation or common saying. But the allusion may be to the play itself, which was revived at the Restoration.[4]

Several other modern editors have quietly emended the text and in their editions the phrase appears unitalicized. Bernard Beckerman and N.W. Bawcutt do not italicize it, nor do they gloss Ford's explanation of it in his dedicatory epistle to John Mordaunt.[5] Ford writes, 'The gravity of the subject may easily excuse the lightness of the title: otherwise I had been a severe judge against mine own guilt' (ll. 15–17). Even though Wiggins also does not italicize the phrase in his New Mermaids edition, he does explicate Ford's epistolary allusion, suggesting that the 'lightness' refers not to frivolity, which is the traditional reading of Ford's word choice, but to amoral sexual conduct. For Wiggins, Ford seems to be saying he 'would not have approved the use of a licentious title in a less serious play' (p. 43, n).

Several critics have noted that another complication concerning the title is the character who utters it. The Cardinal is a morally compromised man amid this morally compromised society, and his blithe condemnation of Annabella expresses, as Thelma Greenfield describes, 'contradictory insight and callousness'.[6] Ronald Huebert reminds us that the final speech in any English Renaissance play is designed to 'put matters to rest'; the Cardinal's 'remarkably pointless question' instead 'invites the emotional impact of the play to continue'.[7] Mark Stavig asserts that the title 'is surely a deliberate assault on tender Puritan moral sensibilities', and speculates that those 'deliberately outrageous' aspects of Ford's plays 'must have appealed to people who were becoming tired of the moralistic preaching of the Puritans'.[8] Because the Cardinal does little to mitigate the devastation that befalls this town, Wiggins adduces that 'we cannot expect to be able to say, with the Cardinal, "'Tis pity she's a whore" and leave the theatre confident in the victory of society over incestuous deviance' (p. 31).

The Cardinal, then, is not viewed as favourably as he might assume. Although he closes the play with the confidence of a highly positioned man of the cloth, he has demonstrated unscrupulous behaviour on at least two prior occasions. The first is when earlier in the play the Cardinal unhesitatingly takes Grimaldi into the Church's protection after he accidentally murders Bergetto, citing his aristocratic standing as obvious justification for this action. Donado, uncle to the unintended victim, is stunned: 'Is this a churchman's voice? Dwells Justice here?' (III.vi.63). Florio answers him, 'Justice is fled to Heaven and comes no nearer' (64). He then cites the futility in pursuing the matter further – 'there's no help in this, | When cardinals think murder's not amiss' (67–68) – and ends by voicing the silent prayer for eventual justice that resides in all of those (and there must have been many in the audience) who have been treated unfairly by those in power: 'Heaven will judge them for 't another day' (70). At the very least, spectators would have been familiar with what Clifford Leech memorably describes as the 'ecclesiastical partiality'[9] that Grimaldi receives due entirely to his noble birth, and would ruefully acknowledge that their only recourse is to hope that heaven will one day mete out parity in compensation for their quotidian disparity. Then, just before the play ends, the Cardinal confiscates 'all the gold and jewels, or whatsoever' (148) for the Pope's personal use. Laurel Amtower argues that

> the irony cannot be mistaken: Annabella may be condemned a "whore" by the cardinal who dismisses her, yet the Catholic church itself – the "Whore of Babylon" – is deemed the same by Protestant critics. Indeed, the framing perspective of the title thus draws attention to the implication of incest within the role of the Catholic religion in the work overall.[10]

Bruce Boehrer finds that the Cardinal's closing couplet 'smacks of the worst sort of glibness',[11] and may, in fact, only foment sympathy for Annabella given that she repented, was blessed by the Friar, and yet is still vilified by another member of that very Church who thinks only of his own needs and that of his superior in the very moment a town is mourning so many lost souls and lives.

For me, the form in which the words appear is less important than the appearance of the words themselves. As Lisa Hopkins notes, the phrase, italicized or not, has 'strikingly little reference to the audience's fundamental experiences' of the play.[12] This has not always been the view held by critics who seem satisfied that the play ends on those words. Roper reproduces excerpts from two historical critics of the play, Gerard Langbaine and David Erskine Baker. Writing in 1691, Langbaine opines that Ford 'paint[ed] the incestuous Love between *Giovanni* and his Sister *Annabella* in too beautiful Colours'. Baker agrees and almost 70 years after Langbaine adds that

> the author himself seems by his title to have been aware of this objection, and conscious that he had rendered the last-mentioned character, notwithstanding all her faults, so very lovely, that every auditor would naturally cry out to himself, *'Tis Pity she's a Whore.*[13]

It seems that Baker is confident that all readers and spectators view the play the same way; therefore, because the audience would give Annabella undue sympathy, the title and final line of the play work to remind them of their obligations to condemn her actions and discourage any sympathy they may have incorrectly engendered towards her.

Rather, closing the play with a pointed reference to Annabella – despite the fact that she is deemed a whore – acts instead to buoy her in the minds of the audience members who would not necessarily side with the Cardinal and conclude that Annabella alone bears the censure of this forbidden consummation. As Lomax reminds us,

> Giovanni instigated the affair, but it is Annabella, the woman who slighted the Cardinal by rejecting the murderer Grimaldi, shamed the immoral Soranzo, and scandalized society by daring to love the best of an unsuitable bunch of suitors, who receives the Cardinal's final condemnation, although there is no indication that the audience is encouraged to agree with him.[14]

Even the most enthusiastic misogynist must pause when he recalls that the last we see of Annabella is when her brother is holding her heart aloft for the men of the town to behold. Surely they shudder when they learn that Giovanni's public display occurs while he calmly reports that first 'this dagger's point ploughed up | Her fruitful womb' (V.vi.31–32) in a sadistic abortion.[15] The Cardinal does cite 'incest and murder' in his closing speech, which are clear references to Giovanni's behaviour, but they refer to what Giovanni has committed and do not criticize him personally or pass judgement on his fallen stature in society as does the female-specific epithet 'whore'. Moreover, the acts of incest and murder are not condemned; the Cardinal observes merely that 'never' have the two 'so strangely met'. This stands in pointed opposition to the final line which alludes to a particular individual, Annabella, denounces her actions (''tis pity') and concludes unquestioningly that she is a 'whore' even though she had sincerely repented by the end of Act III.

There is yet another level of complexity concerning the play's title and final line: its attribution. In her probing examination of the appearance of the word 'whore' throughout the plays of Shakespeare, Kay Stanton notes that it is employed as a 'male-initiated inscription onto the female as scapegoat'.[16] Thus, it is logical to assume that the Cardinal is bestowing his pity and the epithet of whore on Annabella alone. However, there are two other female characters who qualify to be so labelled. The most obvious, perhaps, is Putana, whose very name means whore and whose speech acts confirm her unscrupulous *mores*. When Annabella gushes to her tutress in forbidden post-coital bliss, 'O guardian, what a paradise of joy | Have I passed over!' (II.i.43–44), Putana bawdily corrects her with, 'Nay, what a paradise of joy you have passed under!' (45). She then declares that any woman should pursue sleeping with anyone she desires regardless of blood ties: 'if a young wench feel the fit upon | her, let her take anybody, father or brother, all is one' (48–49). Putana vows to keep the siblings' affair a secret even while she encourages Donado into believing that she is promoting his nephew Bergetto's suit with Annabella: 'Truly, I do commend him to her every night before | her first sleep, because I would have her dream of him' (II.vi.14–15). No doubt Donado is also compensating Putana for the pains she is supposedly taking on his behalf.

But Putana's swagger soon wavers when she discovers that Annabella is pregnant with Giovanni's child. It is a distraught Putana who enters in III.iii, bemoaning to Giovanni, 'O sir, we are all undone, quite undone, utterly undone, | and shamed forever; your sister, O your sister!' (1–2). She goes on to curse 'that ever I was born to see this day!' (4) and concludes despondently, ''tis | too late to repent, now Heaven help us!' (8). It is important to note that she includes herself in what is happening, stating 'we' are all undone and pleading to heaven to help all of 'us'. It is her own inevitable damnation of which she is convinced, and that may prompt her to implement Giovanni's plan to keep Richardetto – Hippolita's estranged husband who has returned to town pretending to be a physician – away from Annabella. It may even be her own persuasive tongue that leads him to misdiagnose Annabella's condition (or, his utter lack of medical experience may have taken care of that small point) as 'a fullness of her blood' (III.iv.8). Sadly, Putana's mouth is also the same vehicle by which the whole affair is unwittingly revealed, and this is due entirely to her concern for her erstwhile charge. Putana enters IV.iii crying because she has witnessed Soranzo's cruelty towards Annabella when he discovers that his new bride is pregnant by another man. She asks Vasques if Soranzo is often this abusive. He suggests that the only way she can save Annabella is to reveal the identity of her lover. If she supplies a name, Putana will 'both relieve her present discomforts, pacify my | lord, and gain yourself everlasting love and preferment' (202–03). Vasques taps into her fear that her soul is damned as well as her worries concerning Annabella's happiness and welfare; she is ready to acquiesce. Once he promises not only to protect her but reward her too – sealing it with that harbinger of deceit throughout all of literature, 'trust | me' (210–11) – Putana gives up Giovanni. Vasques asks why he should believe her; she incriminates herself further with 'I have known their dealings too long to belie | them now' (IV.iii.222–23). With that admission of collusion, she sets into motion Vasques and Soranzo's plans for revenge and her own unexpected and, I would suggest unwarranted, demise.

Hippolita, too, experiences a similar progression from confidence to painful and unforeseen death, also through Vasques's machinations and forsworn promises. Hippolita first appears in II.ii, wearing a widow's black dress and cursing Soranzo for pursuing Annabella in marriage when she assumed he would be marrying her. Her compromised morals are evident when she admits that she was having an affair with Soranzo while still married to Richardetto and that further, she arranged for what she hoped would be her husband's demise by sending him on a dangerous journey to Ligorne to retrieve her niece. This, then, would open the way for her to marry Soranzo, who made a 'vow | When he [Richardetto] should die to marry me' (72–73). That is why she is there, pointedly reminding Soranzo of their affair, his promises, and 'the grossness | Of my abuses' (II.ii.47–48). Stanton importantly notes that the term 'whore' can be applied to any woman, usually by a man, as a reaction to her attempts, successful or otherwise, to take control of her own sexuality (98–99). Hippolita did just that when she took Soranzo as her lover. Now she discovers that he is arranging to marry Annabella instead, whom she superciliously calls 'Madam Merchant' (49) and she is baffled that he would perjure himself this way: 'forget'st thy vows, and leav'st me to my shame' (83). Unsuccessful in his attempts to mollify her, Soranzo correctly points out that any prior contract between them was 'wicked and unlawful' (87) since she was still married to Richardetto at the time, a man 'so noble in his quality, condition, | Learning, behaviour, entertainment, love' (93–94). He dismisses her with a scornful 'Learn to repent and die; for by my honour | I hate thee and thy lust; you have been too foul' (100–1), leaving Vasques alone with the stunned and spurned Hippolita to collaborate on a plan for revenge.

Clearly, Hippolita has learned nothing from her dealings with Soranzo as she quickly enters into a contract with Vasques that is almost identical to the one Soranzo broke moments earlier. If Vasques conspires with Hippolita in her plans to take revenge on Soranzo for wronging her, then Hippolita will make Vasques 'lord of me and mine estate' (155). The scene ends with Vasques vowing to 'be a special actor therein, but never disclose it till it be | effected'

(161–162) and Hippolita deliciously imagining that her 'revenge shall sweeten what my griefs have tasted' (166). In III.viii we see how thorough Vasques is in his duplicity. In this short scene, he reports to Hippolita that Soranzo and Annabella are engaged to be married two days hence. She wishes his wedding day were sooner so she could 'send him to his last and lasting sleep' (5). She preens to her presumed co-conspirator, 'Vasques, thou shalt see, I'll do it bravely' (6). Hippolita's victory, of course, is short-lived and when she unmasks herself at Annabella and Soranzo's wedding feast in IV.i it is she who dies, not Soranzo. Vasques, ever the loyal servant, switches the cup of poison, stating 'know now, mistress she-devil, your own mischievous | treachery hath killed you' (68–69), and ends with the insult, 'I must not marry you' (69). All of the wedding guests are delighted with Vasques's deception, unanimously declaring it 'wonderful justice' (88), and Florio queries if there has ever been 'so vile a creature?' (101). Unlike Putana, Hippolita is allowed a final speech in which she presciently describes Soranzo's future, cursing him with 'May'st thou live | To father bastards' (97–98) and hoping that Annabella's 'womb bring forth | Monsters' (98–99). But her demise, like Putana's, is disproportionate to her crime. She is guilty of attempted murder and is put to death by Vasques who, by the end of the play, will have in fact succeeded in torturing one person and killing several more. His punishment will not be death but exile: the Cardinal will order Vasques to leave Italy. There seems to be nothing approaching 'wonderful justice' in any of this.

The same can be said for Annabella, whose licentious pursuits end with her death at the hands of her brother/lover Giovanni, who disembowels her. Although Giovanni is passionate throughout his opening conversation with the Friar, having 'unclasped my burdened soul' (I.i.13) by declaring his unnatural love for his sister Annabella, nothing presages or justifies the violence he will inflict on her. When the siblings see one another in the next scene, Annabella hardly recognizes her brother, so tormented is he by his feelings for her. She asks Putana 'what blessed shape | Of some celestial creature now appears?' (I.ii.131–32). Putana confirms it is Giovanni not once but twice, yet Annabella resists this identification, stating 'Sure 'tis not he: this is some woeful thing | Wrapped up in grief, some shadow of a man' (136–37).[17] Either because she is so shaken by her brother's altered appearance or because she is embarrassed about her own feelings towards him, Annabella's speech acts suggest that she does not rush into Giovanni's arms once Putana leaves. While there are no stage directions describing her actions, Annabella does not seem to acquiesce when Giovanni asks her to 'lend your hand, let's walk together. | I hope you need not blush to walk with me' (176–77). Annabella then asks, 'How's this?' (179), which implies that she has taken up some position *near* him but has not extended her hand. That would explain why Giovanni follows with 'Faith, I mean no harm' (180). It does not take long for Giovanni to reveal his desire for Annabella, and he offers the following reassurance:

> I have asked counsel of the holy Church,
> Who tells me I may love you, and 'tis just
> That since I may, I should; and will, yes will.
>
> (241–43)

While it is true that Bonaventura did give Giovanni permission – 'Yes, you may love, fair son' (I.i.20) – he also made it absolutely clear throughout I.i that his permission was not proffered with Annabella in mind. The Friar even urges Giovanni to 'Leave her, and take thy choice, 'tis much less sin' (62), which is rarely a position on pre-marital sex that the Catholic Church has endorsed then or now. It is at this moment, according to Leech, that Giovanni's 'wooing becomes seduction' (59). Assured by her brother that a man of the cloth has condoned their feelings, Annabella resists no longer and confesses that 'what thou hast urged, | My captive heart had long ago resolved' (245–46). The siblings drop to their knees and exchange forbidden oaths before hurriedly leaving to consummate their desires.[18]

Scholars rarely note that Giovanni lies to Annabella in order to sleep with her, just as Soranzo lied to Hippolita about marrying her and Vasques lied to Putana about protecting her.[19] For Wiggins, the issue comes down to performative matters: 'it depends on the characterization of Giovanni whether it is a deliberate lie or a tendentious refashioning of the truth by someone who honestly believes in the power of human reason to change reality' (p. 14). Boehrer contends that 'Giovanni has of course not told the truth, but neither has he violated it completely'; therefore, 'the lie to Annabella is both nonexistent and double' (p. 356). While it cannot be denied that Annabella is eager to sleep with her brother and is not coerced to enter into a sexual relationship with him, she clearly does so under false pretences. This is an important point because, of Florio's two children, it is Annabella more than her brother who apprehends their requisite roles in society to strengthen family lines and assets and to continue them by procreating with someone other than each other. Dorothy Farr describes Annabella as a 'realist', and 'while her deepest instincts prompt her to respond to Giovanni's love, she understands, with a clarity he will not permit himself, the facts of their predicament' because of 'the breeding she has received as the daughter of an important family'.[20] Surprisingly, it is Giovanni himself who will remind Annabella of this familial duty. During their post-coital pillow talk, he says 'You must be married, mistress' (II.i.22). Annabella wants to deny the painful reality – she would rather choose her brother as the man to marry, opining 'how all suitors seem | To my eyes hateful' (29–30) – but she knows that is impossible. She then vows to stay faithful to Giovanni even though she is conscripted to marry another. When Giovanni leaves to return to the Friar for an undisclosed period of time, Annabella soliloquizes, 'Go where thou wilt, in mind I'll keep thee here, | And where thou art, I know I shall be there' (39–40). She says only that they will be joined mentally and emotionally; Annabella knows, even if Giovanni wants to deny it, that she must marry someone else.

Ironically, Giovanni seems to express more concern over Annabella's marital status than Florio, whose reminders throughout the play of Annabella's filial duty are constant but not suffocating. Although he makes his preference for Soranzo clear, at no point does Florio force Annabella to choose a mate.[21] For example, when Donado is making a case for his nephew Bergetto to marry Annabella, Florio informs him that 'I would not have her marry wealth, but love, | And if she like your nephew, let him have her' (I.iii.11–12). Florio will later commend Annabella for successfully shaking 'the fool [Bergetto] off' (II.vi.125), and Donado is so grateful for Annabella's direct dealings in response to his nephew's buffoonery that he leaves a costly jewel with Annabella in honour of her forthcoming marriage. Florio takes the opportunity to remind her that Soranzo 'is the man I only like: | Look on him, Annabella!' (127–128), but he provides no further mandates. It is not unusual for Ford to depict fathers who allow their daughters this level of agency; one year later, Ford's historical drama *Perkin Warbeck* would be published (like'*Tis Pity*, its date of composition is in dispute). In that play, another understanding and amenable father, Huntly, provides this same enviable space for his daughter Katherine.[22] She chooses to marry the title character and stand by him during his disgraceful fall from public approval, even declaring herself forever a widow after he is executed. Wiggins correctly notes that in *'Tis Pity* 'the only excessive pressure on Annabella comes from the Friar and his alarming account of eternal torment' (p. 22) in III.vi, a powerful scene in which the Friar details in descriptive and unflinching terms what happens to those souls who do not repent for their sins (III.vi.7–23). He even suggests that Giovanni would eventually turn on Annabella for sleeping with him:

Then you will wish each kiss your brother gave
Had been a dagger's point; then you shall hear
How he will cry, 'O would my wicked sister
Had first been damned, when she did yield to lust!'

(27–30)

This is the same man of the cloth that Annabella believes endorsed
her relationship with Giovanni in the first place. Now he is urging
her to repent and predicting that Giovanni will one day abandon
her. Given what Giovanni has led her to believe, it is logical that
Annabella unhesitatingly follows the Friar's recommendation: she
resolves to marry Soranzo, much to her father's delight and her
brother's opprobrium.[23]

In fact, it is Annabella herself, not her father, who causes the
wedding date to be brought forward. She faints at the end of III.ii
because, as is revealed in the next scene, she is pregnant with
Giovanni's child. Florio sends Richardetto to examine Annabella,
and in III.iv he reports to Florio that 'Her sickness is a fullness of her
blood' (8), which is an allusion to Annabella's sexual appetite
awakening. Of course he is correct but not in the way he imagines.
Florio nevertheless catches Richardetto's implication and orders that
the wedding be set 'within these few days' (10), an alteration to the
plan that Annabella does not resist.[24] It is only Giovanni once again
who refuses to acknowledge that reality has impinged upon his
dreams. Annabella finds herself imprisoned in her chamber in V.i.
She is now completely repentant and writes a letter to her erstwhile
lover Giovanni. In it, as she tells the Friar, she alerts Giovanni that
she now 'blush[es] at what hath passed' between them (V.i.51) and
encourages him to repent as well. The Friar delivers the letter to
Giovanni, but he does not accept it. Giovanni acknowledges that the
handwriting is his sister's, but that is the only aspect of the letter he
confirms. He ardently disagrees with Annabella's written warning
that their love affair has been discovered – 'The devil we are! which
way is 't possible?' (V.iii.37) – and refuses to believe she has repented
voluntarily. Instead, he accuses the Friar of writing the letter,
sneering that it 'is your peevish chattering, weak old man' (40).
Having been ignored and insulted for the last time, the Friar takes
his leave of Giovanni, of Soranzo's obvious plot to entrap him and
of the diseased town of Parma for good, promising Giovanni that
'the wildness of thy fate draws to an end, | To a bad, fearful end'
(64–65). When the Friar leaves, according to Stavig, 'the symbol of
true religion leaves the city, corruption and hypocrisy go
unchallenged, and the powerful Cardinal is made a kind of symbol

of the society's venality'.[25] Now alone on stage both literally and spiritually, Giovanni closes the scene by chiding his soul to 'Be all a man' (74) and vowing that 'with me they all shall perish' (79). Not long after this soliloquy, Giovanni will appear with Annabella's heart impaled on the end of his dagger. He admits that he pillaged it from her body and that his own heart is 'entombed' (27) within hers. Moments later, the whole affair is revealed: Giovanni is dead, as is his father and Soranzo, and the Cardinal closes the drama, 'almost flippantly belying the complexity of the tragic situation with his final judgmental quip' as Larry Champion pointedly describes,[26] censuring Annabella as the whore alluded to in the title of the play.

All three townswomen, whether by verbally endorsing sexual independence or actively orchestrating adulterous or unlawful lovers to enter their beds, die for their pursuits. Yet despite their fallen moral standings, Putana, Hippolita and Annabella come to ends that I contend are unwarranted by and disproportionate to their given crimes. Collectively, they find themselves poisoned, dismembered, burned and imprisoned because the men in their lives mislead them, abandon them, or double-cross them. Vasques coaxes Putana into revealing Giovanni's identity with assurances that she will be protected and rewarded. Immediately upon receiving that coveted information he orders the Banditti 'take me this old | damnable hag, gag her instantly, and put out her eyes' (IV.iii.226–27). When it is clear that the Banditti are not moving fast enough for his satisfaction, he gags Putana himself, meanly declaring, 'I'll help your old | gums, you toad-bellied bitch!' (231–232). Vasques is still not done: if she complains, the Banditti are ordered to 'slit her nose' (234) as well. In the play's final scene, Vasques readily reveals to the Cardinal that he ordered Putana to be bound, gagged and have her eyes plucked out. The Cardinal does not balk at this, and enacts what Lomax observes is the 'undercurrent of violence running just below its [Parma's] respectable surface' (p. xvii) by proclaiming Putana to be 'chief in these effects' (V.vi.132). Therefore, he determines that she deserves the most severe punishment 'for example's sake' (134), which is 'to be burnt to ashes' (135). He then mandates that this immolation should occur 'out of the city' (134), which appears to compromise his hope that burning her would be an example to deter similar behaviour in others. Donado rejoices inexplicably with ''Tis most just' (135); perhaps he is recalling how Putana duped him into thinking that she was helping his nephew Bergetto win Annabella's hand. Nevertheless, Putana's roles as governess and nursemaid do not tally to make her 'chief' in this affair, and they certainly do not justify the cruelty she experiences at the hands of a fellow servant and member of the Church.

Hippolita, as well, suffers public humiliation, double-crossing and invectives on her deathbed. It cannot be denied that she hoped the trip to retrieve Philotis would kill her husband, but she did not arrange for anything more concrete to occur. Richardetto does not die and, as he reveals in a conversation with his niece in II.iii, he has retaliated by deliberately misleading Hippolita into thinking he has perished – 'as I have caused it to be rumoured out' (10) – so he can return to Parma and watch Philotis's 'wanton aunt in her lascivious riots' (7). Hippolita devised this scheme in the first place so she could be free to marry Soranzo, who abandons her in favour of pursuing Annabella. Then it is Vasques's turn: he does not merely hand her the poisoned cup instead of Soranzo, but further takes it upon himself to denigrate her publicly. He describes Hippolita as being 'like a firebrand, that hath | kindled others and burnt thyself' (IV.i.72–73), and calls her a 'thing of malice' (77) and a 'vile woman' (86). Of all of Hippolita's unscrupulous plans – arranging for the death of her husband, killing Soranzo for abandoning her and marrying Vasques in gratitude – not one of them actually materializes. In fact, she accomplishes nothing more than cuckolding her husband which, while not admirable, certainly does not justify being poisoned in public while the assembled townspeople chant their approval. She hopes that Richardetto dies; he does not. She presumes that Soranzo will marry her; he decides not to. She contracts Vasques to poison Soranzo; he poisons her instead. This is in stark contrast to Vasques's plans, all of which he successfully completes. Vasques initiates a quarrel with Grimaldi, which prompts him to seek his revenge on Soranzo; that is when Grimaldi accidentally kills Bergetto instead. In quick succession Vasques kills Hippolita, maims and tortures Putana, imprisons Annabella and murders Giovanni. His punishment, meted out by the Cardinal – that 'protector of well-born criminals' as Roper quips (p. lv) – is to be exiled from Italy. Vasques leaves, life intact, haughtily crowing, 'I rejoice that a | Spaniard outwent an Italian in revenge' (V.vi.145–46).

Then there is Annabella, whose brother initially misrepresents the Friar's words in order to sleep with her, and ultimately ignores her words so as to kill her. It has been Annabella throughout this play, not Giovanni, who has keenly felt the palpable conflict between her personal desire and familial duties, and she finally cedes to the latter. When brother and sister meet for the last time in V.v, Giovanni is unremitting in judging Annabella, calling her 'a faithless sister' (V.v.9) and denouncing her actions as filled with 'malice' and 'treachery' (10). He refuses to acknowledge that she has any commitment that supersedes the one they have made to each other and he resists repenting because he does not regret his love for her. Giovanni kisses Annabella one last time and, reminiscent of Othello, stabs his beloved. It is no surprise that Annabella, like Desdemona before her, devotes her last breath to the man she loves, calling on heaven for mercy: 'farewell, | Brother, unkind unkind – mercy, great Heaven! – O – O!' (92–93). As with Hippolita, Annabella's sexual preferences are inappropriate and she should not, as Putana declares, sleep with her brother or any man to whom she is related simply because she finds herself attracted to them. Nevertheless, Annabella's crime does not warrant being stabbed to death, having her heart removed and her womb mutilated, all after repenting and having that repentance endorsed and blessed by the Friar.

There is one other female character in the play – the only one who remains alive in fact – and that is Philotis. Although a minor participant in the affairs of Parma, she nevertheless deserves some attention.[27] Philotis begins as little more than a plot device: it is she whom Richardetto travels to Ligorne to retrieve, thus affording Hippolita the opportunity to plan a future with Soranzo. When she arrives in Parma she is presented to Florio as 'a maid, for song | And music, one perhaps will give content' (II.i.66–67). Philotis is warmly received into his house. Now it is her uncle's turn to use Philotis for his own means: in II.iii, Richardetto interrogates her on the subject of Annabella's marital affairs. Once she laconically confirms that Florio prefers that Annabella should marry Soranzo, Philotis is dismissed so that Richardetto can scheme with Grimaldi as to how to kill Soranzo. Both men would benefit from his death: Grimaldi would have dispatched a rival for Annabella's hand, and Richardetto would have killed the man who slept with his wife. By the time she returns to the stage in III.v, Philotis has become the object of Bergetto's affection; now she is used as a site of recovery from Annabella's (albeit justified) dismissal of his suit in II.vi. Bergetto suddenly wants to marry Philotis instead; Richardetto does not object. Indeed, the only thing he objects to is Bergetto kissing Philotis, and the scene ends with Richardetto chastising Bergetto to check his passion until they are married: 'when we have done what's fit to do, | Then you may kiss your fill, and bed her too' (50–51). Philotis has no lines here. On their way to the Friar's cell in III.vii, Grimaldi fatally stabs Bergetto, whom he mistook for Soranzo. In the wake of her betrothed's slaying, Ford provides Philotis with merely three lines that amount to little more than commentary for those audience members sitting in seats located some distance from the stage: 'What ails my love?' (10), 'Alas, some villain has slain my love!' (13), 'O, he is dead!' (34). It was Richardetto of course who, as the physician, supplied Grimaldi with the poison for his rapier, so in effect he is responsible for the death of her fiancé and her future plans to be a wife. In IV.i Philotis's name is listed among those present for Soranzo and Annabella's wedding feast, which means she also witnesses her aunt's death, but she has no lines. It is not until the next scene that she will once again speak, and it is to acquiesce, with little protest, to her uncle's pronouncement that she is to become a nun.

Immediately following Hippolita's demise, Richardetto announces his plans to send Philotis away from Parma. He poignantly describes his wife's public poisoning as making her 'more wretched in her shame | Than in her wrongs to me' (IV.ii.1–2) and he accurately predicts that 'vengeance hover[s]' (4) over Soranzo and the town. Therefore, 'in tender love and pity of your youth' (14) he advises Philotis that she 'should free your years | From hazard of these woes' (15–16) and 'vow your soul | In holiness a holy votaress' (17–18). No doubt Philotis is stunned and more than a bit angry when she asks, 'Uncle, shall I resolve to be a nun?' (22). He confirms this decision and pathetically asks her 'in your hourly prayers | Remember me, your poor unhappy uncle' (23–24). Philotis does not debate the point further, and departs, bidding farewell both to 'worldly thoughts' (29) and men, yielding instead to 'chaste vows' (30). Bawcutt points out that 'All the love-affairs in the play end in disaster, including the comparatively innocent one between Bergetto and Philotis, and it would even be possible to read the play as a series of warnings against the destructive effects of passion' (p. xv). Whatever the reason, Philotis agrees to leave Parma saying nothing further on the matter. Once again, a woman comes to an unexpected end in this play.

Philotis's exit is certainly unforeseen, but her future as a nun does not wholly separate her from the other sexualized women in the play. That is, Putana, Hippolita and Annabella all became whores because they stayed in Parma. There is an implication (and Bawcutt's observation above certainly speaks to this) that if Philotis were to remain in Parmesan society, especially given that her chosen mate has recently been killed, she too would inevitably become a whore. Parma is a city inscribed as promoting 'unbridled individualism',[28] to employ G. F. Sensabaugh's apt description, so although Philotis has escaped a direct connection with the term whore, she is always already associated with that invective. 'All women', suggests Laurie Finke, 'are objects, defined solely by their sexuality[;] they are also all potentially sexual threats because they are all potentially false lovers'. The play's hostility towards female sexuality, then, reduces 'all women to whores or potential whores'.[29] Moreover, while Ford's audience would not have condoned Putana's assertion that women should pursue incestuous relationships, Annabella's participation in such a relationship and Hippolita's orchestration of a plan to marry her lover after sending her husband on a journey she hoped would kill him, they would not necessarily have approved of Philotis's forced vocation as a nun either. As I have argued elsewhere, chosen celibacy is a means by which women control their sexuality separately from men.[30] Therefore, women who remain virgins not only abstain from society's expectations that they will marry and procreate but, as Theodora Jankowski argues, 'their virgin condition marked them, paradoxically, as "deviant" as well'.[31] Thus, by not participating in patriarchally-determined roles, women could be perceived as, at the very least, irresponsible and at the very worst dangerous and subversive to the male-constructed social order.

This is why I have nominated the post-lapsarian city of Parma as the only whore to which the title should refer. She establishes a slatternly ethos that allows for the creation of a whorish dystopia, exposing her inhabitants to what Martin Butler describes as a lifestyle of 'radical incoherence',[32] and causing catastrophic and widespread destruction of family lines, personal lives and public reputations. Stanton concludes that the appearance of the word 'whore' in the plays of Shakespeare (45 times, and that number refers only to the singular form of the word) 'demonstrates that Shakespeare considered men's failure to accommodate themselves to the idea of female sexual choice and integrity to be particularly instrumental in war, violence, and, ultimately, societal suicide' (p. 98). This is precisely what occurs in Ford's Parma, a place filled with reprehensible and violent individuals who dissemble and torture fellow townspeople – mostly women – and usually get away with it. Parma can be read as a site marked by 'a code of violence', according to Verna Foster, which 'suggests that the revenge ethic is ingrained in the society itself. The decision to avenge one's honour by murder is apparently almost reflexive'.[33] The younger generation of Parmesan men has been decimated, as Bergetto, Giovanni and Soranzo all die at the sword points of others even when, as in the case of Bergetto, wholly undeservedly. The women, as this chapter has detailed, are either dead or have been forced to leave town and thus avoid becoming ensnared in the endless revenge plots Parma's decadence encourages. The elder townsmen are also afflicted by the reckless sexual proclivities of the young people. Florio dies with the full and cruel knowledge that his children slept together and that one

stabbed and dismembered the other.[34] Donado's family line is, like
Florio's, terminated due to the untimely and unkind death of his
nephew Bergetto. Richardetto, too, is bereft, as his family line will
also die out because his one living relation, Philotis, has had her soul
and her sexuality encaved in a convent in Cremona. And those
visiting the town have already left (the Friar, in response to
Giovanni's assiduous refusal to repent) or will be leaving soon either
because they have no further business to conduct (Grimaldi, who
will presumably return to Rome in the Cardinal's company) or are
required to (Vasques, who is ordered to leave not just Parma but all
of Italy).

Given the deplorable and unceasing acts of revenge that occur
within the town limits, an incestuous affair between a brother and
sister is the least of Parma's woes. Amtower even implicates the
town herself as being responsible for their relationship in the first
place because Parma is so morally inadequate;

> thus two potentially "savable" individuals find themselves
> contaminated by a surrounding culture whose spiritual
> depravity prevents the individual from achieving spiritual
> transcendence on his or her own. In turning toward each
> other, Annabella and Giovanni each provide for the other the
> only other 'good' member of society.[35]

Nor is there any indication, given that the play ends on a question
posed by a representative of an institution 'grossly stained by crime
and impropriety', as Champion describes it,[36] that these various
deaths – spiritual, familial, corporeal – will cleanse the city and
ensure for it a morally upstanding future. Parma has failed to remind
her townsmen and women alike of their duties to society at large,
which in turn has allowed these private acts of carnal perversion,
marital infidelities and ugly revenges to occur. It is Parma, therefore,
whose women are not faithful in their marriages, whose men are
killed by outsiders, whose older generation is left to mourn the
tattered remains of their families, and whose Church figures are
ineffectual leaders, that is the real whore of the play. Her past
neglect and bleak future prospects dictate that our pity should lie
with her above all others.

Notes

1   John Ford,*'Tis Pity She's a Whore*, ed. Martin Wiggins (London: A&C Black,
     2003), p. 11.

2   While there is no dispute surrounding *'Tis Pity*'s year of publication, there is little consensus as to when it was actually written. Many accept the period of 1629–33; Derek Roper helpfully details differing opinions on the matter in the Introduction for his edition of the play (London: Methuen & Co., 1975), pp. xxxvii–xli. He is one of several critics to suggest that 'it may quite easily have been a Jacobean play in fact as well as in spirit' (p. xli).

3   *'Tis Pity She's a Whore*, ed. Derek Roper (London: Methuen & Co., 1975), V.vi.9 sd. All further quotations from the play will be taken from this edition and reference will be given in the text.

4   *'Tis Pity She's a Whore*, ed. Derek Roper, p. 4, n.16.

5   *Five Plays of the English Renaissance*, ed. Bernard Beckerman (New York: Penguin Books, 1993); *'Tis Pity She's a Whore*, ed. N.W. Bawcutt (Lincoln, NE: University of Nebraska Press, 1966).

6   Thelma N. Greenfield, 'John Ford's Tragedy: The Challenge of Re-Engagement', in *"Concord in Discord": The Plays of John Ford, 1586–1986*, ed. Donald K. Anderson (New York: AMS Press, 1986), pp. 1–26, p. 20.

7   Ronald Huebert, *John Ford: Baroque English Dramatist* (Montreal: McGill-Queen's University Press, 1977), p. 88.

8   Mark Stavig, *John Ford and the Traditional Moral Order* (Madison, WI: University of Wisconsin Press, 1968), p. 187.

9   Clifford Leech, *John Ford and the Drama of His Time* (London: Chatto & Windus, 1957), p. 60.

10   Laurel Amtower, ' "This idol thou ador'st": The Iconography of *'Tis Pity She's a Whore*', *Papers on Language and Literature* 34.2 (1998), pp. 179–206, pp. 202–3.

11   Bruce Boehrer, ' "Nice Philosophy": *'Tis Pity She's a Whore* and the Two Books of God', *Studies in English Literature, 1500–1900* 24.2 (1984), pp. 355–71, p. 371.

12   Lisa Hopkins, *John Ford's Political Theatre* (Manchester: Manchester University Press, 1994), p. 114.

13   Quoted in Roper, Appendix III, p. 132.

14   *'Tis Pity She's a Whore and Other Plays*, ed. Marion Lomax (Oxford: Oxford University Press, 1995), Introduction, p. xviii.

15   While many critics have written at length on the appearance of and symbolism behind Annabella's heart, Lisa Hopkins is one of the few who lingers over what is for me the more disturbing violation of Annabella's womb. In her essay 'Marlowe, Chapman, Ford and Nero', *English Language Notes* 35.1 (1997), pp. 5–10, Hopkins asserts that 'the incestuous ripping of the womb would serve to align Giovanni unmistakably with Nero, one of the most notorious of the Roman emperors, and would thus situate his actions immediately, recognizably, within an unmistakable framework of power-mad monstrosity and, as was the case with Faustus and as Bonaventure warns Giovanni at the beginning of the play, of an unholy and destructive curiosity' (p. 9).

16   Kay Stanton, ' "Made to write 'whore' upon?": Male and Female Use of the Word "Whore" in Shakespeare's Canon', in *A Feminist Companion to Shakespeare*, ed. Dympna Callaghan (Oxford: Blackwell, 2001), pp. 80–102, p. 95. As has long been noted by critics, Ford is not much removed from Shakespeare when it comes to his subject matter. This is why I am taking the liberty of applying Stanton's readings of Shakespeare to this later Ford play.

17   In his Introduction to the play Roper opines that Ford 'could have solved or avoided' this inexplicable mistaken identity 'by emphasizing Giovanni's long absence at Bologna' (p. xlv).

18   Bruce Boehrer importantly notes that when Giovanni and Annabella exchange vows and a ring in this scene, they 'both have formally entered into matrimony as specified by Renaissance law' (p. 367). Given 'this scheme of things Giovanni, not Soranzo, is the cuckolded husband' (p. 368). Boehrer reminds that 'as a student and long-time resident of Middle Temple, he [Ford] must have been aware of legal tradition on this point' (p. 369).

19   In his essay 'Shakespeare and Dekker as Keys to Ford's *'Tis Pity She's a Whore*',

Studies in English Literature, 1500–1900 7.2 (1967), pp. 269–76, Sidney R. Homan explains away Giovanni's misleading word choice as an expression of how deeply he loves Annabella: 'To say that his resorting to tricks or secrecy shows a weakness of character and thus a man too lazy or selfish to change his ways ignores the fact that the urgency of Giovanni's desires forces him to use such measures: he does not love Annabella simply as a lark' (p. 273).

20   Dorothy M. Farr, *John Ford and the Caroline Theatre* (London: MacMillan, 1979), p. 47.

21   For disagreement see Lisa Hopkins who, in her marvellous book *The Female Hero in English Renaissance Tragedy* (Basingstoke: Palgrave 2002) takes issue with Florio's choice of Putana as Annabella's tutress. For Hopkins, Florio's selection seems to be based on the assumption 'that all women need to know is sex and that women even of the Renaissance need know no more than the members of the generation which preceded them' (p. 133). Mark Stavig also does not view Florio in wholly benevolent terms and predicts in his book, *John Ford and the Traditional Moral Order* that Annabella would not 'have been able to hold out very long against his indirect but powerful maneuverings' (p. 190).

22   For an examination of Katherine's agency throughout that play, see my 'Katherine Gordon and the Art of Marriage Brokering in *Perkin Warbeck*', *Rocky Mountain Review of Language and Literature* 53.2 (1999), pp. 11–29.

23   Critics often express a less favourable view of the Friar in this particular scene and in the play as a whole. See, for example, Richard S. Ide, 'Ford's *"Tis Pity She's a Whore* and the Benefits of Belatedness', in *"Concord in Discord": The Plays of John Ford, 1586–1986*, ed. Donald K. Anderson (New York: AMS Press, 1986), pp. 61–86 , who suggests that in this scene the Friar 'terrorizes her with threats of Dantesque tortures in hell' (p. 77). Dorothy M. Farr goes even further, and in her book *John Ford and the Caroline Theatre* (London: Palgrave Macmillan, 1979), claims that throughout the play the Friar is 'conceived and deliberately presented as a destroyer of the human spirit' (p. 46). In *'Tis Pity She's a Whore*: The Overall Design', *Studies in English Literature, 1500–1900* 17 (1977), pp. 303–16, A.P. Hogan dismisses the Friar as a figure who 'fumbles and stumbles' (p. 306) throughout the play, spouting 'crabbed and frozen orthodoxy' (p. 305) and who possesses a 'stupid and naive trust in the institution of marriage' (p. 315). For a persuasive and judicious defence of the Friar, see Stavig, *John Ford*, pp. 110–21. In his essay ' "Ignorance in Knowledge": Marlowe's Faustus and Ford's Giovanni', *Modern Philology* 57.3 (1960), pp. 145–54, Cyrus Hoy thoughtfully offers the following: 'Since after I, 1, Giovanni never makes even the slightest pretense of heeding the Friar's words, the Friar comes to seem accordingly ineffectual' (p. 153).

24   Roper states that 'Florio's prescription [of moving up the wedding date] is orthodox' (p. 65, n11).

25   Stavig, *John Ford*, p. 120.

26   Larry S. Champion, 'Ford's *'Tis Pity She's a Whore* and the Jacobean Tragic Perspective', *PMLA* 90.1 (1975), pp. 78–87, p. 84.

27   Philotis is rarely discussed at length or even mentioned in passing in the scholarship of this play. A notable exception is Lisa Hopkins, who views Philotis's principal role 'as a bringer of happiness to those who have apparently no chance of it, such as Richardetto and Bergetto, and when she makes her final exit at the end of Act IV, scene ii an important potential source of consolation and healing has vanished' (*John Ford's Political Theatre*, p. 84).

28   G. F. Sensabaugh, *The Tragic Muse of John Ford* (Palo Alto, CA: Stanford University Press, 1944), p. 175.

29   Laurie A. Finke, 'Painting Women: Images of Femininity in Jacobean Tragedy', *Theatre Journal* 36.3 (1984), pp. 356–70, p. 359.

30   Corinne S. Abate, 'Missing the Moment in *Measure for Measure*', in *Shakespearean Performance: New Studies*, ed. Frank Occhiogrosso (Madison, NJ: Fairleigh Dickinson University Press, 2008), pp. 19–39.

31 Theodora Jankowski, ' "Where there can be no cause of affection": Redefining Virgins, their Desires, and their Pleasures in John Lyly's *Gallathea*', in *Feminist Readings of Early Modern Culture: Emerging Subjects*, ed. Valerie Traub, M. Lindsay Kaplan and Dympna Callaghan (Cambridge: Cambridge University Press, 1996), pp. 253–74, p. 255. See also Jankowski's essay 'Pure Resistance: Queer(y)ing Virginity in William Shakespeare's *Measure for Measure* and Margaret Cavendish's *The Convent of Pleasure*', *Shakespeare Studies* 26 (1998), pp. 218–55; and the book in which this work culminates, *Pure Resistance: Queer Virginity in Early Modern English Drama* (Philadelphia, PA: University of Pennsylvania Press, 2000).

32 Martin Butler, '*Love's Sacrifice*: Ford's Metatheatrical Tragedy', in *John Ford: Critical Re-Visions*, ed. Michael Neill (Cambridge: Cambridge University Press, 1988), pp. 201–31, p. 228.

33 Verna Foster, '*'Tis Pity She's a Whore* as City Tragedy', in *John Ford: Critical Re-Visions*, ed. Michael Neill (Cambridge: Cambridge University Press, 1988), pp. 181–200, p. 192. Foster goes on to say that Ford's Parmesan society is one in which 'it is demonstrably impossible to live uncorrupted' (p. 193).

34 In his essay 'The Adaptation of a Shakespearean Genre: *Othello* and Ford's *'Tis Pity She's a Whore*', *Renaissance Quarterly* 48.3 (1995), pp. 582–92, Raymond Powell blames Annabella wholly for her father's broken heart (p. 588). While he may do this in order to find another connection between this play and Shakespeare's tragedy, Powell's complete disregard of Giovanni as being the sole means by which Florio is notified of Annabella's behaviour presents an incomplete and arguably troubling portrait of events.

35 Amtower, ' "This Idol Thou Ador'st" ', p. 204.

36 Champion, 'Ford's *'Tis Pity She's a Whore*', p. 84.

CHAPTER SIX

New Directions: The Confessional Identities of *'Tis Pity She's a Whore*

Gillian Woods

I have unclasped my burdened soul,
Emptied the storehouse of my thoughts and heart,
Made myself poor of secrets, have not left
Another word untold which hath not spoke
All what I ever durst or think, or know.[1]

As exposition scenes go, John Ford's opening to *'Tis Pity She's a Whore* is particularly exposing. In conversation with his 'confessor' (I.i.46), Giovanni has undertaken the total excavation of self requisite to the Catholic Sacrament of Penance: every half-formed thought, lust and sensation has been disclosed. And this incestuous disclosure is certainly sensational. It is appropriate that Giovanni's highly taboo desire for his sister should be divulged within a sacramental space that is both utterly exposing and intransigently secret. The confessional revelation itself retains a degree of opacity, having taken place before the scene opens. The first words we hear are an instruction to be quiet: 'Dispute no more in this' (I.i.1.). Despite the imperative to 'speak fully' (*confiteri*), confessional strictures on speech delimit the speaker's self-representation. Two more times in this scene Friar Bonaventura tries to silence the importunate Giovanni: 'No more! I may not hear it' (I.i.12); 'Have done' (I.i.35). In its form and content, this first confession stages the play's central conflict between will and repression, the force of which is moral, intellectual and dramatic (hungry for details, we want Giovanni to keep speaking). Furthermore, Giovanni disputes within a disputed Catholic practice, which had been stripped of its sacramental meaning and which remained the 'most broadly controversial' Catholic sacrament in post-Reformation England.[2]

Religious controversy is integral to the dynamic of the play from its very first word. The incestuous subject matter locates 'Tis Pity at an ideological disjunction between God's prohibition and Nature's sanction. In sermons published just four years prior to 'Tis Pity's first appearance in print, the moderate Anglican Bishop Arthur Lake identified the 'first degree' of the sin of incest as the failure of 'absolute obedience to GODS commands'.[3] In the play, Friar Bonaventura does not refute Giovanni's contentions that the laws of nature endorse incest, but rather reasserts God's legal pre–eminence (II.v.29–34). Thus, as Bruce Boehrer has shown, the play severs what was understood in medieval and early Renaissance times as an absolute congruence between nature and scripture.[4] Obedient faith in God meets with sceptical empiricism. The drama of Giovanni's and Annabella's incest interrogates the relations of the individual with other human beings, with the universe and with God. Confession is a meeting point for these ideas.

The idea of confession resurfaces at crucial moments in 'Tis Pity. Giovanni's first scene confession is echoed by the scene of Annabella at shrift in Act III (when the Friar convinces her to marry Soranzo). The sacrament also maintains an allusive hold on other scenes, as in II.v when Giovanni gloats about the consummation of his love in a private conversation with the Friar (who offers unheeded spiritual instruction), and in V.i when Annabella articulates her repentance and is overheard by the Friar (who then blesses her). Providing, as it does, a structure for the interactions between man, God and society, confession is a dramatically useful venue for the tensions of 'Tis Pity, particularly since the meaning of that structure was itself controversial. A brief synopsis of confessional procedure might be helpful: the confessant examines his/her conscience, discovering sins of the heart as well those actually enacted; sins of commission and omission are then confessed privately to a clerical confessor; the priest gives absolution and imposes penance (usually prayers and pious deeds). Confession was not completely lost to the reformed Church, but its significance and practice was altered: the Elizabethan Prayer Book no longer stipulated the necessity for private confession of sins, instead translating confessional revelation into a generalized formula spoken by the whole congregation.[5] Inward sins were a matter of and for private guilt, whereas sins that harmed the social order were punished publicly via ecclesiastical courts which did not claim to offer God's forgiveness.[6] Luther, who recognized the potential emotional benefits of individual confession, banned the imposition of penance and insisted that confession should be made to another layperson rather than to a priest presuming a Christ-like authority. Such presumption was the major theological accusation against Catholic confession. Calvin claimed that 'the Papists are trecherous traitours in that they beare vs in hande that they are succeeded in the roome of Iesus Christ, to iudge the spirituall leprosie'.[7] The political vocabulary 'trecherous traitours' identifies a usurpation at the heart of confession, whereby priests forgave sins in place of Christ and sinners thought salvation could be procured with penance. William Perkins explained: 'The Scriptures mention no other satisfaction but Christs, and if his be sufficient, ours is needles: if ours needfull, his imperfect'.[8] Though confession formalized the sinner's obedient subjection to God, its sacramental dynamic apparently granted a salvific agency to both priest and penitent that reformers found (to different degrees) unacceptable.

However, not only reformers but Catholics themselves were troubled by the manner in which the sacrament blurred divine and human agency.[9] Brian Cummings's analysis of the drafts of the Tridentine Canons concerning the confession reveals Catholics wrestling with these problems. The final decrees balance contrary impulses, so that statements of human passivity (justification begins in the 'predisposing grace of God' and proceeds without 'any merits on the part of the sinner') take surprisingly active turns. Cummings explains a deliberate ambiguity:

> in the space of the same sentence, the passive construction (*ab eius vocatione ... vocantur*) is abandoned for the active description of the sinners converting themselves 'to their own justification by freely assenting to and cooperating with that grace.[10]

Hence those writing for the Catholic laity indicated that penance did not earn salvation but was nevertheless necessary to it:

> the death and passion of Iesus Christ, is a price sufficient to ransom and redeeme a thousand worlds, yet is it beseeming the iustice of God, that now in delinquents and transgressors, where the crimes are personall [...] they should be made partakers againe of the merits of Christ, by their owne personall cooperation, reconciling them selues before reuolted from him, and taking vp their owne Crosse, haue part in the burthen with Christ, and groane with Cyreneus vnder the

heauie waight thereof, to the cancelling, extinguishing, and full satisfying for their sinnes.[11]

Here, the Sacrament of Penance is not needed for the action of salvation itself, but is required to help make up some of the logical deficit that remains if Christ's sacrifice is unmatched by any action on the part of the sinner who necessitated it. But God nevertheless enables this 'personall cooperation'. Individual selfhood is emphasized through the stress placed on the significance of each secret sin: 'God in the next world will not goe by generall chapters, but will haue an accompte of all our proper woorkes and misdedes, till it come to our idle woords & vaine thoughtes', cautioned William Allen.[12] However, confessional guides asserted that comprehensive self–understanding was extremely difficult to achieve: 'it is very hard for a man to know himselfe in deade, and to serch throughly all the secret places of his conscience'.[13] Confession articulates accountability in an enactment of agency (repentant participation in the drama of salvation) that is always delimited. Thus in one anecdote an 'ould brother' prayed for help in remembering any forgotten and unconfessed sin; answered by a heavenly 'voyce', he then confessed the sin back again.[14] Allen relates self-knowledge to self-abasement: 'it is exceeding commodious to breake the pride of mans harte, & to make him knowe him self'.[15] Confessional speech itself is a declaration of a 'submission of our selues' to the laws of God and the Church.[16] Confessional self-centredness subdues the self.

Confession, then, is concerned with the same dilemmas as tragedy: what makes an individual unique? How much responsibility do humans have for their actions? How much control does a person have over his/her own destiny? It usefully dramatizes a character's introspection (an ideologically loaded alternative to soliloquy) and clarifies his/her agonistic relation with society. Repentance is a key theme in this play, even for its more minor characters: in casting off Hippolita, Soranzo claims a penitential motive (II.ii.85–88) and instructs his former lover 'Learn to repent and die' (II.ii.99); in seeking the identity of the father of Annabella's baby, Soranzo feigns repentance for his anger (IV.iii.133); and at the close of the play Vasques brags 'I repent nothing' (V.vi.120).[17] The dilemma of *'Tis Pity* is not whether Giovanni will fall in love with his sister – his desire is established fact at the beginning of the play[18] – but rather whether the siblings will choose to reject this love and opt for repentance over romance. The play asks how repentance is possible and whether it is desirable. Giovanni and Annabella characterize paradoxical ideals of agency and responsibility, defiance and submission. Even after the

Reformation, confession had retained a place in early modern dramatic diction, intelligible both as a sacramental imperative for Catholic characters (see the dread of Webster's Cariola: 'If you kill me now | I am damned! I have not been at confession | This two years')[19] and as a shorthand signal of hypocrisy in plot devices and jokes for reform–conditioned audiences. But Ford is unusual among early modern dramatists in implicating the theology of confession in the development of his plot. For example, confession enables the plot of Ford's source, *Romeo and Juliet*: the lovers get married under cover of 'leave to go to shrift' and Juliet solicits the Friar's help to avoid bigamy while supposedly going to him 'To make confession and to be absolved' for displeasing her father.[20] This opportunistic use of confession is differently meaningful from Giovanni's and Annabella's sacramental examination of their sins. In *Romeo and Juliet*, anti-Catholic assumptions about confessional scheming and lechery ambiguously translate into romantic plots that prize chaste marriage. While recourse to shrift might hint at both sinfulness and piety, the sacramental activity of confession – the controversial process of repentance itself – does not impinge on the action as it does in *'Tis Pity*, where had Giovanni's penance been successful, incestuous consummation would not have taken place, and where had Annabella's repentance failed, Giovanni would not have been roused to revenge.

Confession is also integrated in the generic organization and meaning of *'Tis Pity*. The play's multiple plots mostly revolve (and unspool) around revenge: Hippolita's against Soranzo, Richardetto's against Soranzo and Hippolita, Vasques's against Hippolita etc. As early as the second scene Grimaldi declares, 'I'll be revenged, Soranzo' (I.ii.47). For most of the play incest seems to mark Giovanni and Annabella out as likely victims of revenge, though Giovanni ultimately snatches the title of revenger. Concerned as it is with forgiveness, confession might seem to be wholly antithetical to the retributive logic of revenge. However, the first mention of vengeance in *'Tis Pity* is uttered in the penitential promise of Giovanni in confession: 'All this I'll do, to free me from the rod | Of vengeance' (I.i.83–84). The sacrament helps generate the play's generic momentum, and this makes theological sense. As a variety of confessional literature made clear, the Sacrament of Penance sought to forestall God's rightful and inevitable revenge against sinners. 'Satisfaction' was glossed as 'a reuenge and punishment taken of ones self for his offences'[21] and penitents were instructed that sins should be confessed in a manner showing 'we are desirous to be reuenged of our selves'.[22] Far from opposing the concept of revenge, confession both confirmed and cautioned that divine order operated according to its brutal logic. William Stanney warned that 'God neuer leaueth the offence without reuenge and punishment, for either the sinner must punish his owne offence in himself, by doing Penance, or else God in his wrath wil chastice it'.[23] The play's primary revenge plot, then, is the one established through the confessional first scene.

But of course while reformers firmly opposed the notion of 'satisfactory' penance appeasing divine vengeance, Calvinists as well as more moderate Protestants also cast God in the role of revenge,[24] and all denominations agreed that revenge usurped God's wrathful authority. Early twentieth-century critics disputed the extent to which this broad Christian condemnation of revenge dictated contemporary responses to revenge tragedy. Lily B. Campbell argued for the likely moral disapprobation of action that infringed God's right to revenge, whereas Fredson Bowers maintained that secular practice upheld the individual's right to take private revenge in certain circumstances.[25] Such debates were sidelined in favour of provocative feminist and political readings of the drama.[26] However, religion has returned in recent years with an increased sensitivity to the sectarian complications of the post–Reformation situation. (Thus Alison Shell detects a pervasive anti-Catholicism in the corrupt Italian courts of revenge tragedies.)[27] Theology is insepar-able from the literary and ideological meaning of the drama. The sectarian difficulties exploited by *'Tis Pity* participate in its tragic dynamic but are not reconciled into an answer about Ford's personal confessional identity. Ford engages anti-Catholic ideas (this is a play in which 'cardinals think murder's not amiss' [III.ix.67]) but also questions the possibility of a Catholic dynamic. Tragedy tends to articulate problems rather than console us with answers and Ford's paradoxes create meaning through contention not resolution. In identifying God as primary revenger, Giovanni's penitential promise announces a tension running throughout the play: is God the author of, an actor in, or simply absent from this tragic universe?

Confessional Dispute: Giovanni at Shrift

In several ways, Giovanni seems to miss the point of the sacrament he goes to receive. Sinners were told that their confessions should 'be plaine and simple, not artificially composed: without excuse, couering, or diminishing anie thing at al'.[28] As Romeo is reminded, 'Riddling confession finds but riddling shrift' (II.ii.56). Excess speech opposes the spirit of the sacrament, hence Friar Bonaventura's attempts to silence the argumentative Giovanni. Primarily, confes-

sion was meant to be an expression of profound regret for sin: 'he
that maketh his Confession, must necessarily haue [. . .] sorrow and
detestation of sinne committed.[29] Penitents were to begin their
confessions with a prayer that admitted they had sinned: '*through
my fault, my fault, my most grieuous fault*'.[30] Giovanni rather seeks
'comfort' (I.i.18) from the Friar and a way to 'dispute' the sinful
categorization of his love. The nearest he comes to 'sorrow and
detestation' for his incestuous desires (rather than sorrow that he is
barred from enacting them) is in his fear of God's anger: 'O, do not
speak of that, dear confessor' (I.i.46); 'All this I'll do, to free me
from the rod | Of vengeance' (I.i.83–84). Theologians such as
Sylvester had long thought that sinners 'who so lack displeasure for
sins and the will to change that they wish, positively, not to amend'
committed mortal sin 'by the very act of seeking absolution'.
Nevertheless, it was thought proper for such hardened sinners to
attend confession to rouse more appropriate emotions. Since as early
as the twelfth century the practice had been to admonish these
sinners while encouraging them on the path to true repentance by
setting them pious tasks, not as satisfactory penance, but to ignite
true contrition.[31] This is Friar Bonaventura's method. He prescribes
a seven-day course of ascetic behaviour ('Weep, sigh, pray | Three
times a day, and three times every night' [I.i.76–77]) that is in
keeping with Catholic '*remedies against Leachery and vncleannes*'
recommending sinners to 'chasten and exercise the bodies with
labours & painful thinges'.[32] Giovanni submits to these instructions
with a willingness tempered by his concluding (and conclusive?)
preparedness to fail: 'else I'll swear my fate's my God' (I.i.84).[33] Ford
establishes an ambiguous test of Giovanni, God and a ritual of
repentance.

Oddly, Giovanni seems to think that the verbalization of
sinfulness merits its redemptive redefinition. After stressing the
completeness of his confession (I.i.13–17, quoted above) he
complains 'And yet is here the comfort I shall have? | Must I not
do what all men else may – love?' (I.i.18–19);[34] and after his week of
weeping he declares 'I thoroughly have examined, but in vain'
(I.ii.145), as if the primary step of examination of conscience rather
than sorrow for what is found therein equalled repentance. (He
seems to share the suspicions of anti-Catholics that confession
awards dispensation for sins about to be committed.) The confession
of his desires translates them into available action. Drawing on
Lacan, Dennis Foster argues that confession enacts a major
epistemological reorganization: 'No matter how one's experiences
may be present in memory, the events of these narratives are

understandable only when they are transformed into objects for consciousness, into histories rather than sensations'.[35] Once Giovanni has 'objectified' the 'sensation' of his incestuous desire in the confessional, its reality is unavoidable and the inevitable next step is to enact sin perversely (in both senses) after confession.

Far from breaking his pride, Giovanni's experience of confession and confessional tasks shores up his sense of self:

> I have even wearied Heaven with prayers, dried up
> The spring of my continual tears, even starved
> My veins with daily fasts: what wit or art
> Could counsel, I have practised. But alas,
> I find all these but dreams, and old men's tales
> To fright unsteady youth: I'm still the same.
>
> (I.ii.148–53)

His lack of spiritual regeneration takes the form of an awareness of self-consistency. Though he opens this soliloquy bemoaning 'Lost, I am lost' (I.ii.140), he ends it like a Marlovian hero:

> Keep fear and low, faint-hearted shame with slaves!
> I'll tell her that I love her, though my heart
> Were rated at the price of that attempt.
>
> (I.ii.156–58)

This bravura intensifies throughout the play as Giovanni's self-belief becomes increasingly imperial. Exulting in his incestuous consummation, he boasts:

> Thus hung Jove on Leda's neck
> And sucked divine ambrosia from her lips.
> I envy not the mightiest man alive,
> But hold myself, in being king of thee,
> More great than were I king of all the world.
>
> (II.i.16–20)

His 'regal' authority is precariously predicated on his sister's role as subject (his magisterial rhetoric ends with the doubtful 'But I shall lose you, sweetheart' [II.i.21]), but it is expressed with growing certainty. The man who in Act I declared that he might be forced to 'swear my fate's my God' (I.i.84) by Act III claims to be 'regent' of the 'Fates' (III.ii.20).

We might expect an unrepentant sinner to avoid confessional

confrontation, but Giovanni seeks it out (we learn that he had 'gone' to the Friar in act two and not the other way round [II.vi.2]). In this second 'confession' (its sacramental dimensions are unclear but as a private conversation between sinner and Friar it echoes I.i) the Friar once again tries to silence Giovanni:

> Peace! Thou hast told a tale whose every word
> Threatens eternal slaughter to the soul;
> I'm sorry I have heard it.
>
> (II.v.1–3)

Although Friar Bonaventura rebukes Giovanni for content rather than style in referring to the 'tale' told, the term matches the proscription against tale-telling repeated in confessional guides. Time and again penitents were warned not to turn themselves into the heroes of their own confessional stories. For example, Laurence Vaux explains:

> we confesse our sins with shamefastnesse and confusion, not as though wee did brag or vaunt of our sinnes, nor tell them, as one that told some story, or tale of thinges happened in our life: but that wee remember and consider well, before whome wee stand and confesse the same.[36]

And an anonymous guide dictates:

> our sins are not to be spoken of as though we bragged thereof, (as those vse to do, who reioyse when they haue done amisse) neyther are our sinnes to bee vttred in such sort, as if we tolde a tale to delyte those that heare vs talk: But our sinnes must be spoken of with such a mynde, that delyts in accusing of one his selfe.[37]

This intriguing prohibition against tale-telling perhaps responds to narrative embellishment as a verbal re-creation of sin too close to recreation: a repeated indulgence in the pleasure of sin. Allowing the penitent both authorial and characterological status might generate a sense of agency that contradicts the submission central to confession. Though we do not hear Giovanni's tale-telling he does turn himself into the Marlovian literary type.

Where confession seeks to break the self to an admission of its reprehensive weakness, Giovanni instead gains an increased belief in his own agency. Far from being the obedient penitent, he regards himself as the authority that others are wrong to cross. Hence he rather oddly 'fear[s] this friar's falsehood' (III.vi.49) when he sees his sister's penitential tears and employs Calvin's political metaphor when Annabella's repentance sticks: 'Are we grown traitors to our own delights?' (V.iii.38); 'What danger's half so great as thy revolt?' (V.v.8). That this is overblown in literary as well as theological terms is clear from other characters' lack of interest in Giovanni. While the admiring Friar has followed his gifted student from Bologna to Parma and Annabella selects him as her unlikely romantic lead, no one else notices that Giovanni is the play's protagonist until the very end (when they are bewildered as well as horrified). Of course, it is not unusual for the revenger to pass for marginal for most of the play, but in *'Tis Pity* everyone is far more interested in their own (more conventional) revenge tragedies and the opportunity for romantic comedy with Annabella. Even his own father writes him off/out: 'I doubt his health. | Should he miscarry, all my hopes rely | Upon my girl' (I.iii.6–8). Thus Giovanni's self-importance is dangerously out of kilter with both theological strictures and the play's social organization.

Ford is decidedly ambivalent about the attractiveness and validity of his protagonist's wilfulness. Giovanni's confidence grows, but he remains explicitly 'the same' (I.ii.153) in other ways, and this represents both stability and limitation. He cannot perceive, or rather accept, the reality of change in others. In celebrating the sexual consummation of their love, he says to Annabella:

> I marvel why the chaster of your sex
> Should think this pretty toy called maidenhead
> So strange a loss, when, being lost, 'tis nothing,
> And you are still the same.
>
> (II.i.9–12)

The change in Annabella's social, emotional and spiritual being is significant, despite Giovanni's nominalist dismissiveness. Annabella's ironic "Tis well for you; | Now you can talk' (II.i.12–13) hints both playfully and poignantly at a richer epistemological grasp of the situation. Susannah B. Mintz argues that the different attitudes of the siblings are gendered. Giovanni denies 'the import of Annabella's newly realized sexuality', since to acknowledge it might recognize something threateningly uncontainable about her.[38] To his own surprise Giovanni finds that Annabella's marriage to Soranzo does not alter the terms and experience of his (pointedly sexual) relationship with his sister:

but I find no change
Of pleasure in this formal law of sports.
She is still one to me, and every kiss
As sweet and as delicious as the first.

(V.iii.6–9)

Giovanni's 'sameness' is a spiritual stagnation that the play implies is both laudable continuity and reductive limitation. For a literary type Giovanni has marked problems with narrative progression. He locks himself into one moment of incestuous consummation (hence 'every kiss' is like 'the first'). The intensity of his devotion is necessarily blinkered. He boasts 'My world and all of happiness is here, | And I'd not change it for the best to come' (V.iii.14–15). Giovanni cannot repent because he cannot imagine a heaven better than the one with Annabella. Despite his love of hypotheticals he cannot properly conceive of anything other than his personal experience of 'now' (as was evident when he first appended doubt to his promise to try out penance).

Earlier, when the Friar pleads that 'time is left', Giovanni interrupts, 'To embrace each other; | Else let all time be struck quite out of number' (II.v.65–66). But time already is 'out of number' for Giovanni. When in his first confession he questions why the 'peevish sound' of 'brother and of sister' should 'be a bar | 'Twixt my perpetual happiness and me?' (I.i.24–27) it is unclear whether 'perpetual happiness' refers to heavenly eternity or romantic bliss with Annabella. The idea surfaces again when Putana reveals the incest to Vasques: 'O, they love most perpetually' (IV.iii.212–13). The incest takes place in an endless present tense that ruptures the narrative development of sin-repentance-forgiveness. Appropriately, the Friar describes the torment of eternity in hell as an interminable present where sinners suffer 'never-dying deaths' (III.vi.15) and the murderer is 'forever stabbed, | Yet can he never die' (III.vi.20–21). Arthur Lake warns that 'All men sinne, but they that haue grace take heed of *doing* sinne'.[39] Giovanni's incest is not an act of sin that recedes into the past tense, or even an act of sin that is repeatedly performed, but rather a 'perpetual' sinful state. The grammatical difference between sinning and 'doing' sin is the theological difference between being subject to sin and being the (over)active subject of the verb sin. Giovanni is the agent, the author even, of this incestuous moment – but only as long as Annabella remains in it with him:

Why, I hold fate
Clasped in my fist, and could command the course
Of time's eternal motion hadst thou been
One thought more steady than an ebbing sea.

(V.v.11–14)

His wilfulness is both exciting and confused (his own statements declare him to be alternatively servant and master of fate) just as his incest is both radical and a form of retrograde autoeroticism (Annabella is doubly possessed as both his sister and lover). That Annabella should feel or act differently from him is aberrant to his understanding. Hence while he initially objects to Annabella marrying, he happily gives Bonaventura 'leave' to 'shrive' her: 'At your best leisure, father; then she'll tell you | How dearly she doth prize my matchless love' (II.v.43–46). Here he seems to expect Annabella to share his enjoyment of verbalizing their incest, but Annabella is markedly different.

Penitent Queanes: Annabella at Shrift

Where Giovanni remains ontologically stuck, Annabella is profoundly fluid. Physically, she changes from virginity to pregnancy; socially, from maid to wife to whore; and spiritually, from innocent to sinner to redeemed penitent. For all that Giovanni attempts to put a neoplatonic spin on his love for Annabella, he also sees her as a source of theological corruption: 'Such lips would tempt a saint; such hands as those | Would make an anchorite lascivious' (I.ii.197–98). Though the comments have a self-justificatory edge they also alert us to Annabella's religious significance. Indeed the dilemma of repentance at the heart of the play concerns not just Giovanni but also Annabella; Bonaventura worries about 'a pair of souls' (II.v.69). Annabella exemplifies an alternative confessional identity. Act III, scene vi repeats the confessional situation of the first scene, with Annabella replacing Giovanni as a very different confessant. The stage direction describes ideal confessional decorum with emblematic precision:

Enter the FRIAR *in his study, sitting in a chair,*
ANNABELLA *kneeling and whispering to him,*
a table before them and wax-lights; she weeps, and
wrings her hands.

(III.vi)

Physically subordinate to the seated Friar, her whispering is as inaudible as Giovanni's offstage confession, but is pointedly distinct from his 'disputing'. The lines she does speak are mostly orthodoxly short exclamations, just long enough to emphasize her sinful culpability and necessarily passive receptiveness to redemption: 'Wretched creature!' (III.vi.6); 'Mercy, O mercy!' (III.vi.24); 'Ay me!' (III.vi.39); 'I am' (III.vi.42). Such verbal diminution records her minimized agency and the pleased Friar encourages her to 'Weep faster' (III.vi.5). But this perfect confessional performance is theatrically opaque. Critics often argue that having been made newly-vulnerable by her pregnancy, Annabella is easily manipulated by the Friar rather than genuinely repentant. Nathaniel Strout is convinced by Annabella's sincerity but interprets it as an act of social conformity instead of a sublime reformation;[40] similarly Alison Findlay sees her as unable to resist the patriarchal pressure of the Friar.[41]

Annabella's continued relationship with Giovanni and her subsequent taunting of Soranzo indicates that her first confession is far from perfect in its effects, but she is not necessarily feigning or uninterested in III.vi. The confession is certainly replete with sectarian ironies. Richard McCabe points out that whereas Shakespeare's Friar Lawrence plotted to save Juliet from bigamy, Bonaventura recommends a 'questionable' marriage to the pregnant Annabella.[42] This plot is put 'First, for your honour's safety' before the penance that comes 'next, to save your soul' (III.vi.36–37). Even Protestants (who defended a private relationship between sinner and God) regarded incest as a public sin for which reparation needed to be made to the Church community (hence the context of Lake's incest sermons). That Bonaventura should seek to cover up this sexual sin without scruple for the 'safety' of Soranzo's 'honour' speaks to the moral pragmatism often associated with the closed Catholic confessional.

Such ideas were familiar on the post-Reformation stage where Catholic confession is often associated with sex. For example, in *The Roaring Girle*, Neatfoot's announcement that the disguised Mary Fitzallard has arrived to deliver an 'auricular confession'[43] complements his other double entendres, implying the revelation of sexual sins; while in *1 Henry VI*, Alanson's joke 'Doubtless he shrives this woman to her smock'[44] uses the confessional verb as a conventional synonym for intercourse itself. Having heard Mistress Wagtail listing possible fathers for her unborn child, the Page in Nathan Field's *A Woman is a Weather-coke* puns: 'I haue ouer hearde your Confession, and your casting about for a Father'.[45] Such allusions perpetuate pre-Reformation jokes (about sexual irregularities not only revealed but also enacted in confession) in a more sectarian context: bawdy humour both belittled Catholic piety and relabelled chastity as perverse hypocrisy. But there was a particular fascination with the figure of the female confessant. Dramatic confession often performs an epistemological fantasy in which the hidden sexual truth (or rather falsity) of a woman is exposed. Of course, confessional voyeurism is not always directed at women: in *Measure for Measure* the disguised Duke's desire to spy on and manipulate his citizens scandalously involves his attempts to confess them. But the figure of the female penitent is more frequent in Renaissance drama. Robert Davenport's *The City Night-Cap* sees Lodovico disguise himself as a friar to hear his wife's confession and 'know the very core of her heart' (which proves to be adulterous).[46] In addition, confessional language locates guilt. In Thomas Heywood's *The Second Part of the Iron Age*, Thersites jeers at the self-condemning Helen: '*Hellen* at shrift: alas poore penitent Queane'.[47] The anachronistic confessional vocabulary emphasizes the sexual nature of the crimes of this 'Quean'. Later in the scene Helen declares 'I must confesse, my inconsiderate deed | Haue made a world of valiant hearts to bleed' (F3v). Taking on spousal, national and international responsibility, Helen's 'confession' misogynistically tropes culpability and acknowledges her absolute blame for all worldly corruption.[48]

The confessions in *'Tis Pity* are not anti-Catholic clichés of bawdy friars and naive confessants (or sexual sinners and disguised voyeurs) but representations of sacramental struggle. Ford's female penitent conventionally confesses a sexual sin. But although Annabella participates in confession like the model penitent, her subsequent behaviour refuses to conform to dramatic type. When Soranzo rages at the discovery of her pregnancy, an unrepentant Annabella boasts about the superiority of her baby's unnamed father:

> This noble creature was in every part
> So angel-like, so glorious, that a woman
> Who had not been but human as was I,
> Would have kneeled to him, and have begged for love.
> You – why you are not worthy once to name
> His name without true worship, or indeed,
> Unless you kneeled, to hear another name him.
>
> (IV.iii.36–42)

As both Lisa Hopkins and Alison Findlay point out, Annabella rewrites incest in the unlikely terms of the immaculate conception.[49] This self-identification with the Virgin Mary completely rejects the culpability found in other dramatizations of female penitence. Ford confronts us with an uncomfortable paradox in which Annabella's shocking blasphemy doesn't necessarily feel wholly false. Earlier, the usual frisson of the confessional scene is missing since the sexual story is already known. Instead the dramatic interest lies in Annabella's will: does she want to be in confession? Does she feign her sorrow? Rather than being laid bare (like Giovanni) Annabella is difficult to read. In one of her longest lines in III.vi she asks the Friar: 'Is there no way left to redeem my miseries?' (33) and thus expresses attrition ('feare of the paines of hell') rather than contrition ('perfect sorrow, and horrour' felt because of a 'soueraigne and singular loue' for God).[50] Self-concerned, she readily takes the Friar's advice to marry Soranzo, and her confessional repentance seems at best short-lived when she later gloats over her cuckolded husband. But the gloating also passes and she subsequently kneels to Soranzo in sorrow. Unlike Giovanni, Annabella has the capacity to think beyond her own present existence and understand that her actions have hurt another. This, not fear of a patriarchal cleric or husband, initiates her repentance.

In V.i Annabella begins a soliloquy that ends as a confession. Theologically speaking she now exhibits contrition instead of attrition.[51] That is, her self-awareness is now less ethically self-centred. Critics have been reluctant to credit this repentance with spiritual significance, instead regarding it as her final capitulation to the pernicious social forces that entrap her. As Mintz has demonstrated, Annabella's incest is more 'revolutionary' than Giovanni's: unlike her brother she does not seek religious validation for her desire and insists on 'their filial connection' and 'pledges first in their exchange of vows.[52] But in its own way Annabella's repentance is also radical. Ford redraws the distinctions between will and submission. In the first ten lines of soliloquy Annabella explains that 'My conscience now stands up against my lust | With depositions charactered in guilt' (V.i.9–10). She exerts control over her own desire in an 'independent' repentance, achieved by her own efforts.[53] (Giovanni lacks such self-possession.) This is Annabella's first and last soliloquy. However, the entrance of the Friar transforms it as Annabella says 'Now I confess' (V.i.11). The denominational connotations of the scene are conflicting. John Wilks convincingly contends that the entrance of the Friar conforms to a providential, Calvinist structure whereby Annabella wins grace denied the reprobate Giovanni.[54] But the Friar is also definitively Catholic. The presence of a priest was said to be 'a distinctiue note of the catholickes from hereticks who vse noe confession to a preist [*sic*]'.[55] (Bonaventura's importance is marked by his headline position in Ford's dramatis personae, above his theatrical, ecclesiastical and social superiors.) In having the Friar overhear half of Annabella's soliloquy Ford blurs the boundaries between independent and sacramentally assisted repentance. Annabella is given institutional support on her own terms. Her soliloquy becomes like a Catholic confession (repentance heard and blessed by a friar) but is pointedly different from the ritual ideal of Act III (not least in its visual appearance whereby Annabella is now seen '*above*' the Friar instead of kneeling by his seat). She also clearly continues to love Giovanni even as she now forswears her 'lust' (V.i.9) and her submission takes an active force as she seeks to rescue him from hell and suffer 'alone [...] The torment of an uncontrolled flame!' (V.i.22–23). In fact Annabella's repentance is specifically conditional on heaven 'grant[ing]' her the means to send her letter of pious encouragement to Giovanni (V.i.31–37). This letter translates satisfactory obedience into instructive authority, written as it is in the penitential ink of 'tears and blood' (V.i.34). Confessional guides banned storytelling, but Annabella is insistently literary when she categorizes the action according to her centrality: 'A wretched, woeful woman's tragedy' (V.i.8). The scene of her death maintains this tragic equilibrium between will and obedience as she talks with Giovanni on a bed, and repeatedly kisses him. She has achieved a level of repentant confidence unbound by confessional conventions.

'Tis Pity?

Annabella's newfound spirituality proves incompatible with worldly survival and understanding. Her repentance motivates Giovanni's wrath, though the very idea of repentance is now so far beyond his comprehension that he misreads it as change of sexual preference for her 'new sprightly lord' (V.v.1) or a 'fit' of female caprice (V.v.4).[56] Giovanni cannot let go of the incestuous moment that has kept him the 'same' throughout the play. Discussing the possibility of heaven he demonstrates a need for the other world to reproduce his here and now: 'May we kiss one another, prate or laugh, | Or do as we do here?' (V.v.40–41). As the incestuous moment breaks down Giovanni commands 'Be dark, bright sun, | And make this midday night' (79–80), collapsing time into a single instance of destruction. If he is here arrogantly imperative by the next scene he is totally deluded about the power of his will, and confuses literary hyperbole with reality: 'The glory of my deed | Darkened the midday sun, made noon as night' (V.vi.21–22). His ontological stagnation is symptomatic of his inflated sense of will. He plans to kill Annabella, therefore her physical liveliness is mere deceit, she is already dead:

> How sweetly life doth run
> In these well-coloured veins! How constantly
> These palms do promise health! But I could chide
> With Nature for this cunning flattery.
>
> (V.v.74–77)

No longer in thrall to fate, Giovanni understands his intentions as fait accompli. And yet, for a brief moment before he dies, Ford teases us with the possibility of Giovanni's 'perpetuation', as if his will really could triumph over all. It proves oddly difficult to kill Giovanni, a circumstance to which Vasques calls attention in temporal language as he stabs at him: 'No, will it not be yet? If this will not, another shall. – Not yet? I shall fit you anon.' (V.vi.78–79). In this pause Giovanni continues in the 'same' living state.

But this is only temporary. Giovanni's 'glory' is aberrant, not just morally but also in literary terms. That the denouement should be shaped by Giovanni's revenge instead of Soranzo's is structurally surprising and thematically unconventional. Early modern narratives more familiarly told of cuckolded husbands taking revenge; 'Fully cognizant of Soranzo's revenge plot against Giovanni and Annabella, Ford's audience cannot but expect that God will use Soranzo as the instrument of retribution against the incestuous couple'.[57]

Giovanni has changed from seeing himself as the subject of God's 'vengeance' attempting to avoid a revenge story (I.i.84) into a blasphemous actor of revenge: 'Thus die, and die by me, and by my hand. | Revenge is mine' (V.v.85–86). When killing Annabella, Giovanni places tautological emphasis on his own agency; the early attempts at confessional obedience are replaced by a forceful assertion of will. For Richard S. Ide this problematizes any providential view of the play which would put God in ultimate control: Giovanni's will has narrative pre-eminence.[58] But this reflects only one part of Ford's paradox. The ending validates God's power which punishes the reprehensible Giovanni and simultaneously asserts his surprisingly successful will. In the first act Giovanni sought to forestall God's vengeance; from one angle the fifth act stages a degraded repetition of this intent as he now merely forestalls Soranzo's vengeance. The Friar had warned Annabella that once in hell 'you will wish each kiss your brother gave | Had been a dagger's point' (III.vi.27–28). Annabella dies confident of her salvation, but like a good penitent suffers a measure of her hellish due in life rather than eternity, since her brother's final kisses are accompanied by the stabbing of a dagger's point. In theological terms, revenge usurps God's right to punish, but Giovanni enacts the very providential design he also thwarts. Having 'unclasped' (I.i.13) his inner secrets in his first confession, Giovanni here plays the brutal confessor and rips out Annabella's heart.[59] Early modern discourses of penance regularly drew on bodily analogies and metaphors. Confessors are

> surgeons of our soules as to whom the serching, the cutting, the burning, the harde griping, the opening or the closing of euerie of oure woundes, and sores of conscience doth aperteine.[60]

The physical dimensions of many forms of penance translates actual bodies into metaphorical vehicles: physical pain imperfectly registers a metaphysical hope of salvation. Giovanni parodies and participates in this process, just as his feasting imagery gives Annabella's heart a Eucharistic resonance:

> I came to feast too, but I digged for food
> In a much richer mine than gold or stone
> Of any value balanced.
>
> (V.vi.24–26)

Ford establishes intellectual oppositions that are binary in nature but humanly blurred in practice. Thus this wilful intellectual Giovanni should stand for atheism, but he commands Annabella to pray four times before he kills her (V.v.63, 66). He cannot escape the discursive structures of religion and the penitent Annabella cannot be contained by them. The end result for both is alienation.

The play's title offers us a provocatively ambiguous theological and critical judgement that we necessarily question (pity is a religious virtue and an Aristotelian ideal). Taken from the play's last couplet, the title is voiced by the Cardinal: 'Of one so young, so rich in Nature's store, | Who could not say, 'Tis pity she's a whore?' (V.vi.158–59). The casual tone of the redundant question is as glaringly inadequate to the tragic experience as the term 'whore' is inappropriate to the complexity of Annabella's crime. But it does confirm Annabella's contention, noted above, that this is finally a 'wretched, woeful woman's tragedy' (V.i.8). In other works by Ford, 'pity' alternatively holds salvific potential ('My *Bloody sweate* won pitie in your eyes [...] Take *life eternal*, for your due reward',[61] and is a disgrace to be avoided ('It is better to be envied then pittied, pity proceeding out of a cold charitie towards the miserable; envie out of a corruption of qualitie against the virtuous').[62] In *'Tis Pity* itself the word appears on ten other occasions: twice as a shunned emasculating softness (IV.iii.78; V.ii.22); three times as part of a feigned sensitivity (IV.iii.131; IV.iii.200; IV.iii.209); twice as religious sympathy (I.i.39; II.v.47); and three, possibly four, times as sexual sympathy (I.ii.248; II.ii.37; II.v.47; and perhaps I.i.39 again). The title is freighted with these cynical, sexual and theological connotations. Pity is etymologically linked to piety, though the Cardinal's trite rhyme is closer to sanctimony. That it should be a Catholic cleric who is so oblivious to Annabella's absolution emphasizes the totality of her estrangement even as she is made central to the action's meaning. A few lines earlier the Cardinal had ordered:

> First, this woman, chief in these effects,
> My sentence is that forthwith she be ta'en
> Out of the city, for example's sake,
> There to be burnt to ashes.
>
> (V.vi.132–35)

Whether 'woman' refers to Annabella or Putana is unclear (the vagueness speaks to the generalization of misogyny), but if Annabella, it would augment the conventional blame of the female penitent implicit in the title (it is also a pity that he is a seducer and a murderer). Confession is a ritual of inclusion that keeps penitents within the ecclesiastical fold, but this Church spokesperson excludes Annabella. Claiming in the present tense that ''Tis pity she's a whore' denies the reality and efficacy of her repentance and locks her into Giovanni's perpetual incestuous moment (though the incest itself is elided). And this is the moment into which we are locked, unable to 'view' (V.vi.107) the real Annabella, whose identity has finally eluded family, society and Church.

Acknowledgements

I am grateful to Emma Rhatigan and Emma Smith for their judicious comments on earlier versions of this work.

Notes

1 John Ford,'*Tis Pity She's a Whore*, ed. Martin Wiggins (London: A&C Black, 2003), I.i.13–17. All further quotations will be taken from this edition and reference will be given in the text.

2 See Brian Cummings, *The Literary Culture of the Reformation* (Oxford: Oxford University Press, 2002), p. 347 and John Bossy, 'The Social History of Confession in the Age of Reformation', *Transactions of the Royal Historical Society* 25 (1975), pp. 21–38.

3 Arthur Lake, *SERMONS With some Religious and Diuine Meditations* (London: 1629), Dddd5r.

4 Bruce Boehrer, '"Nice Philosophy"': '*Tis Pity She's a Whore* and The Two Books of God', *Studies in English Literature* 24 (1984), pp. 355–71.

5 Ramie Targoff, *Common Prayer* (Chicago: University of Chicago Press, 2001), pp. 31–33.

6 See Anthony Low, 'Sin, Penance, and Privatization in the Renaissance', *Ben Jonson Journal* 5 (1998), pp. 1–35, p. 7.

7 John Calvin, *THE SERMONS OF M IOHN CALVIN VPON THE FIFTH BOOKE OF Moses called Deuteronomie*, trans. Arthur Golding (London, 1583), p. 849.

8 William Perkins, *A Golden Chaine* (Cambridge, 1600), pp. 761–62.

9 In the concluding stanzas of Ford's *Christes Bloodie Sweat* (1613) the narrator affirms his repentance by listing what he will 'offer up' to Christ: 'Contrition | My penance; the confession I reveale, | My guilt; my Hope the comforts of fruition; | His spirit my Confessor; Faith the gift, | Which must absolve mee, and his Love my shrift' (L. E. Stock, Gilles D. Monsarrat, Judith M. Kennedy and Dennis Danielson, eds, *The Nondramatic Works of John Ford* [Binghamton, NY: Medieval & Renaissance Texts & Studies in conjunction with Renaissance English Text Society, 1991], ll.1471–76). A Catholic sacramental vocabulary provides the vehicle for a salvific metaphor. But the metaphor itself reforms the Catholic sacrament: 'Contrition' is collapsed into 'penance', the revelation of 'confession' is ambiguously unfolded in 'guilt' rather than through formal rehearsal before a priest, indeed the 'Confessor' is Christ's 'spirit' not a mediating Catholic cleric, and absolution takes the form of a 'gift' of 'Faith'. The metaphorical confessant does not intervene in the process of salvation, but actively chooses to make himself available for the 'shrift' of Christ's 'Love'.

10 Cummings, *The Literary Culture of the Reformation*, pp. 344–45.

11 Anon., *A TREATISE OF AVRICVLAR CONFESSION* (St Omers, 1622; facsimile edn, Menston: Scolar Press, 1976), pp. 23–24.

12 William Allen, *A TREATISE MADE IN DEFENCE of the lauful power and authoritie of Priesthod to remitte sinnes* (Louvain, 1567; facsimile edn, Menston: Scolar Press, 1972), p. 208. Protestants thought this exposure of non–social secret sins a counterproductive infringement of the sinner's private conscience (see T. N. Tentler, *Sin and Confession on the Eve of the Reformation* [Princeton, NJ: Princeton University Press, 1977], p. 109).

13 See Anon., *A short and absolute order of confession* (1575–78; facsimile edn, Menston: Scolar Press, 1969), Av; see also Anon., *AN INTRODVCTION TO THE CATHOLICK FAITH* (1633; facsimile edn, Menston: Scolar Press, 1973), p. 152 and Anon., *A TREATISE OF AVRICVLAR CONFESSION*, p. 246.

14 Anon.., *A TREATISE OF AVRICVLAR CONFESSION*, p. 246.

15 Allen, *A TREATISE MADE IN DEFENCE*, p. 247.

16 Laurence Vaux, *A CATECHISME OR CHRISTIAN Doctrine* [. . .] *Wherevnto is adioyned a briefe Forme of Confesion* (1599; facsimile edn, Menston: Scolar Press, 1969), p. 195.

17 For comment on this, see Gilles D. Monsarrat, 'The Unity of John Ford: '*Tis Pity She's a Whore* and *Christ's Bloody Sweat*', *Studies in Philology* 77 (1980), pp. 247–70, p. 256.

18 See Cyrus Hoy, '"Ignorance in Knowledge": Marlowe's Faustus and Ford's Giovanni', *Modern Philology* 57 (1960), pp. 145–54, p. 153.

19 John Webster, *The Duchess of Malfi*, ed. Brian Gibbons (London: A&C Black, 2001), IV.ii.242–44.

20 William Shakespeare, *Romeo and Juliet*, The Riverside Shakespeare 2nd edn, ed. G. Blakemore Evans and J. J. M. Tobin (Boston, MA: Houghton Mifflin, 1997), II.v.66, III.v.233. All further quotations from the play will be taken from this edition and reference will be given in the text.

21 Anon., *AN INTRODVCTION TO THE CATHOLICK FAITH*, p. 37.

22 Anon., *A short and absolute order of confession*, B6r.

23 William Stanney, *A Treatise of Penance* (1617; facsimile edn, Menston: Scolar Press, 1972), p. 110.

24 See Lily B. Campbell, 'Theories of Revenge in Renaissance England', *Modern Philology* 28 (1931), pp. 281–96, p. 282.

25 Fredson T. Bowers, *Elizabethan Revenge Tragedy 1587–1642* (Princeton, NJ: Princeton University Press, 1940).

26 See Stevie Simkin, John Peck and Martin Coyle, eds, *Revenge Tragedy* (Basingstoke: Palgrave Macmillan, 2001).

27 Alison Shell, *Catholicism, Controversy and the English Literary Imagination, 1558–1660* (Cambridge: Cambridge University Press), pp. 23–55.

28 Anon., *AN INTRODVCTION TO THE CATHOLICK FAITH*, pp. 82–83.

29 Anon., *AN INTRODVCTION TO THE CATHOLICK FAITH*, p. 81.

30 Anon., *AN INTRODVCTION TO THE CATHOLICK FAITH*, p. 91.

31 Tentler, *Sin and Confession on the Eve of the Reformation*, pp. 121–22.

32 Vaux, *A CATECHISME OR CHRISTIAN Doctrine*, p. 235.

33 For comment on this, see Hoy, '"Ignorance in knowlede"', p. 148.

34 For comment on this, see Lisa Hopkins, *John Ford's Political Theatre* (Manchester: Manchester University Press, 1994), p. 148.

35 Dennis A. Foster, *Confession and Complicity in Narrative* (Cambridge: Cambridge University Press, 1987), p. 10.

36 Vaux, *A CATECHISME OR CHRISTIAN Doctrine*, pp. 199–200.

37 Anon., *A short and absolute order of confession*, BVv–[BVIr].

38 Susannah B. Mintz, 'The Power of "Parity" in Ford's *'Tis Pity She's a Whore'*, *Journal of English and Germanic Philology* 102 (2003), pp. 269–91, p. 287.

39 Lake, *SERMONS*, Aaaa2v.

40 Nathaniel Strout, 'The Tragedy of Annabella in *'Tis Pity She's a Whore'*, in *Traditions and Innovations*, ed. D. G. Allen and R. A. White (Newark, DE: University of Delaware Press, 1990), pp. 163–76, p. 173.

41 Alison Findlay, *A Feminist Perspective on Renaissance Drama* (Oxford: Blackwell, 1999), pp. 28–29.

42 Richard A. McCabe, *''Tis Pity She's a Whore* and Incest', in *Early Modern English Drama*, ed. Garrett A. Sullivan, Jr, Patrick Cheney and Andrew Hadfield (Oxford: Oxford University Press, 2006), pp. 309–20, p. 313.

43 Thomas Middleton and Thomas Dekker, *The Roaring Girle* (London, 1611), Bv.

44 William Shakespeare, *Henry VI, Part One*, The Riverside Shakespeare, 2nd edn, ed. G. Blakemore Evans and J. J. M. Tobin (Boston, MA: Houghton Mifflin, 1997), I.ii.119.

45 Nathan Field,, *A Woman is a Weather-coke* (London, 1612), E2r.

46 Robert Davenport, *A Critical Edition of Robert Davenport's The City Night-Cap*, ed. W. J. Monie (New York: Garland Publishing, 1979), l. 1324.

47 Thomas Heywood, *The Second Part of the Iron Age* (London, 1632), E4r.

48 For a different reading of the figure of the female penitent in Renaissance drama see Heather Hirschfeld, 'Confessing Mothers: The Maternal Penitent in Early Modern Revenge Tragedy', in *The Impact of Feminism in English Renaissance Studies*, ed. Dympna Callaghan (Basingstoke: Palgrave Macmillan, 2007), pp. 53–66.

49 Lisa Hopkins, 'John Ford's Annabella and the Virgin Mary', *Notes and Queries* 42 (1995), p. 380; Findlay, *A Feminist Perspective on Renaissance Drama*, pp. 29–30.

50 Anon., *A TREATISE OF MENTAL PRAYER* [...] *Togeather with a Dialogue of CONTRITION and ATTRITION* (1617; facsimile edn, Menston: Scolar Press, 1970), p. 329.

51 For comment on this, see also A. P. Hogan, *"Tis Pity She's a Whore*: The Overall Design', *Studies in English Literature* 17 (1977), pp. 303–16, and Monsarrat, 'The Unity of John Ford', p. 254.

52 Mintz, 'The Power of 'Parity' in Ford's *'Tis Pity She's a Whore'*, pp. 279, 284–85.

53 McCabe, *"Tis Pity She's a Whore* and Incest', p. 316.

54 John S. Wilks, *The Idea of Conscience in Renaissance Tragedy* (London: Routledge, 1990), pp. 260–61.

55 Anon., *A TREATISE OF AVRICVLAR CONFESSION*, p. 174. See also Hopkins, *John Ford's Political Theatre*, p. 171.

56 See McCabe, *"Tis Pity She's a Whore* and Incest', p. 316.

57 Richard S. Ide, 'Ford's *'Tis Pity She's a Whore* and the Benefits of Belatedness', in *"Concord in Discord"*, ed. D. K. Anderson, Jr (New York: AMS Press Inc., 1986), pp. 61–86, p. 72.

58 Ide, 'Ford's *'Tis Pity She's a Whore* and the Benefits of Belatedness', p. 72.

59 See Michael Neill, ' "What Strange Riddle's This?": Deciphering *'Tis Pity She's a Whore'*, in *John Ford Critical Re-Visions*, ed. Michael Neill (Cambridge: Cambridge University Press, 1988), pp. 153–79, pp. 167–8.

60 Allen, *A TREATISE MADE IN DEFENCE*, p. 220.

61 John Ford, *Christes Bloodie Sweat*, in *The Nondramatic Works of John Ford*, ed. L. E. Stock, Gilles D. Monsarrat, Judith M. Kennedy and Dennis Danielson (Binghamton, NY: Medieval & Renaissance Texts & Studies in conjunction with Renaissance English Text Society, 1991), ll. 805–10.

62 John Ford, *The Golden Mean*, in *The Nondramatic Works of John Ford*, ll. 593–95.

CHAPTER SEVEN

New Directions: The Deconstructing *'Tis Pity*?: Derrida, Barthes and Ford

Mark Houlahan

At the famous climax of *'Tis Pity*, Giovanni enters the last scene of the play and, as he knows, his life, *'with a heart upon his dagger'*, with which be-hearted implement he stabs his enemy and brother-in-law Soranzo, before himself being fatally stabbed in the ensuing melée. The heart, it seems, is Annabella's, removed from her after Giovanni's loving, surgical sacrifice of his pregnant sister/wife in the scene before. The 'seems' here is crucial, for at first this is not clear, neither to the onstage audience, waiting for Giovanni to arrive at the banquet, nor to an audience watching the play or those reading it. The eloquent Giovanni exults in providing the explanation to both groups. To begin, he sounds like a dilettante who has read rather too many poems by John Donne, whose *Songs and Sonets* was also published in 1633: '[...] I digg'd for food | In a much richer mine than gold or stone | Of any value balanc'd [...]';[1] Giovanni's rhetoric here is close to Donne's at the opening of 'Loves Alchymie': 'Some that have deeper digg'd loves Myne then I, | Say, where his centrique happinesse doth lie: I have lov'd, and got and told [...]'.[2]

  Giovanni's proclamation is obscure, so he clarifies the referent, in a gestic moment aligning his gruesome prop with the following: ''tis a heart, | A heart, my lords, in which is mine entombed [...] | 'Tis Annabella's heart, 'tis; why d'ye startle?' (V.vi.24–30). This is perhaps the most over-determined, over-signifying moment in a play redolent with its debts to the prior tradition of revenge and love tragedy on the Renaissance stage. As Quentin Tarantino assumes that postmodern viewers will recall the Hong Kong crime epics and 1970s blaxploitation films he obsessively quotes, so Ford assumes his first audience will readily recall Shakespeare's Othello (who kills his wife for love), Romeo (who dies besides his wife for love) and Hamlet, whose eloquence is never more abundant than when speaking of death and love. Giovanni is all these. He is Titus, arriving at a Thyestean feast, determined to kill and so feast upon his enemies. He is also Hieronimo, Kyd's great anguished, revenging hero in *The Spanish Tragedy*, a play that no one who saw it in early modern London, it seems, ever forgot. Hieronimo stabs his enemy, and then excises his own tongue. Giovanni does not go that far, but then in conventional moral terms having slept with, impregnated, killed and anatomized his sister, he hardly needs further outrage to sensationalize his story for the audience. His verbal and visual excess can be seen to fulfil the potential unleashed by all these prior tragic scenarios, which Giovanni himself appears to have included in all the reading for which Friar Bonaventura chastises him at the beginning of the play: 'Dispute no more in this, for know, young man, | These are no school points. Nice philosophy | May tolerate unlikely arguments, | But Heaven admits no jest [...]' (I.i.1-4). Giovanni's excess is such, however, that fulfilling that potential seems to result in those scenarios referencing multiple source plays from the early modern theatre collapsing on top of each other amidst the frenzy of blood and signification which Giovanni himself unleashes. Things are by no means what they so luridly appear to be. The more Giovanni calls them into being through language, the more 'words' and 'things' are severed one from the other. The obvious point to begin thinking about this process is the tip of Giovanni's dagger. Here, he tells us, is now perched Annabella's heart.

He needs to explain this heart for a range of reasons. Firstly, he is proud of his Caligula-like skill at carving up his sister. Weirdly enough, he seeks the approval of his enemies. Secondly, if presented with one in its disembodied state, which of us (cardiac specialists aside) could tell one human heart from another? Thirdly, whatever we are led to gaze upon, either 'live' on stage, or in the stage imaginary of reading the play, cannot surely be what Giovanni insists it is, unless that is, as Catherine Silverstone remarks in her chapter in this volume, we are to imagine a truly repugnant snuff theatre.

If not the 'real' thing, what would serve as its simulation? Either a mammalian but not human heart, fresh and dripping blood, I suggest, or a complete simulation, a harmlessly lurid synthetic prop. The more you think about either kind of prop the less 'real' either will seem, and the more cognitive dissonance will appear between

Giovanni's words and deeds. He promises to the Friar to make himself and Annabella 'One soul, one flesh, one love, one heart, one all?' (I.i.34). Michael Neill has brilliantly expounded the potential resonance between the play's cardiac obsession, early modern anatomy and Catholic doctrines of the sacred heart.[3] From Neill's perspective, Ford fulfils the potential of anatomy theatre, bringing emblems of the heart to vivid stage life. From the perspective of deconstruction, however, it can be seen that Ford only appears to do so. Rather it can be seen that, in a further move, Ford turns those terms inside out, rendering them incompatible. The very brilliance of Ford's staging and rhetoric undoes itself. One heart is played by no heart at all. The score becomes 'nil all'. This then is the truly 'strange riddle' (V.vi.29) inquired into by Vasques (Soranzo's serving man); and is then the real basis for the mocking, tendentious hollowness of the Cardinal's lines, now so famous as the title of the play itself. The first published text of the play uses the emerging capacity of print culture to gesture towards this, literally unspeakable, hollowness. I will come back to these lines, as well as to the play's very thorough preparing of the grounds of its own undoing. But first I will deal with the issue of what we might mean by 'deconstruction'.

To 'deconstruct' a text, *OED* tells us, is 'to analyse and reinterpret in accordance with the "strategy" associated with Jacques Derrida',[4] in other words to follow through the implications of the epochal readings of philosophical and ethnographic texts Derrida initiated in *Writing and Difference* and *Of Grammatology* in the 1960s.[5] Deconstruction, since the 1960s, has become a fashionable all-purpose signifier. As the first *OED* citation for 'deconstructionism' remarks as long ago as 1980, 'the coincidence of vulgar with erudite deconstructionism is a circumstance worth remarking'.[6] I will call these two forms 'weak' and 'strong' deconstruction. These coexist in current discourse in a way that is emblematic of Derrida's underlying method. For 'weak' deconstruction is lazy, almost flippant, yet prevalent. Strong deconstruction, at its best, in contrast, is unrelenting and exhausting to conduct and to assimilate. Since it can be found in fewer books and articles, it is numerically much weaker than its inferior sibling. Weak deconstruction abounds. Customary users of the term in its weak sense usually intend to deconstruct a sign system or a cultural practice. Their meaning is well summed up by the *Merriam-Webster Dictionary*, the American equivalent of the *OED*, which gives for deconstruct 'to adapt or separate the elements for use in an ironic or radically new way', offering a lovely example from American *Vogue* of someone who 'uses his masterly tailoring to *deconstruct* the classics'.[7] In terms of the fashion industry, Vivienne Westwood is a famous example of someone who thus 'deconstructs' prior styles, adapting, for example, elements of eighteenth-century couture, 'in an ironic or radically new way'. In terms of cultural or semiotic analysis, the essays on French culture Roland Barthes pioneered in his *Mythologies*, or the accounts of global media culture Umberto Eco offers in his *Travels in Hyperreality* work likewise towards a radical, detached, ironic critique of the operations of culture. They 'deconstruct', they disrupt, the bourgeois surface of modern western lifestyles. In this weaker sense, Ford in his play can be said to deconstruct the early modern dynastic family unit, and the hold of the Catholic Church on Renaissance Italy. When literary/aesthetic analysis likewise 'deconstructs', most often it aims to decode, analyse and critique.

In its stronger and more challenging form, however, analysing 'in accordance with the "strategy" associated with Jacques Derrida' requires a good deal more from its practitioners, those attempting, as here, to read in his name. Derrida was a trained philosopher. In his most celebrated and influential 1960s works he approaches key texts in the western philosophical tradition from a linguistic perspective showing how, by paying ruthlessly literal attention to all a text says, and reading its metaphorical figures as intrinsic to its ethical thought, it cannot really mean what it has often been held to mean. This reading procedure is derived from the work of Ferdinand de Saussure's *Course in General Linguistics*, perhaps the most influential linguistics textbook ever written. The linguistic sign, Saussure famously tells us, is divided into two parts: the signifier, or sound concept, and the 'thing', or idea signified. We grasp the signified by decoding the signifier. Signifiers, in turn, can be grasped by their difference from each other. The relationship between the signifier and its signified is arbitrary: there is no fundamental, absolute relationship between signifier and signified. Rather, common understanding within language groups allows meaning to take place or, in Derrida's terms, appear to have done so. A single signifier, such as 'cat', in English, has a comparable signifier in French (*'chat'*), Italian (*'gatto'*) and so on. The relationship between these signifiers is an arbitrary system of differences.

Now one cannot do much with a single arbitrary noun, or even several of them, beyond writing a reader for new entrants in primary schools, as in the famous Dr Seuss book *The Cat in the Hat*. For more complex signification, such as, for example, constructing or enacting a riveting Renaissance revenge/love play, you would obviously need more complex and extensive collections of signifiers. These too operate through readers or audience members locating meaning or 'signification' by understanding the difference between the terms made available to them.

In the 'real' world, where, for example, one must call and feed cats reliably lest they suffer, the system of linguistic difference Saussure specifies is arbitrary yet fixed. That is, we allow it to appear to be fixed in order to allow common-sense communication to take place. Derrida begs to differ. In his rereading of Saussure he shows that the relationship between signifier and signified is perpetually unreliable, perpetually opening a gap, aporia or abyss between the two halves of the sign. The inevitable difference between the two halves of Saussurean signs means that meaning is perpetually deferred or differed. Hence Derrida's famous coinage

> 'difference' (*différence* in French, combining the meanings of difference and deferral) to characterize those aspects of understanding, [which he] proposed [...] lay at the heart of language and thought, at work in all meaningful activities in an elusive and provisional way.[8]

One of the things that makes *'Tis Pity* especially available or open to a deconstructive reading is the way it attempts to literalize or embody what lies at the 'heart of language and thought', what, in another context, Graham Greene named *The Heart of the Matter*, or what in *The Wasteland* T. S. Eliot evokes as being 'the heart of light the silence'.[9]

At this 'heart' Derrida perceives not ultimate, fixed meaning but only 'elusive and provisional' *différence*, a realm something like that depicted in the opening of the Book of Genesis before the creation of the world, when, in the words of the King James Bible, the 'earth was without form and void, and darkness was upon the face of the deep' (Gen. 1:2). These verses are a crucial zone of *différence* in Derrida's reading practice, for they enunciate within the zone 'without form and void' an interface between speech and text, between the written and the oral. Genesis 1 is one of the oldest *written* texts in the Judeo-Christian tradition we possess, passed down from scroll to parchment, into print and now cyberspace in a process continuous since the first manuscripts were produced around 900 BC. Yet this written text, which the 'peoples of the book' (adherents to Judaic and Christian cultures and faith) have preserved for so long, privileges speech over the written word, for it is speech which, in the voice of God, creates the world. The word is spoken, then, before it is committed to text. The spoken word is primary and essential; the written is the secondary, proliferating afterglow of speech, the speech which promises 'full presence'. Derrida traces this dynamic not through scripture directly, but rather through Plato's *Pharmakon*. Writing, he insists, is prior to speech; the written underpins the oral, and not the other way round, as so long had been supposed. Writing, unlike speech, will not guarantee full 'presence'; rather it is governed by forms of absence. 'The precondition of discourse [...] the disappearance of any originary presence, is *at once* the condition of possibility *and* the condition of impossibility of untruth'. And this paradox is the always shifting heart of writing, governed in turn by the '*graphics of supplementarity*, which supplies, for the lack of a full unity, another unit that comes to relieve it, being enough the same and enough other so that it can replace by addition'.[10]

Writing and speech, 'absence' and 'presence', in Derrida's terms, are linked, dynamic binaries. As this approach invites us to disrupt the smoothly untroubled play of difference Saussure evokes, so, over the last 40 years, it has seemed, Derrida has invited us to disrupt 'truly', to deconstruct the orderly surface of classical writing. The 'disappearance of the good-father-capital-sun is thus the precondition of discourse'.[11] Disrupting the power of the father-sun-god complex which has governed western assumptions about the priority and divinity of speech might lead then also to Roland Barthes's famous proclamation of the 'Death of the Author', whose demise would reveal that 'Writing is that neutral, composite, oblique space where our subject slips away, the negative where all identity is lost, starting with the very identity of the body writing'.[12] Barthes wrote these words within the same cultural moment as Derrida was 'deconstructing' Plato, when Barthes was transforming himself into a proto-deconstructionist, nearly 15 years before the *OED* caught sight of the term in print in an English text.

The core metaphors Derrida links together in the phrase quoted, the form of the good, the father, the capital (or head, from the Latin *caput*) and the sun come under sustained attack throughout *'Tis Pity*. The play, in these terms, can be seen to inhabit something like the spirit of vehement play (often called Nietzschean) which both Barthes and Derrida bring to their playful yet earnest rereading and rewritings of literary and philosophical tradition, in which 'no moment, no mark (grapheme) is too small for examination [... and ...] conflicts between speaking and writing are insinuated [...] legalistic [...] casuistic'.[13] Like Ford's Giovanni they aimed to deconstruct the world of texts so comprehensively that they would come to seem part of a world turned upside down. Thirty years before Derrida and Barthes, the French theatre practitioner and theorist Antonin Artaud in his 1938 essay 'Theatre and the Plague' had divined a comparable spirit in Ford's play when he claimed it as one that 'upsets our sensual tranquillity, releases our repressed subconscious, drives us to a kind of potential rebellion', opening the doors of perception out to a realm where 'all true freedom is dark, infallibly identified with sexual freedom, also dark, without knowing exactly why'.[14] Artaud of course proposes a fully potent, essentializing reading of the play. When he describes the play he has, as it were, become Giovanni. Giovanni is a 'deconstructor', one who deconstructs the social facades of Parma, his father's ambitions and his sister's body. Yet in terms of the binary proposed earlier, Giovanni is a 'weak' deconstructor; the play that contains him, I suggest, has a wider ambit, deconstructing in turn Giovanni's own powerful deconstructing energies. To see this, we can return where we began, with Annabella's heart.

This climactic cardiac moment is carefully overprepared for throughout the play, its texture constantly gesturing towards what we are about to see for which, the play anticipates, we will be duly ungrateful, no matter how we keep our eyes fixed on what the 'unspeakable' Giovanni takes such gleeful pains to enunciate. Before the play begins, Giovanni, in his confession to the Friar, has '[e]mptied the storehouse of [his] thoughts and heart' (I.i.14), equating here 'heart' with 'soul'. He seeks to replenish the heart thus 'emptied' through his union with Annabella, so that joined together they may be '[o]ne soul, one flesh, one love, one heart, one all' (I.i.34). Here again Giovanni sounds like someone who has read early modern love poetry very attentively. His anatomizing at the end of the play shows that he has conducted his reading in an obsessively literal way, linking tenor with vehicle, the literal and metaphorical. The seizure of Annabella's heart is something she rapturously consents to, as she surrenders to him her 'captive heart' (I.ii.266). This follows the gestic moment where Giovanni offers her the prior right to anatomize him:

> GIOVANNI: Here!   *Offers his dagger to her*
> ANNABELLA: What to do?
> GIOVANNI: And here's my breast; strike home!
>   Rip up my bosom; there thou shalt behold
>   A heart in which is writ the truth I speak.
>
>   (I.i.228–31)

The procedure he urges here is precisely that he practises later, and which his enemy (and double)[15] Soranzo threatens when he discovers Annabella is pregnant; to find the name of her lover, he cries, 'I'll rip up thy heart, | And find it there' (IV.iii.52-53).[16]

In the fiction of the play, Giovanni thus rips up Annabella's heart on behalf of all three of them, emptying her storehouse both of heart and the embryo it was supporting, the better to express the vengeful anguish of his own 'heart'. This proves to be too extreme a testing of the links between poetic metaphors of the heart, the theology of the sacred heart of Jesus (which, as Michael Neill shows, Ford draws on) and the 'heart' 'itself'. The terms engaged in Giovanni's final gest, his tableau-like entrance into V.vi, collapse on top of each other. If the point of the anatomy was to bring things to light, then Giovanni's gesture results in obscurity. Giovanni's exit from the scene before hints towards this disassemblage: 'Shrink not, courageous hand; stand up, my heart, | And boldly act my last and greatest part!' (V.v.105–6). The terms Giovanni uses here fold back upon themselves. 'My heart' invokes the use of heart as a term of endearment and companionship available in the period, as when, much earlier in the play, Giovanni instructs Anabella to 'keep well my heart' (II.i.32). As his 'heart' companion or dear friend, she should keep well; as his heart, she should keep well, for where would he be without his heart? Her heart is his to use, which is the riddle couched within 'stand up my heart'; he will shortly bring this phallic command to his self-devised theatre of revenge, entering '*with a heart upon his dagger*', holding it before him as his weapon. This non-heart unmakes his enterprise to achieve fullness of meaning and self-actualization in his own play's last scene. For the oneness Giovanni sought through the language and action of the heart is rather a return to blankness and nullity. Crashaw suggests as much with his epigraph for Ford: 'Thou cheats't us *Ford*, mak'st one seeme two by Art. | What is *Loves Sacrifice*, but *the broken Heart?*'[17] Crashaw riddles with the titles of two other Ford plays which revolve around sacrificial love and gruesomely-staged deaths, implying that Ford has outdone his own ingenuity, with all three plays articulating one and the same thing. The mammalian (or otherwise contrived) heart Giovanni is then compelled to proffer as a metonymic substitute for a 'real' one serves to undo all this furious verbal and embodied playmaking, making bare also the emptiness of the play's (and Giovanni's) devices for readers and audiences alike. Giovanni is too flushed with his triumphs to be aware of this, but the play coolly frames his adolescent excess. Perhaps this is the 'real' reason why Tom Stoppard framed his hit 1982 comedy *The Real*

Thing around a sub-plot where his heroine Annie travels to Glasgow to star as Annabella in a production of *'Tis Pity*. This seems to play partly as a joke against the Scottish hinterlands.[18] In Scotland, Ford might play as the 'real' thing, real quality theatre, 'real' emotion and love; in London, where most of the play is set and where of course it was first staged, audiences would know better. In Derridean terms they would perceive there could be things proffered as props, but these could never be 'real'; and this thing called 'love', the pursuit of which both Ford and Stoppard make so central, would remain elusive also, no matter how poetically or viscerally their invented characters appear to strive for it.[19]

Threading so profusely through the play and the cast the rhetoric of the heart serves to underline that elusiveness. The play makes and then unmakes its central verbal premise. What remains is a scenario that is repugnant if you take Giovanni at his word for what he claims to have done to Annabella's corpse; or ridiculous if you attend to the gap between these claims and the enfeebled means by which any stage production must gesture towards them. The capacity of the text to make and unmake itself runs all the way to the play's last couplet, which I will discuss later. It makes the play seem like a splendid theatrical example of the kind of seventeenth-century text Stanley Fish calls *Self-Consuming Artifacts*. In his terms, 'to read' (or watch) the play 'is to use it up', creating an interpretation 'in which the work disappears',[20] since working through the work creates a process whereby the work confounds its own premises. In this reading, Ford, not Giovanni, emerges as the stronger deconstructor. Neither Ford nor Giovanni may have read William Harvey's famous treatise published in 1628 as *Exercitatio Anatomica de Motu Cordis et Sanguinis in Animalibus* (*Anatomical Exercises on the Motion of the Heart and Blood in Animals*, it was published in England in 1653), but the coincidence is suggestive. For in demonstrating for the first time how blood really did circulate from the heart and through mammalian bodies, Harvey initiates an epoch of literal, empirical exploration and verbal description of the heart and its function within the body machine. This new scientific perspective then made redundant the previous metaphorical grasp of the 'motion of the heart'.[21] Giovanni tries to unite both perspectives. The play, published five years after Harvey's treatise, shows this to be unsustainable.

The reactions depicted from his father and sister (the only family the play gives him) suggest a stronger grasp on the way the undoable might register also as the unsayable, either eschewing words altogether or using them to work beyond them to what words, whether written or spoken, could not possibly fully say. Where Giovanni continues to be profuse in his eloquence to the last, Annabella expires with a dense, deconstructive pun: 'Brother unkind, unkind' (V.v.93). He is unkind, having been not gentle in his stabbing of her. Then too he has 'unkinned' her, in a literal sense, since killing her eliminates her as his sister. He has taken one of his two kin away. Giovanni thinks not so, of course, here literalizing the vows they made earlier: 'Love me, or kill me brother. | [...] Love me, or kill me, sister' (I.i. 276, 279). Ford clearly assumed his first audiences would know both how incest narratives unfold in fiction and would recall the fates of Othello and Desdemona and Romeo and Juliet. Loving and killing fold one into the other. Giovanni is then an 'unkind' brother and the closest kin imaginable. Annabella then reacts to the unspeakable with a line that is unsayable and perhaps not playable; how could an actor utter so many contradictions at once? At this point the publication of the play for the eager reading 'audience' of Caroline London might be read as a gesture towards that unplayability, for contradictions which may not be staged may more easily be weighed by readers.

The cancellation of his father Florio is rhetorically simpler. He dies mid-line: 'Cursed man! – Have I lived to—' (V.vi.61). With the evidence of 'Annabella' now paraded before them, the onlookers are in no doubt as to what causes Florio's demise: 'see what thou hast done, | Broke thy old father's heart!' (V.vi.63). Florio's death is the inverse of the riddle of Annabella's heart. For Florio may indeed be heartbroken, and the pathological cause of death may indeed be cardiac arrest. The characters onstage can 'see' Florio is dying, but they cannot see his breaking heart. They make the obvious metaphorical link; that it is Giovanni who has broken his father's heart, just as he gleefully informs them that his 'hands have from her bosom ripp'd this heart' (V.vi.59). The proclamation of this previous 'unkind' action leads to Florio's 'unkind death'. With his father's death Giovanni becomes fully 'unkinned', having no kin left in Parma. His own death cancels the family completely. Giovanni's assumption of patriarchal control, that it is his destiny to love, kill and revenge, undoes his patriarchal family from within, a self-deconstructing triumph made the more complete because of the fact that their mother is mentioned ('even by our mother's dust I charge you' [I.ii. 277]) in such a way that makes clear she is dead long before the story begins. Florio dies mid-line to make clear his death is to be very sudden, and to underline the forms of unmeaning Giovanni's 'unkind' actions bring the family to. Not even the verse of the father can make sense, so radical is the attack of the son upon the family, conducted, mistakenly, to advance its glory. John Lanchester characterizes such a deconstructive moment as like the action of

> a snake permanently and necessarily eating its own tail. This process is fluid and constant, but at moments the perpetual process of deferral stalls and collapses in on itself. Derrida called this moment an 'aporia,' from a Greek term meaning 'impasse'.[22]

In terms of Giovanni's impulses, this fluid process is in train as the play begins. The death of his entire family, including his brother-in-law, arrests that impasse, momentarily. Again though Ford takes a wider view; the conclusion to his play offers a wider aporia that encompasses the play as a whole, suggesting a structure just like that Lanchester figure evokes. Just as the snake swallows its own tail, so the end of the play envelops the rest. It happens this way.

As is customary in a Renaissance play, order is restored at its end. The audience is invited to view the ruins of Soranzo's feast, with Giovanni, Florio and Soranzo lying dead on the stage. Beyond these deaths a sense of calm needs to prevail. The Cardinal takes charge, dispensing justice and, in being given the last lines of the play to speak, summarizing what the audience has witnessed. He orders that Putana, Annabella's servant, be burnt to death for her complicity in the crimes committed, and banishes Vasques on pain of death. He then confiscates 'all the gold and jewels, or whatsoever' from the family estate 'to the Pope's proper use' (V.vi.157–59). With a quatrain of two heroic couplets (rhymed iambic pentameter), the Cardinal then closes the play:

> We shall have time
> To talk at large of all; but never yet
> Incest and murder so strangely met.
> Of one so young, so rich in Nature's store,
> Who could not say, *'Tis pity she's a whore.*

> (V.vi.164–68)

Here the Cardinal's blandly rhymed assurance projects a confidence that the audience will agree with his judgement of the case, but his credibility is questionable. Catholic friars and priests (as with Friar Laurence in *Romeo and Juliet* and Bonaventura in Ford's play) are frequently sympathetic figures in early modern playtexts. Catholic cardinals, however, are treated more harshly, projected as symptomatic of both the Roman Catholic Church and the morass of iniquity and sexual impropriety which is integral to the way the English in the seventeenth century imagined Italy to be. Excellent examples of such cardinals include those in Webster's two great tragedies, *The White Devil* and *The Duchess of Malfi*, which Ford clearly knew well, and *The Cardinal* in Shirley's 1640 tragedy of that name. The justice the Cardinal dispenses demonstrates harshness towards unwitting victims, as in his demand that Putana be burnt: she must be punished by transference for Annabella's crimes, as Giovanni has taken his sister beyond the realm where the Cardinal can pass judgement. Moreover, his confiscations of the family's estate suggest the greed for which the Catholic Church was notorious, and which was a point of contention throughout Europe from the beginnings of the Reformation in the early sixteenth century.

The Cardinal's last phrase, *'tis pity she's a whore*, envelops the play, since this last half line is also the title of it, and this would seem to suggest that if the Cardinal endorses the play's title then, in return, the play endorses the Cardinal's perspective, one being complicit with the other. Yet this catchphrase (so memorable as a title for a play) makes a contradictory kind of sense. The Cardinal insists that Annabella was a 'whore'. Technically this judgement would be correct, since she committed adultery and incest. But reading this judgement over against the presentation of Annabella suggests its limitations. Ford establishes Annabella as a sympathetic figure, dominated by helpless pathos and, in her last moments, the unwitting victim of her brother's grandiose desires. The model here is Shakespeare's Desdemona, whose tragic death became an often repeated archetype on the London stage. The Cardinal assumes the audience will agree with him, but it is questionable how complete that assent is, though of course they are liable to remember his memorable catchphrase. Ford himself seems to have registered this as problem, in his dedication protesting that the 'gravity of the subject may easily excuse the lightness of the title' (19–20).

The Cardinal treats his phrase as irrefutable: 'who could not say [...]'. The question rather seems to be, if they did say it, what could they possibly mean? If you took the harsh moral line of the Cardinal, you would consider her a whore. But if you did so think of her, how could you pity her? You would rather eagerly condemn her to her fate, with as much relish as the Cardinal sentences Putana. If Annabella is a whore, then it is not a pity. If on the other hand you pity her, recalling in particular her untimely, underplayed death, then you would not think of her as a whore. In this sense, Ford takes advantage of the rhyming couplet which breaks each line so readily into two, with a clear caesura or cut between 'who could not say' and ''tis pity'. The second half of the line breaks equally into two components, each in turn governed by the verbal clause which precedes them: ''tis pity | she's a whore'. Who could not say 'tis pity. Who could not say she's a whore.

At first the line is seamless, and then it reads against itself. She is a whore and not a whore. She is an object of pity and yet not an object of pity. The phrase of course draws us back into the play as a whole, returning us to its beginning. Here in a few surviving copies of the first published quarto of the play, we find a commendatory verse by Thomas Ellice, which seems to grasp the paradox of the Cardinal's claim, and its relationship to the play which that claim appears to govern:

> With admiration I beheld this Whore
> Adorn'd with beauty [...]
> Thy name herein shall endure
> To th'end of age; and Annabella be
> Gloriously fair, even in her infamy.
>
> (1–2, 8–10)

The play (and Annabella) both are and are not whores. They both are and are not admirable. The play, Ellice's early reading suggests, refuses to take the Cardinal's side, finding both play and heroine 'gloriously fair'; yet he refuses to take away the title. It undoes then what it most eagerly seeks to assert. In some of his writings, Derrida subjects words to what he calls 'erasure', striking a line through a word he cannot dispense with, reminding readers that the word does/not represent what it appears to.

The 1633 text of the play represents this undecidability in visual form, using italics and capital letters for the phrase *'Tis pitty shee's a Whoore*.[23] It is quite common for early modern printed texts to use capitals in the middle of lines where modern usage would not. It is common too for a word or phrase to be placed in italic for emphasis over against the roman typeface which, by 1633, had become standard. Ford provided dedications and other ancillary matter for his plays, so we know he had some involvement in seeing the text into print. Modern editors of his plays concur that the way the first printed texts use italics and capitals for emphasis suggests authorial involvement. 'Such use of italic emphasis has a distinctively authorial stamp', A. T. Moore suggests, 'and is an outstanding feature of several early texts of Ford's works. It is the mark of a dramatist who gave some thought to the literary form of his plays'.[24] Derek Roper concurs, pointing out that of all the playtexts Nicholas Okes printed between 1628 and 1635, it is only his edition of *'Tis Pity* that uses italic type in a striking way.[25] It is very likely that Ford oversaw the setting of the play into type, and that the play's final words appeared thus in print at Ford's request; and were thus made available to the wider audience of readers beyond the Phoenix in Drury Lane where the play was first performed, for the publication of Ford's text is part of the newly-expanding market for printed playtexts in the 1630s.[26]

On a first reading, you can grasp the visual presentation of the phrase as a self-referential joke, arcing back through the play you just read. Wilde's famous 1895 farce repeats this device, proclaiming its theme and its title in its last line as 'the importance of being earnest'. Wilde's text too is wilfully deconstructive. In Ford's case the phrase reads as self-refuting. This is partly because of the internal contradictions within the Cardinal's claims. Partly too this has to do with the gap or aporia between the written and the oral, which Derrida has explored so searchingly. For a playtext is an amphibious printed object. Words on the page are presented as they might have been said on stage, or as they might be in future performance. The script can give you the look of the words, but not their sound. The gap between 'look' and 'sound' is unbridgeable. In these terms the italics granted to the Cardinal's phrase are unsayable. Readers will take them to be both his clever dismissal of Annabella and the title of the play. You could say (or read) these lines suavely, urbanely, even sadly, but you could not say them both as the title and the dismissal. That is, audience members could not distinguish the sound of one from the other. Either the title of the play erases the Cardinal's remarks, or the Cardinal's remarks cancel the title of the play. Readers of the 'written' text are privileged over those who merely hear it, since in reading you can entertain the possibility of both readings at once. They occupy the same half line of space on the printed page, but suggest radically different readings of the text encountered. The effect is then to cancel the savage illumination Giovanni strives to bring to bear in the last scene of the play, and follow the path back from the last line to the title page and the first lines, to attempt yet once more the impossible yet rewarding task of resolving the undecidable, a task never completed because its terms come to us in the constant flux of deferral.

Acknowledgements

Thanks to Michael Neill, for his exemplarity, to Sophie Tomlinson, to Sonia Massai and Catherine Silverstone, who first invited me to rethink Ford, to the members of the *'Tis Pity* seminar at the 2006 SAA meeting in Philadelphia; and to the Faculty of Arts and Social Sciences at the University of Waikato, who funded the conference travel to that SAA.

Notes

1   *Selected Plays of John Ford*, ed. Colin Gibson (Cambridge: Cambridge University Press, 1986); *'Tis Pity*, s.d. following line 9; V.vi.24–30. All references to the play are from this edition.

2   Text from *Poetical Works*, ed. Sir Herbert Grierson (Oxford: Oxford University Press, 1968 (1933), p. 35.

3   See his ' "What Strange Riddle's This?": Deciphering *'Tis Pity She's a Whore*', in *John Ford: Critical Revisions*, ed. Michael Neill (Cambridge: Cambridge University Press, 1988), pp. 153–81. This volume is an excellent example of contextualized formalist and historicist readings of Ford which the essays here by myself and Catherine Silverstone seek to disrupt. For an excellent recent approach to reading the 'heart' in this period through literary, cultural and historical lenses, see William Slights's *The Heart in the Age of Shakespeare* (Cambridge: Cambridge University Press, 2008).

4   *OED* online 'deconstruct' s.v. 1.a.

5   For an excellent introduction to Derrida's work, see the entry 'Jacques Derrida' in the *Stanford Encyclopedia of Philosophy*, online: http://plato.stanford.edu/entries/derrida/.

6   *OED* online, 'deconstructionism' s.v. 1.b, citing R. M. Adams.

7   *Merriam-Webster* online, 'deconstruct'.

8   Derek Attridge and Thomas Baldwin, 'Obituary: Jacques Derrida', *Guardian Weekly* (15–21 October 2004), p. 30.

9   T. S. Eliot, *The Complete Poems and Plays* 1909–1950 (San Diego, CA: Harcourt, Brace, Jovanovich, 1971), l. 41, p. 38.

10 Jacques Derrida, 'Play: from the Pharmakon to the Letter and from Blindness to the Supplement', in *The Norton Anthology of Theory and Criticism*, ed. Vincent B. Leitch (New York: Norton, 2001), p. 1875. All direct citations from theorists are from this volume. Students are highly recommended to consult the readings in this volume, along with the consummately helpful introductions and suggestions for further reading.

11 Derrida, *Norton Anthology of Theory and Criticism*, p. 1875.

12 Barthes, *Norton Anthology of Theory and Criticism*, p. 1466.

13 Andrew DuBois, 'Introduction', *Close Reading: the Reader*, ed. Frank Lentricchia and Andrew Dubois (Durham, NC: Duke University Press, 2003), p. 35.

14 Antonin Artaud, *The Theatre and Its Double*, trans.Victor Corti (London: John Calder, 1985), pp. 19, 25.

15 They are both 'husband' and 'lover' to Annabella.

16 See Michael Neill's essay, pp. 156–57, for anecdotes of anatomized hearts from the period which it is claimed could be read in just such ways.

17 Richard Crashaw, '*Vpon* Ford's *two Tragedyes* Loves Sacrifice *and* The Broken Heart', in his *Steps to the Temple 1646, together with Selected Poems in Manuscript* (Menston: Scolar Press, 1970), p. 45.

18   This might also draw on the reputation of Glasgow's Citizens' Theatre for its 'strongly visual and visceral form of theatre, particularly suited to the production of the classic plays of the European repertoire', 'University of Glasgow Special Collections: Citizens' Theatre', online: http://special.lib.gla.ac.uk/STA/citzcat/index.html.

19   For more on Stoppard's appropriation of Ford, see my 'Postmodern Tragedy: Returning to John Ford', in *Tragedy in Transition*, ed. Sarah Annes Brown and Catherine Silverstone (Oxford: Blackwell, 2007), pp. 248–49.

20   Stanley Fish, Self-*Consuming Artifacts: the Experience of Seventeenth-Century Literature* (Berkeley, CA: University of California Press, 1972), p. 3. Fish's earlier *Surprised by Sin: the Reader in Paradise Lost* is another exemplary application of deconstructive rhetoric strategies to a canonical early modern text.

21   For a concise assessment of Harvey's experiments and their significance, see Andrew Gregory, *Harvey's Heart: The Discovery of Blood Circulation* (Cambridge: Icon Books, 2001).

22   John Lanchester, 'Melting into Air', *The New Yorker* (10 November, 2008), pp. 80–84, p. 84.

23   This line is from the Scolar Press facsimile of the play *John Ford: 'Tis Pity She's a Whore 1633* (Menston: Scolar Press, 1969).

24   A. T. Moore, in his edition of *Love's Sacrifice* (Manchester: Manchester University Press, 2002), p. 273.

25   See Derek Roper's edition of *Tis Pity She's a Whore* (London: Methuen, 1975), p. lxiii. For a summary of evidence for Ford attending so carefully to the visuality of his printed playtexts, se R. J. Fehrenbach's 'Typographical Variation in Ford's Texts: Accidentals or Substantives', in *'Concord in Discord': the Plays of John Ford, 1586–1986*, ed. Donald K. Anderson, Jr (New York: AMS Press, 1986), pp. 265–94.

26   For more on this audience and its reading practices, see Martin Butler's 'The Caroline Audience', in his *Theatre and Crisis 1632–1640* (Cambridge: Cambridge University Press, 1984), pp. 101–40.

CHAPTER EIGHT

New Directions: *'Tis Pity She's a Whore* and the Space of the Stage

Lisa Hopkins

The English Renaissance stage was a location characterized above all by the fluidity with which it could be used. As Sir Philip Sidney tartly observed in *An Apology for Poetry*,

> Now ye shall have three ladies walk to gather flowers and then we must believe the stage to be a garden. By and by we hear news of shipwreck in the same place, and then we are to blame if we accept it not for a rock. Upon the back of that comes out a hideous monster with fire and smoke, and then the miserable beholders are bound to take it for a cave. While in the meantime two armies fly in, represented with four swords and bucklers, and then what hard heart will not receive it for a pitched field?[1]

In *A Midsummer Night's Dream*, Peter Quince cheerfully collapses the distinction between reality and illusion when he says, 'Pat, pat; and here's a marvellous convenient place for our rehearsal. This green plot shall be our stage, this hawthorn-brake our tiring-house'.[2] In *The Tempest*, the stage can represent a ship; in Chapman's *Memorable Masque* it is a gold mine in Virginia. Elsewhere in Renaissance drama there are scenes in prisons, convents, brothels, fairs, palaces and private houses. Indeed it is hard to think of any terrestrial location which the Renaissance stage was never called upon to represent, and even heaven and hell, or at least possible approach routes to them, could be gestured at, as for instance in *Doctor Faustus* (a play by which *'Tis Pity* is clearly influenced – Cyrus Hoy says that 'Ford's Giovanni is a young Faustus, dabbling in forbidden love as Marlowe's hero has dabbled in forbidden knowledge'[3] – in ways to which I will return), in which 'Hell is discovered'.[4] In this chapter I want to explore one specific aspect of the representation of space in 'Tis Pity She's a Whore, awareness of which is heightened by a recognition of the play's rootedness in a long series of earlier explorations of the logic of dramatic space: the way in which throughout the play a thinly and vaguely understood sense of the space of the spiritual world consistently fails to compete with our far more fully realized awareness of the resonances and politics of domestic and civic space. The strong predominance of the secular over the spiritual simultaneously undercuts the already flagging authority of the Cardinal, whose flippant verdict supplies both the play's title and the nearest it comes to any sort of moral compass, and at the same time hollows out a moral vacuum, into which the audience are perforce invited to step to consider their own perspective on events – a perspective inevitably honed and sharpened by the care taken by the play to create an illusion of a coherent social state to which they can readily relate.

By the time he came to write 'Tis Pity, Ford had served a dramatic apprenticeship involving co-authorship of plays with such seasoned dramatists as Dekker, Rowley, Webster and, almost certainly, Fletcher, and he was also clearly extremely familiar with the plays of Shakespeare and Marlowe. One product of these earlier collaborations is The Witch of Edmonton, which he co-wrote with Dekker and Rowley in 1621, and Sidney R. Homan Jr has proposed using this and Romeo and Juliet as ways of understanding 'Tis Pity, suggesting that

> Perhaps the reason for the variety of critical responses to 'Tis Pity lies in the fact that in this play Ford had either reversed or complicated the notions of human responsibility which inform the early Shakespearean tragedy and the collaboration of 1621 that both directly and indirectly influenced him.[5]

The Witch of Edmonton is also the most useful play for my own purposes, especially since it is in itself steeped in memories of earlier plays: Mother Sawyer, like Sycorax in The Tempest, is 'like a bow buckl'd and bent together';[6] Susan badgering Frank to know what's the matter is like Portia badgering Brutus (II.ii.66–81) in Shakespeare's Julius Caesar; Mother Sawyer is referred to as 'Mother Bumby' (IV.i.200) and 'Gammer Gurton' (IV.i.256), both titles of earlier plays about old women; Frank, Don-Quixote, like, speaks of 'Some windmill in my brains' (IV.ii.87); and Cuddy thinks he could recommend the dog to 'Moll Cutpurse' (V.i.174), heroine of *The Roaring Girl*. In IV.i, the grounds on which the locals suspect Mother Sawyer of witchcraft are clearly mere superstition and are recognized as such by the more educated members of the community; however, though later in the scene she puts up a magnificent self-defence, she is then quite clearly confirmed to be in fact guilty, in a pattern reminiscent of Vittoria Corombona in *The White Devil*.

In particular, *The Witch of Edmonton*, like *'Tis Pity*, remembers *Doctor Faustus* – Cuddy says of his horse, 'Give him oats, but water him not till I come' (III.i.20), echoing Doctor Faustus's instruction to the Horse-Courser, 'ride him not into the water, at any hand' (A-text, IV.i.124–25; the episode is also present in the B-text, though there the wording is slightly different), and a spirit disguises himself as Katherine (III.i.72) as one does as Helen of Troy in V.i. of *Doctor Faustus* (A-text; the episode is also present in the B-text). It also recalls *A Midsummer Night's Dream*, which, like *'Tis Pity*, gives us a character named Hippolita who seems to be not altogether comfortable with the constraints of marriage, an echo underlined when the Hippolita of *'Tis Pity* proves to have a niece who espouses the vocation of nun with which Hermia is threatened in *A Midsummer Night's Dream*. Moreover Louis Montrose has persuasively argued that the conception of Hippolytus, son of Theseus and Hippolyta and future victim of the incestuous passion of his stepmother Phaedra, is proleptically glanced at in *A Midsummer Night's Dream*, so that

> sedimented within the verbal texture of *A Midsummer Night's Dream* are traces of those forms of sexual and familial violence which the play would suppress: acts of bestiality and incest, of parricide, uxoricide, filicide, and suicide.[7]

In *The Witch of Edmonton*, as in *A Midsummer Night's Dream*, some country people meet to rehearse an entertainment and one of them asks to see an almanac (II.i.55); one of them also gets involved with a magic figure, who tells him to 'turn to the west' (II.i.233), also a location of symbolic importance in *A Midsummer Night's Dream*; and Cuddy (whose name in fact means 'donkey') suggests that he might be called ass (III.i.111), as Bottom in *A Midsummer Night's Dream* acquires an ass's head.

Finally, *The Witch of Edmonton*, like *'Tis Pity*, is also interested in the politics of domestic space, as seen in the following exchange:

SIR ARTHUR: Alone? Then I must tell thee in plain terms
   Thou hast wrong'd thy master's house basely and lewdly.
FRANK: Your house, sir?
SIR ARTHUR: Yes sir. If the nimble devil
That wanton'd in your blood rebell'd against
All rules of honest duty, you might, sir,
Have found out some more fitting place than here
To have built a stews in.

(I.i.76–82)

Here Sir Arthur, as we shall see, anticipates *Tis Pity*'s Florio, who is similarly concerned about trouble coming too close to his doors, as well as ironically recalling Shakespeare's Lady Macbeth. Another note which we will hear in *'Tis Pity* is also sounded here when Frank says to Winnifride 'While we together are, we are at home | In any place' (III.ii.19–20); later, he declares, 'All life is but a wand'ring to find home; | When we are gone, we are there' (IV.ii.31–32), and later still says that 'He is not lost | Who bears his peace within him' (V.iii.73–74). This psychologized perspective on space, in which its meaning for the individual is radically divorced from actual locality, is one to which I shall return later in connection with *'Tis Pity She's a Whore*.

After such an apprenticeship, it is no surprise that by the time he comes to write *'Tis Pity* Ford shows himself extremely well aware of how to use to the full the rich potential of the stage to figure and suggest different possible locations. As Verna Foster observes,

> In *'Tis Pity* Ford creates the sense of a tightly knit urban community by focusing on three 'houses' – the homes of Florio and Soranzo and the Friar's cell – and by moving his characters singly or in small groups from one house to another. He particularizes these important places of his drama through his use of the physical possibilities of his stage and through properties and stage business.[8]

'Tis Pity was first staged at the Phoenix, which appears to have had two doors leading out from the tiring-house and a discovery space in between them, allowing for the possibility of flexible creation of a series of different locations. It is also clear that it had an upper stage,[9] and of the spaces available to him, this is the one which Ford invests with the greatest symbolic meaning. In his later *Perkin Warbeck*, the figure of the dreamy, ineffectual would-be king seems to glance at Shakespeare's *Richard II*, in which there is a highly significant descent from a balcony:

Down, down I come, like glist'ring Phaëton,
Wanting the manage of unruly jades.
In the base court? Base court where kings grow base
To come at traitors' calls and do them grace.
In the base court? Come down? Down court, down king!
For night-owls shriek where mounting larks should sing.[10]

In *'Tis Pity*, Annabella first appears on a balcony. From it, she sees and admires Giovanni, and then descends; shortly afterwards, she embarks on an incestuous affair with him. Later, she repents and reascends to the balcony, from which she throws a letter of warning to the Friar for him to pass on to Giovanni.

On one level, this is clearly readable as a descent from the moral/spiritual high ground, and then a subsequent return to it. In *'Tis Pity*, the heaven/hell polarity is established from the outset, when the Friar warns Giovanni that

Heaven admits no jest; wits that presumed
On wit too much, by striving how to prove
There was no God, with foolish grounds of art,
Discovered first the nearest way to Hell.

(I.i.4–7)

For the Friar, Hell is a physical place that can be reached by a concrete route, as it was on the medieval stage in a tradition that is still being gestured at as late as *Arden of Faversham*:

SHAKEBAG: Oh Will, where art thou?
BLACK WILL: Here, Shakebag, almost in hell's mouth, where I cannot see my way for smoke.[11]

At the same time, though, it is worth paying attention not only to the open acknowledgement of the possibility of atheism in the Friar's speech but also to the fact that the 'wits' who espoused that idea might well be supposed to have included Marlowe, arguably the most celebrated Renaissance figure to be publicly identified as an atheist, and indeed Cyrus Hoy describes the Friar as 'warning him against what amounts to the fate of Faustus'.[12]

The Friar's own view, however, is unwavering. Later, he tells Giovanni,

Nay, then I see th'art too far sold to Hell;
It lies not in the compass of my prayers
To call thee back.

(II.v.37–39)

At least one other character shares the Friar's literalized view of Hell: Richardetto says,

All human worldly courses are uneven;
No life is blessed but the way to Heaven.

(IV.ii.20–21)

It is also clear that we should read the two poles of heaven and hell in conventional above/below terms, as in *Doctor Faustus* where the Old Man tells Faustus that 'I see an angel hovers o'er thy head' (A-text, V.vi.54; also present in B-text with a very slight difference of wording): the Friar warns Giovanni that 'thou hast moved a Majesty above | With thy unrangèd almost blasphemy' (I.ii.44–45), and Richardetto declares 'there is One | Above begins to work' (IV.ii.8–9). What is up, then, should be good, and what is low should not.

However, the logic of Annabella's pattern of descent and reascension does not readily adhere to this paradigm, for the issues are not quite so clear-cut. Firstly, it is when Annabella is at the lower of the two poles between which she moves that the highest metaphorical associations accrue to her, when, her pregnancy detected, she declares to Soranzo that the man who got her pregnant was 'So angel-like, so glorious' (IV.iii.37). This has obviously Marian echoes, with a pregnant woman assuring her outraged husband that her baby is of supernatural origin:[13] in the mystery play *Joseph*, for instance, the pregnant Virgin Mary says exactly this, and her outraged husband replies,

An aungel! Allas! Alas! Fy for schame!
Ye syn now in that ye to say
To puttyn an aungel in so gret blame.[14]

This episode may also encode a recollection of *Doctor Faustus*, specifically the episode in which Mephistopheles brings grapes for the Duchess of Vanholt (A-text, IV.iii; the episode is also present in the B-text), since the idea of the pregnant Virgin craving (and duly receiving) out-of-season fruit is a staple of the many variants of the Cherry Tree Carol, of which clear traces can be found as early as the medieval Coventry Corpus Christi plays (Mystery VIII). Faustus could thus appear as a parodic version of Joseph just as Annabella can resemble a blasphemous version of Mary.

Annabella's literal descent thus proves not to debase her in the ways that might have been imagined. Even when the idea of coming down does present itself in Annabella's exchange with Soranzo, it does not work in the ways that might be expected. At IV.iii.64–68, Soranzo says,

> Dost thou triumph? The treasure of the earth
> Shall not redeem thee, were there kneeling kings
> Did beg thy life, or angels did come down
> To plead in tears, yet should not all prevail
> Against my rage: dost thou not tremble yet?

In the wake of the previous Marian imagery, the twin ideas of kneeling kings and treasure seem unmistakably to tap into the iconography of the nativity, as recorded in Matthew 2, reinforcing the sense of an aura of the holy accruing to Annabella rather than of her having been in any way tainted by her descent.

Soranzo's language might well seem also to echo rhetoric such as that of Father Forrest, a Franciscan martyr under Henry VIII, who declared that 'if an angel should come down from heaven and teach "any other doctrine than that which he had received and believed from his youth" he would not believe him', a remark which Roy Battenhouse introduces in connection with his discussion of the Catholic associations of the Ghost in *Hamlet*.[15] The Seraphic Doctor, after whom Ford's Friar is presumably named, was indeed a Franciscan theologian, and Franciscans may be alluded to in *Doctor Faustus* too: the Revels editors' note on the name 'Friar Sandelo' (A-text, III.ii.94; also in the B-text) observes that 'The name Sandelo may suggest "sandal", often spelled *sandell* in the sixteenth century; the Franciscans were the only order permitted to wear sandals'. In *'Tis Pity*, though, it is not the Franciscan friar who uses such language, but the very secular and indeed profane Soranzo, and he does so to dismiss the logic of elevation and debasement which structures the heaven/hell polarity: whether kings look up to him or angels come down to him, it will make no difference.

Conversely, when we first see Annabella on the balcony she is not alone, but accompanied by her venal and amoral 'tut'ress', Putana. She is, therefore, already associated with taint, and despite the fact that there are some obvious points of comparison in some other respects, she is pointedly *not* like Juliet, who uses the balcony as a space for solitary thought and to mark a physical distance between herself and Romeo until after they are married (after which he ascends to her rather than she descending to him). Rather Annabella is more like Bianca in *Women Beware Women*, a play to which Ford obsessively recurs – its sub-plot is echoed in the main plot of *'Tis Pity*, and its Livio is clearly an influence on the Livio of *The Fancies, Chaste and Noble* – for the first time we see Bianca after her initial appearance she too is standing on a balcony where, framed in the window, she is seen by the duke as being as much a marketable commodity as the wares in a shopfront. Bianca's ambiguous positioning enables us to see how she is poised uneasily between the private world inside and the public world outside (the balcony is also a liminal space in another sense, since it has its back to the tiring house and its front to the stage); Annabella's has something of the same effect.

The question Annabella asks when she perceives Giovanni represents a further inversion of the apparent situational logic: 'what blessed shape | Of some celestial creature now appears?' (I.ii.131–32) – what is 'celestial' is below here rather than above. The topsy-turvy logic implicit here is underlined when Annabella and Putana discuss her first sexual encounter with Giovanni:

> ANNABELLA: Go where thou wilt, in mind I'll keep thee here,
> And where thou art, I know I shall be there.
> Guardian!
> *Enter Putana.*
> PUTANA: Child, how is't child? Well, thank Heaven, ha?
> ANNABELLA: O guardian, what a paradise of joy
> Have I passed over!
> PUTANA: Nay, what a paradise of joy have you passed under!
> (II.i.39–45)

Firstly, Annabella riddles the logic of place entirely by effectively refusing to recognize the existence of separate locations (a strategy to which I will return later); secondly, she and Putana doubly invert the over/under paradigm, crudely in Putana's case but more subtly and suggestively in Annabella's, since here too she gestures at a schema in which what is paradisal/celestial is below rather than above. The customary and traditional logic of stage space is thus evoked only in order to be disabled.

In the same way as the use of the balcony plays with both secular and spiritual meanings, an actual border between the secular and the spiritual is both plotted and riddled in the play, when the Watch pursue Grimaldi for the murder of Bergetto but are stopped short when they find themselves trespassing on the domain of the Cardinal:

> Why, how now, friends! What saucy mates are you
> That know nor duty nor civility?
> Are we a person fit to be your host,
> Or is our house become your common inn,
> To beat our doors at pleasure? What such haste
> Is yours as that it cannot wait fit times?
> Are you the masters of this commonwealth,
> And know no more discretion?
>
> (III.ix.28–35)

The Cardinal implies both that the Watch have made a serious mistake about the nature of actual locations, since he affects to believe that they have mistaken his house for an inn, and also that in so doing they have tarnished their civic authority with the taint of savagery and lack of 'civility', inverting the polarities of the border which supposedly separates the one from the other. The more profound violation, however, is the Cardinal's own, for by protecting Grimaldi after his murder of Bergetto he acts against the dictates of both justice and morality. This undermines not only his religious authority but also the basis on which, at the end of the play, he will take it upon himself to police the borders of the civic by expelling Putana from them.

The importance of boundaries and their impact on civic and social existence is also stressed elsewhere in the play, but on every occasion in a way that shows a violation of the boundary in question. Hippolita violates the private space of Soranzo's inner sanctum:

> VASQUES: [*Within*] Pray forbear, in rules of civility, let me give
> notice on't: I shall be taxed of my neglect of duty and service.
> SORANZO: What rude intrusion interrupts my peace?
> Can I be nowhere private?
>
> (II.ii.19–23)

Even the foolish Bergetto is aware of the protocols governing the use of urban space, although he learns his lesson the hard way and is forced to occupy a very undignified space indeed:

> As I was walking just now in the street, I met a swaggering
> fellow would needs take the wall of me; and because he did
> thrust me, I very valiantly called him rogue. He hereupon bade

me draw; I told him I had more wit than so; but when he saw
that I would not, he did so maul me with the hilts of his rapier,
that my head sung whilst my feet capered in the kennel.

(II.vi.69–75)

And Soranzo shows a similar awareness when he says to the
Cardinal: 'Most reverend lord, this grace hath made me proud |
That you vouchsafe my house' (V.iv.48–49), although the Cardinal's
arrival at his house will in fact prove the precursor to his own death.
Most interesting is Florio's demand:

What mean these sudden broils so near my doors?
Have you not other places but my house
To vent the spleen of your disordered bloods?
Must I be haunted still with such unrest
As not to eat or sleep in peace at home?

(I.ii.21–26)

This not only reflects on the politics of urban space and provides a
further instance of their disruption but also broadens out their
implications, since it foreshadows *Perkin Warbeck*, which opens
with the line 'Still to be haunted, still to be pursued' (I.1.i), which
has in turn been seen as echoing the opening line of *Henry IV, Part
One*, 'So shaken as we are, so wan with care'.[16] Thus the apparently
domestic suddenly opens up to reveal a far greater resonance.

The border between the private and the public more generally is
also important. In Thomas Heywood's domestic tragedy *A Woman
Killed with Kindness*, a scene rich in its exploration of the symbolic
connotations of household space culminates in frustration as Master
Frankford's prolonged penetration of the multiple layers of his
house, which we are invited to suppose will end in the bedroom, in
fact stops short at the threshold of it:

This is the key that opes my outward gate,
This is the hall door, this my withdrawing chamber.
But this, that door that's bawd unto my shame,
Fountain and spring of all my bleeding thoughts,
Where the most hallowed order and true knot
Of nuptial sanctity hath been profaned.
It leads to my polluted bedchamber,
Once my terrestrial heaven, now my earth's hell,
The place where sins in all their ripeness dwell.
But I forget myself; now to my gate.[17]

This titillating approach in fact balks us, and even when Frankford actually reaches the right door, he enters without us: the characters inside the room may in due course come out to us, but we cannot go inside to them. In *'Tis Pity*, where the title of *A Woman Killed with Kindness* seems to be remembered when Vasques remarks of Soranzo that 'he will go near to kill my lady with unkindness' (IV.iii.181–82), the logic of Heywood's sequence is reversed by the stage direction which opens V.v, 'Enter Giovanni and Annabella lying on a bed'. As Zenón Luis-Martínez has it,

> the movement from the street into the house, from the house into the bedroom, from the bedroom into the bed, from the bed into Annabella's bleeding womb, and from the womb to the heart, propose a topography of incest which compels the gaze to an endless progress toward the profanation of the very limits of privacy.[18]

In *A Woman Killed with Kindness* we are made aware of where we cannot go; in *'Tis Pity*, there is nowhere we cannot go, and yet this is the scene in which Giovanni and Annabella, for all their physical intimacy, are at their furthest from each other in emotional terms, for Annabella is beginning to repent and to believe in a heaven which to Giovanni is no better than a myth. Later in the play, structures of in/out and public/private are further riddled when hired banditti prove welcome guests at a private birthday party and when Putana, who has been the most intimate confidante of Annabella, is cast out entirely from civic space. In each of these cases, the usual logic of in/out is destabilized just as that of up/down is, robbing the audience of their usual bearings and implicitly inviting them to supply their own.

The one area of the stage of which Ford does *not* make use is also worth considering. *'Tis Pity* in many ways recalls *Hamlet*: as the Revels editor notes, Vasques's 'Work you that way, old mole? Then I have the wind of you' (II.ii.146–47) is 'a mixed metaphor which probably conflates two phrases from *Hamlet*: "Well said, old mole! canst work i'th'earth so fast?" (I.v.162) and "Why do you go about to recover the wind of me [...]?" (III.ii.337–39)', and Soranzo when planning to drink from the poisoned cup declares:

> Hippolita, I thank you, and will pledge
> This happy union as another life:
> Wine there!

(IV.i.63–65)

Both the reference to a 'union' and the idea of the innocent person quaffing from the poisoned cup echo *Hamlet*, especially when Vasques, like Claudius, tells him not to drink. Most notably, the Ghost's 'But soft, methinks I scent the morning air' (I.v.58) seems to be directly echoed in the Friar's 'But soft, methinks I see repentance work' (III.vi.31), and the two characters are also linked by the fact that both offer graphic visions of hell. (Cyrus Hoy also compares the Friar's description of hell with the view of hell in *Doctor Faustus*.)[19] In *Hamlet*, the Ghost declares,

> I am thy father's spirit,
> Doom'd for a certain term to walk the night,
> And for the day confin'd to fast in fires,
> Till the foul crimes done in my days of nature
> Are burnt and purg'd away. But that I am forbid
> To tell the secrets of my prison-house,
> I could a tale unfold whose lightest word
> Would harrow up thy soul, freeze thy young blood,
> Make thy two eyes like stars start from their spheres,
> Thy knotted and combined locks to part,
> And each particular hair to stand on end
> Like quills upon the fretful porpentine.
> But this eternal blazon must not be
> To ears of flesh and blood.
>
> (I.v.9–22)

In *'Tis Pity*, the Friar echoes this closely when he tells Annabella,

> There is a place –
> List, daughter! – in a black and hollow vault,
> Where day is never seen; there shines no sun,
> But flaming horror of consuming fires;
> A lightless sulphur, choked with smoky fogs
> Of an infected darkness: in this place
> Dwell many thousand thousand sundry sorts
> Of never-dying deaths: there damnèd souls
> Roar without pity, there are gluttons fed
> With toads and adders; there is burning oil
> Poured down the drunkard's throat, the usurer
> Is forced to sup whole draughts of molten gold;
> There is the murderer forever stabbed,
> Yet can he never die; there lies the wanton

On racks of burning steel, while in his soul
He feels the torment of his raging lust.

(III.vi.8–23)

However, no scene in *'Tis Pity* calls for or would permit the use
of an understage area, as the ghost scene in *Hamlet* does – 'you hear
this fellow in the cellarage'[20] – or as is needed later to bury Ophelia
in. Indeed the stage direction which heads this particular scene (and
Ford is normally careful in such matters) says that it takes place in
the Friar's study (III.vi.0 sd), with the Friar sitting in a chair and
Annabella kneeling before him. Roper's note adds that 'It is
uncertain where Ford meant this impressive scene to be located',
because at line 44 of the scene Giovanni says of Soranzo that 'He
stays below'; this specifically disables any suggestion that the space
'below' might be in any sense a spiritual rather than a physical one,
since 'below' must be a part of the house to which Soranzo can gain
access (and also suggests that we may in fact be once again seeing
Annabella on the balcony).

Wherever it is located, moreover, this speech is in fact
significantly different from the apparent equivalent in Shakespeare.
Not only does it opt for the clunkily defined rather than the
suggestively sketched in its presentation of a vision of hell, but there
is no suggestion that that vision is born from actual experience:
indeed, several features of it are clearly derived from emblem books,
with such classic and well-established images as molten gold being
poured down the throat of the money-lover. Even odder are some of
the little linguistic peculiarities into which the Friar's flowing
rhetoric leads him: the murderer 'can [...] never die', yet surely, if he
is in hell, he is already dead? And how can the wanton be said to feel
anything 'in his soul' when he presumably no longer has a body to
oppose it to? There is no sense of reality or possibility here, nothing
of the power of a Marlovian or Miltonic vision of hell, and in fact is
is clearly second-hand: as the Revels editor notes,

> The Friar's part in this scene has many echoes of the
> penitential poem *Christes Bloodie Sweat* (1613), by 'I. F.',
> who was almost certainly Ford himself [...] For the
> description of Hell, where the parallel is closest, an anterior
> source may be Nashe's *Pierce Pennilesse*.

Indeed, a study is in some sense the only appropriate setting for
such a speech, since it smells so strongly of the study, a point which
will be underlined twice more, first when Giovanni says 'Let poring

book-men dream of other worlds' (V.iii.13) and next when he muses that 'The schoolmen teach that all this globe of earth | Shall be consumed to ashes in a minute' (V.v.30–31). And a study, as we have seen in *Doctor Faustus*, is not a location whose pleasures can easily compete with those of direct sensory experience; indeed, it is a place which, in one sort of spatial logic, proves to be a staging-post to hell.

In '*Tis Pity She's a Whore* no character is borne off to hell: the worst fate to befall anyone, other than death itself, is what happens to Putana, which is expulsion from civic space. Throughout the play, Ford evokes Marlovian and Shakespearean drama, but he also reminds us that in the years which intervene between their plays and his the theatre has effectively shrunk and diminished in its resonance, showing us now only this world rather than shades or hints of the next. Our sense of this is heightened by '*Tis Pity*'s repeated reminders of the Marlovian model which it both imitates and deviates from, and which Ford indeed renders inherently divided by the fact that he seems to display a distinct preference for the spatial aesthetic of the A-text in particular rather than the significantly different one of the B-text. In B, Faustus orders,

> Ashtaroth, Belimoth, Mephistopheles!
> Go horse these traitors on your fiery backs,
> And mount aloft with them as high as heaven;
> Then pitch them headlong to the lowest hell.
>
> (IV.ii.78–81)

Later, Mephistopheles tells him "'Twas I that, when thou wert I'the way to heaven, | Damned up thy passage' (V.ii.98-9), and finally a stage direction assures us that '*Hell is discovered*' (V.ii.121 sd). This physicality is, however, notably eschewed in the A-text; there none of these passages is present, and instead we find the very different logic of the Old Man's injunction to the devils 'Hence, hell!' (V.vi.119), in which location is specifically figured as dependent on and produced by the human mind. That is also the idea which lies behind the line spoken by Mephistopheles, 'Why this is hell nor am I out of it' (A-text, I.iii.77) (though that is present in the B text too), and in fact that line is closely echoed in '*Tis Pity* when Soranzo exclaims 'I carry Hell about me, all my blood | Is fired in swift revenge' (IV.iii.149). Equally Hippolita, like Mephistopheles, appears to experience a hell on earth:

> I feel my minute coming; had that slave
> Kept promise – O, my torment! – thou this hour
> Hadst died, Soranzo. – Heat above hell-fire! –
> Yet ere I pass away – cruel, cruel flames! –
> Take here my curse amongst you: may thy bed
> Of marriage be a rack unto thy heart –
> Burn, blood, and boil in vengeance; O my heart,
> My flame's intolerable!
>
> (IV.i.90–97)

Such concreteness and certainty contrast tellingly with the language used about hell elsewhere in the play. Giovanni says:

> But 'twere somewhat strange
> To see the waters burn: could I believe
> This might be true, I could as well believe
> There might be Hell or Heaven.
>
> (V.v.32–35)

Even the Friar can at least consider the claims of natural philosophy against those of religion:

> Indeed, if we were sure there were no Deity,
> Nor Heaven nor Hell, then to be led alone
> By Nature's light – as were philosophers
> Of elder times – might instance some defence.
> But 'tis not so: then madman, thou wilt find
> That Nature is in Heaven's positions blind.
>
> (II.v.29–34)

Actually, though, what the play appears to dramatize might be said to be rather the converse: that heaven is in nature's positions blind, or at any rate that what we learn or are told about both heaven and hell is far less compelling than what we experientially understand about earth, for throughout this play an obviously abstract and second-hand description of the world beyond is both tellingly contrasted with a far more concrete and fully realized discourse of civic and household space and also undercut by a careful and informed use of stage tradition and dramatic allusion to underscore the distinctiveness of Ford's vision and the creativeness of his stagecraft, and the extent to which both are used in this play to cut the audience loose from their traditional moral moorings.

Notes

1 Sir Philip Sidney, *An Apology for Poetry*, ed. Geoffrey Shepherd, revised R. W. Maslen (Manchester: Manchester University Press, 2002), p. 111.

2 William Shakespeare, *A Midsummer Night's Dream*, ed. Harold F. Brooks (London: Methuen, 1979), III.i.2–4.

3 Cyrus Hoy, '"Ignorance in Knowledge": Marlowe's Faustus and Ford's Giovanni', *Modern Philology* 57.3 (February 1960), pp. 145–54, p. 146.

4 Christopher Marlowe, *Doctor Faustus*, ed. David Bevington and Eric Rasmussen (Manchester: Manchester University Press, 1993), B-text, V.ii.121 s.d. All further quotations will be taken from this edition and reference will be given in the text.

5 Sidney R. Homan, Jr, 'Shakespeare and Dekker as Keys to Ford's *'Tis Pity She's a Whore*', *Studies in English Literature, 1500–1900* 7.2 (spring 1967), pp. 269–76, p. 276.

6 Thomas Dekker, John Ford and William Rowley, *The Witch of Edmonton*, ed. Simon Trussler and Jacqui Russell (London: Methuen, 1983), II.i.4. All further quotations from the play will be taken from this edition and reference will be given in the text.

7 Louis Montrose, '*A Midsummer Night's Dream* and the Shaping Fantasies of Elizabethan Culture: Gender, Power, Form', *Representations* 2 (1983), pp. 65–87, p. 75.

8 Verna Foster, "*'Tis Pity She's a Whore* as City Tragedy', in *John Ford: Critical Re-Visions*, ed. Michael Neill (Cambridge: Cambridge University Press, 1988), pp. 181–200, p. 184.

9 David Stevens, 'The Stagecraft of James Shirley', *Educational Theatre Journal* 29.4 (December 1977), pp. 493–516, p. 495.

10 William Shakespeare, *King Richard II*, ed. Charles R. Forker (London: Thomson Learning, 2002), III.iii.178–83.

11 Anon., *Arden of Faversham*, in *The Routledge Anthology of Renaissance Drama*, ed. Simon Barker and Hilary Hinds (London: Routledge, 2003), xii, ll.1–3.

12 Hoy, '"Ignorance in Knowledge"', pp. 146–47.

13 For comment on this, see Alison Findlay, *A Feminist Perspective on Renaissance Drama* (Oxford: Blackwell, 1999), pp. 29–30.

14 *Joseph*, in *English Mystery Plays*, ed. Peter Happé (Harmondsworth: Penguin, 1975), p. 224.

15 Roy Battenhouse, 'The Ghost in *Hamlet*: A Catholic "Linchpin"?', *Studies in Philology* 48.1–2 (1951), pp. 161–92, p. 174.

16 William Shakespeare, *Henry IV, Part 1*, ed. P. H. Davison (Penguin: Harmondsworth, 1968), I.1.i.

17 Thomas Heywood, *A Woman Killed with Kindness*, in *The Routledge Anthology of Renaissance Drama*, ed. Simon Barker and Hilary Hinds (London: Routledge, 2003), xii. 8–17.

18 Zenón Luis-Martínez, *In Words and Deeds: The Spectacle of Incest in English Renaissance Tragedy* (Amsterdam: Rodopi, 2002), p. 196.

19 Hoy, '"Ignorance in Knowledge"', pp. 149–50.

20 William Shakespeare, *Hamlet*, ed. Harold Jenkins (London: Methuen, 1982), I.v.159.

CHAPTER NINE

A Survey of Resources

Rhonda Lemke Sanford

In what follows, I hope to present a useful compendium of resources for students and researchers of John Ford and *'Tis Pity*, and for professors and lecturers teaching the play. I have organized this chapter into syllabi (both undergraduate and graduate), databases, online resources and caveats, and editions of the play. Print sources change over time, with more articles and books written and added every year, but internet sources can *change* – change web addresses, or even disappear – overnight. Please do keep this in mind when consulting such resources.

Syllabi

Several of those who include *'Tis Pity She's a Whore*, and others of John Ford's plays, have made their syllabi available through the internet. These syllabi might serve well as models when considering including *'Tis Pity* for the first time in a course, or when thinking about constructing a course from the ground up around a particular theme or motif. Some of the examples here are period-based and others are genre-based (tragedy, revenge tragedy) or culturally-based, such as Jonathan Burton's course on religious performance. Other thematic, critical theory and character approaches might also lend themselves to the teaching of *'Tis Pity*. One could easily imagine a course on 'forbidden love', for example. The following syllabi were found through Google searches. The most useful search words for finding syllabi and teaching suggestions online are likely to be 'John Ford', 'Tis Pity', 'early modern', 'whore' (not to put too fine a point on it), and 'syllabus', in some combination ('Ford whore syllabus' worked very well).

Undergraduate literature courses

Period courses

Meg Powers Livingston, of Penn State Altoona, includes 'Tis Pity in her design of an upper division course for English majors, 'Readings in Earlier Seventeenth-Century British Literature'. This course begins with poetry by John Donne, moves through poetry and drama by Ben Jonson (*Volpone*), Webster's *Duchess of Malfi*, then poetry by Herbert, Crashaw, Vaughn, Mary Sidney, Mary Wroth, Aemelia Lanyer, Margaret Cavendish, Katherine Philips, Herrick and Carew, then to drama with Ford's *'Tis Pity*, Massinger's *The Roman Actor*, then to Rachel Speght, Robert Burton, Hobbes and several writers of civil war polemics. She finishes the course with Milton and Marlowe. Livingston's syllabus includes useful questions along the way and can be found at www.personal.psu.edu/mpl10/17lit.htm.

Daniel Traister's 'Renaissance Drama: Drama of the Tudor and Stuart Periods' (University of Pennsylvania), offered in the autumn of 1998, is an excellent example and includes drama from the medieval through to the Stuart period, including anonymous medieval texts, then Greene, Kyd, Marlowe, the Countess of Pembroke, Elizabeth Cary, Jonson, Webster, Tourneur, Beaumont and Fletcher, Middleton and Ford. Traister includes solid secondary readings and an excellent range of web materials. His syllabus is so thorough, and quite frankly terrific, that it is well worth a look at www.sas.upenn.edu/~traister/syl-rendrama.html.

Edmund M. Taft, of Marshall University, offered a split undergraduate and graduate course in 'Shakespeare's Contemporaries' (English 417/517) in the autumn of 2008. His syllabus begins with *The Second Shepherds' Play*, and moves through *Dr Faustus*, *Edward II*, *The Spanish Tragedy*, *Arden of Faversham*, *The Shoemaker's Holiday*, *The Masque of Queens*, *A Woman Killed With Kindness*, *The Knight of the Burning Pestle*, *The Duchess of Malfi*, *The Changeling* and ends with *'Tis Pity She's a Whore*. His course objectives are well articulated, and his is the only course I found that uses the film version of *'Tis Pity*. See www.marshall.edu/English/courses/fall08/TAFTEng%20417%20517%20Syllabus.pdf.

Genre and themed courses

Blair Hoxby of Stanford offers 'Jacobean Tragedy' (English 240), with the goal of reading 'three [*sic*] types of Jacobean tragedy: revenge tragedies like *Hamlet*, domestic tragedies like *Othello*, tragedies of over-reaching like *Macbeth*, and tragedies of suffering like *Cymbeline*', and to

compare Shakespeare's plays to those of his greatest contemporaries and successors: Beaumont and Fletcher, Webster,
Middleton, Ford. Attention to the significance of carnal,
bloody, and unnatural acts, to the knowledge gained by
suffering, and to the pleasure peculiar to tragedy.

He includes a final unit on 'Hybrid Tragedies: Revenge, Domestic
Violence, Ambition, and Suffering', which includes *The Duchess of
Malfi, Women Beware Women* and *'Tis Pity*. A Google search
brought up his syllabus as both an HTML and a Word document:
www.stanford.edu/dept/english/deptWebFiles/syllabi/2057sylla-
bus.doc.

Norman Boyer, of Saint Xavier University, Chicago, includes *'Tis
Pity* in a combination English and women's studies course (ENGL/
WMSTU 303, autumn 2006), entitled: 'English Renaissance Drama:
The Performance of Gender on the Early Modern Stage'. He
includes *The Spanish Tragedy, The Jew of Malta, Edward II, Arden
of Faversham, The Shoemaker's Holiday, Epicene, Bartholomew
Fair, The Revenger's Tragedy, The Roaring Girl, A Chaste Maid in
Cheapside, The Changeling, The Duchess of Malfi* and *'Tis Pity
She's a Whore*. Using the Norton *English Renaissance Drama,* edited
by David Bevington, as well as supplementary critical material,
Professor Boyer presents an ambitious and interesting syllabus for
the course which can be found at http://english.sxu.edu/boyer/
fall06/303EngRenDrSyF06.pdf.

Professor Katy Staverva of Cornell College presents an ACM
Newberry Library seminar entitled 'Medieval and Renaissance
Drama: Shakespeare's Rivals', in which seminar members study four
plays: *'Tis Pity, Tamburlaine, The White Devil* and *The Roaring
Girl*. This seminar met five days a week for four weeks in April
2009, and afforded advanced undergraduates from the Associated
Colleges of the Midwest (ACM) the resources of the Newberry, as
well as shared living quarters. Professor Staverva's syllabus is an
excellent example for a short intensive seminar, and is posted at
http://people.cornellcollege.edu/kstavreva/Renaissance-Drama/syl-
labus.htm.

Interdisciplinary course
MIT's Open Courseware provides another example of what can be
done in the undergraduate classroom, this time for a course entitled
'Learning from the Past: Drama, Science, Performance', developed
by Diana Henderson and Janet Sonenberg. According to the course
description,

This class explores the creation (and creativity) of the modern scientific and cultural world through study of western Europe in the 17th century, the age of Descartes and Newton, Shakespeare, Rembrandt and Moliere. It compares period thinking to present-day debates about the scientific method, art, religion, and society. This team-taught, interdisciplinary subject draws on a wide range of literary, dramatic, historical, and scientific texts and images, and involves theatrical experimentation as well as reading, writing, researching and conversing.

The course includes a variety of reading and visual materials to accomplish its goals. The course home is at http://ocw.mit.edu/ OcwWeb/Literature/21L-016Spring-2007/CourseHome/index.htm. This syllabus can be found at http://ocw.mit.edu/OcwWeb/ Literature/21L-016Spring-2007/Readings/index.htm. A complete list and index to courses in the Open Courseware, 'LIT @ MIT' is accessible at http://ocw.mit.edu/OcwWeb/Literature/index.htm, and information of the concept and philosophy of the Open Courseware programme is available at http://ocw.mit.edu/OcwWeb/ web/about/about/index.htm.

Graduate literature courses

Wayne Narey, of Arkansas State University, includes 'Tis Pity in a combination upper level and graduate course in 'Renaissance Drama Excluding Shakespeare'; he includes many of the plays we have seen in other courses: *Doctor Faustus*, *The Spanish Tragedy*, *Titus Andronicus* (because of authorship issues), *The Revenger's Tragedy*, *The Duchess of Malfi*, *The Alchemist*, *The Changeling* and *'Tis Pity She's A Whore*. He begins his discussion of *'Tis Pity* with a discussion of *Romeo and Juliet*, with which it is often compared: forbidden love, the garrulous nurse, the advising Friar. He suggests, further, that the rearrangement of similar events in the later play 'influences how we perceive the images, the poetry, and characterization in ways that ironically change the same play it imitates' (email communication). His syllabus is located at http://www.clt.astate.edu/wnarey/Renaissance%20Drama/ sample_syllabus.htm. Some of his course materials are located at http://www.clt.astate.edu/wnarey/Renaissance%20Drama/ renaissance_drama_excluding_shakespeare.htm.

Patricia Cahill, of Emory, has included two Ford plays in her graduate seminar, 'Studies in Renaissance Literature: Revenge on the Renaissance Stage' (autumn of 2006). Her course includes Thomas Kyd's *The Spanish Tragedy*, Shakespeare's *Hamlet* and *Titus*

Andronicus, Elizabeth Cary's *The Tragedy of Mariam*, Tourneur's *The Revenger's Tragedy*, Middleton and Rowley's *The Changeling*, ending with Ford's *The Broken Heart* and *'Tis Pity She's a Whore*, and including Angela Carter's short story.

Jonathan Burton, of West Virginia University, included *'Tis Pity* in his graduate seminar, 'The Performance of Faith: Religion and Difference on the Early Modern Stage' (English 764, Fall 2001). Burton's selection of plays and critical material is wide-ranging and provides an excellent model for a graduate seminar centered on the exigencies of religion in the early modern period. His course description makes clear the range of the materials he has chosen for the course:

> In the twenty-five year period between 1533 and 1558 England's state religion shifted three times, first from Catholicism to Anglicanism, then back to Catholicism, before returning again to Anglicanism. With each change the English were required to abandon their current practice in state-mandated rites of apostasy. At the same time, English sailors in the Mediterranean were converting to Islam in unprecedented numbers. The threat of apostasy combined with the instability of English Christianity made virtually every public occasion for the next 80 years an opportunity to perform the proper faith. In this class we will look at how the public performance of faith both borrowed from and contributed to contemporary theatrical practices. We'll begin by examining Michel de Certeau's The Possession at Loudon (2000) and John Foxe's Acts and Monuments of the Christian Church (1563) to develop an understanding of the interanimation of Reformation politics and Renaissance theatricality. Then, over the course of the semester, we'll refine our models by testing them against a dozen or so plays and civic pageants featuring representations of Protestantism, Catholicism, Puritanism, Judaism and Islam, as well as a range of archival materials concerning apostasy and religious difference.

His syllabus can be found at www.as.wvu.edu/clcold/knowl-edgebase/dept_syllabi/jburton764-F01.html.

'Tis Pity appears on the current graduate reading list for 'Earlier Seventeenth Century British Literature' at UCLA; the full list is at www.english.ucla.edu/academics/graduate/current/readinglist/Early17th1099.htm.

Databases

Most library websites make some sort of distinction between print resources found in the library and resources available through database searches of books held in other libraries worldwide or databases of electronic journals and periodicals. Once one is into the database searching mode, most databases rely on the Boolean logic of 'and', 'or', and 'not' in the advanced searching mode. Searching for 'John Ford' can be problematic because of the Hollywood director, so the 'basic search' mode may not work here; using the 'advanced search', adding the play title or the word 'playwright', 'early modern' or 'renaissance' will help. Advanced searches can be performed by adding various key words such as 'incest', confession' and so on.

For those who have access to the fully digitized journal articles in the databases JSTOR (134 journals in language and literature) or Project Muse (117 journals in literature) through their library's home pages (and usually accessible from home, whether by a direct sign-in or by setting up a proxy server), these are good places to begin research, or to demonstrate online research practices for students. JSTOR and Project Muse give one access to the full text of the journals they catalogue, which include many journals dedicated to the early modern period.

General One File (Gale Cengage Learning) is less helpful than JSTOR and Project Muse, as the resources listed are not all full text, and many are not academic, but one does have the option here to select popular press (magazines – the first tab) and to look up reviews of recent theatrical performances, which, in the case of John Ford, might be useful.

The MLA International Bibliography (Ebsco Host) contains bibliographic as well as full-text items. As with JSTOR and Project Muse, the MLA uses Boolean logic and one can designate fields, such as author, subject, keywords, language and so on.

Wilson OmniFile Full Text Mega (Wilsonweb) has some of the same limitations as General OneFile, in that not everything that is indexed here is available in full text through this source.

World Cat (First Search) can be searched from the home computer for primary sources as well as for current critical essays and books. World Cat shows that the 1633 edition of the play, titled as *'Tis pitty shee's a whore*, printed by Nicholas Okes for Richard Collins, is available on microfische at 87 libraries worldwide through the STC Three Centuries of Drama series. Those who have access to Early English Books Online (EEBO) may also be able to access Ford's works through this digitized version. World Cat lists 13 libraries worldwide that own first edition copies of the 1633 text (though World Cat lists this many, there are certainly more, as it only lists two in the UK, for example, not including the one held at the British Library). Finding books here, and ordering them through inter-library loan is a basic research practice for professors and lecturers, like myself, at smaller schools and universities.

OCLC (the Online Computer Library Center) also hosts World Cat publically (and at no charge) for those who do not have access through their library, at www.oclc.org/us/en/worldcat/default.htm. Once a zip/postal code is entered, World Cat will list the nearest libraries (in miles) for a particular work.

Many of these databases, as well as many libraries, include some sort of optional citation-saving or bibliography-building component, or the capacity to save citations to programmes like EndNote or RefWorks. World Cat offers help with citations (and includes a video of how to download and format citations, with a useful caveat that citations should also be checked manually to see that entries truly comply with format requirements). Downloaded items can be transferred to EndNote and RefWorks, but when I tried to download one source to my own EndNote program, my entire EndNote library entitled 'Ford Resources' (yes, the resources listed here, including notes on each of the editions listed at the end) was replaced by that one source, so beware and be careful. One can also save lists of sources for public view here, so I suspect this might be a place to list electronic reserves for a course.

Some sources are worth keeping an eye on even though presently they do not hold any Ford resources at present: Renascence Editions, hosted at http://darkwing.uoregon.edu/~rbear/ren.htm (perhaps someone reading this may volunteer) and the Perseus Project, hosted by Tufts University (http://www.perseus.tufts.edu).

Online Resources

In beginning a search for study guides and for additional material on John Ford, students are often tempted turn to popular search engines such as Google, Yahoo and Ask.com. The limitations of such searches is well known to professors and lecturers, but because these limitations are not so clear to students, because every course website I looked at had harsh words about plagiarism and because we need to know what's out there, I want to spend a little time on searching through commercial websites and conventional search engines.

Because there are many 'John Fords' around, including the twentieth-century movie director, one must limit one's search in some way (keywords such as 'playwright', 'early modern' or 'Renaissance' are useful delimiters, as discussed above). The web resources generated by such a search are perhaps a rudimentary introductory exercise, but the material can be dated or spurious. Information at Ask.com, for example, is quite dated (M. Joan Seargeaunt's 1935 biography as well as works of criticism dated 1978 or earlier). Wikipedia (that scourge of college teaching) provides similar general information, with a few additional references – but still nothing later than 1978. As with any web search using these popular search engines and websites, the information, and particularly the references listed, may serve well to show the limitations of such searches, if nothing else.

These sites are also commercially sponsored, so when I was led from a Google search to look at 'Bookrags' recently, an ad by 'Glam.com' asked, 'What's your favorite Keira Knightly look? – strapless, backless, short, or long?' There are also ads for current movies, TV shows and perhaps of interest here, two rehab centres, including one called Renaissance Malibu Center, whose website (yes, I looked) features drawings by Leonardo, paintings by Michelangelo and an audio testimonial by Daniel Baldwin (read: expensive); the Center is limited to only 12 clients (read: *very* expensive).

As seems usual in the dot.com world, much information given in these sources is cross-cribbed (with or without proper attribution) and varies in reliability. Again, these sites are most useful as object lessons or cautionary tales in how *not* to do research. Sponsored by Thompson Gale (also known now as Cengage Learning – the publishers of the Arden Shakespeare), Bookrags' 'Research Any-thing' slogan leads one to some free summaries, but many other resources for purchase, either of a specific guide or at various payment or subscription levels. Unfortunately, though the site has stern warnings against plagiarism (don't they all?), one *can* purchase student papers (22,000 at last count) through the site. Teachers' plans are also sadly available, but these are geared toward high-school and middle school teachers (and not available for '*Tis Pity* – which, I think, is *not* a pity). 'E-notes' offers a study guide and essays (also for sale), as well as teacher's guide. There are certainly many other sites out there that prey on students' sense of panic when papers are due; reiterating policies and demonstrating the ease with which it is possible to backtrack to these sites should be ample warning to those who would fall victim to such desperation. My own best cautionary tale is when I received the same paper from four different students in two sections of the same course.

One bright light that shines in the midst of many mundane to mediocre public sites is Luminarium (www.luminarium.org), which has been an excellent medieval and early modern (and now eighteenth century) online resource since 1996. Compiled by Anniina Jokinen, the site includes wide-ranging material on authors in the early modern period. The 'Letter from the Editor' on the site recalls the background and development of the project and Jokinen's purpose in providing material to undergraduate students, like herself 12 years ago, who did not have access through their libraries to JSTOR or Project Muse, or who had to pay for articles, in what she calls 'The Internet Dark Ages'. The site is stunningly beautiful, and though it now carries some advertising, this is necessitated by its sheer size (3,300 pages in 2006) and the volume of visits (1.5 million per month, and over 10 million page views). The adverts are usually related to the site content and generally (though not always) non-intrusive and I think the site remains the 'beacon of light' that Ms Jokinen intended when she first named the site 'luminarium'. It is often referenced in the syllabi that I have examined on the early modern period, and on Ford. The site includes discussion boards for many authors and topics, including John Ford (with no entries at present); readers here might want to get a discussion going.

The John Ford section of the site includes an image of the original title page of *The Witch of Edmonton*, a brief biography (from Grosse and Garnett's 1904 *English Literature: An Illustrated Record*), a link to famous quotations from Ford though Giga Quotes (which touts itself as 'The most extensive collection of quotations on the internet'), and works (through GoogleBooks), including a digitized edition of Ford's works from *The Works of John Ford* (three volumes), edited by William Gifford, with further additions by Rev. Alexander Dyce (London: Lawrence and Bullen, 1895, digitized in 2005). There are also essays, book and more.

The peer-refereed journal *Early Modern Literary Studies* (*EMLS*), founded in 1995, offers consistently high-quality scholarship, including the following two entries on John Ford. An *EMLS* article by Marguérite Corporaal, 'An Empowering Wit and an "Unnatural" Tragedy: Margaret Cavendish's Representation of the Tragic Female Voice', comparing Margaret Cavendish's *An Unnatural Tragedy* to *'Tis Pity She's a Whore*. Go to http://extra.shu.ac.uk/emls/si-14/corpempo.html. An interactive edition of Ford's *The Queene, Or the Excellency of Her Sex*, edited by Tim Seccombe as part of his MA studies at Sheffield Hallam University, can be found at http://extra.shu.ac.uk/emls/iemls/renplays/queencontents.htm.

Editions of the Play

Anthologies that include 'Tis Pity She's a Whore

Bevington, David, Engle, Lars, Eisaman Maus, Katharine and Rasmussen, Eric, eds, *English Renaissance Drama: A Norton Anthology* (New York: W.W. Norton, 2005). This 2,400-page collection spans the drama from Thomas Kyd, *The Spanish Tragedy*, through Ford's *'Tis Pity*. The full table of contents can be viewed at www.wwnorton.com/college/titles/english/bev/contents.htm.

Fraser, Russell and Rabkin, Norman, eds, *Drama of the English Renaissance II: The Stuart Period* (New York: Macmillan 1976). Although this anthology is out of print, it is still readily available second-hand through many sources. The plays in Volume II include Tourneur, Jonson, Middleton, Webster, Beaumont and Fletcher, as well as Ford's *Perkin Warbeck* and *'Tis Pity*. This is an excellent anthology.

Gifford, W., ed., *The Dramatic Works of John Ford* (London: John Murray, 1827). This and the next entry are classics of nineteenth-century criticism and editing.

Gifford, W. and Dyce, A., eds, *The Works of John Ford* (London: J. Toovey, 1869). This edition is also available in a digitized, though marked up, version at 'Google Books' (www.books.google.com). The section of the introduction that deals with *'Tis Pity* begins on p. xxix. Gifford refers to the 'dreadful plot' (p. xxx) of the play, and believes that 'somewhat too much indulgence has been shown to the management of the principal characters' (p. xxxi). The play begins on p. 107. See http://books.google.com/books?id = k4U0AAAAMAAJ&pg = PA107&dq = %27tis + pity + she%27s + a + whore.

Kinney, Arthur F., ed., *Blackwell's Renaissance Drama: An Anthology of Plays and Entertainments* (Malden, MA: Blackwell, 1999). This anthology offers conventional stage plays as well as masques and pageants. Its table of contents is available at www.blackwellpublishing.com/book.asp?ref = 9781405119672&site = 1.

Lomax, Marion, ed., *'Tis Pity She's a Whore and Other Plays*, Oxford World's Classics (Oxford: Oxford University Press, 1995). This collection includes *The Lover's Melancholy*, *The Broken Heart* and *Perkin Warbeck* as well. It is lean on notes (using endnotes) and introductory materials.

Single editions

Barker, Simon, ed., *'Tis Pity She's a Whore*, Routledge English Texts (New York: Routledge, 1997). Barker's introduction includes sections on the author, Ford's theatre, sources and influences; the Italian setting (especially important, he notes, because of English stereotypes of corruption, sexual immorality and revenge); gender, sexuality, and spectacle; productions of the play on stage and in film; and the playtext. Endnotes are provided for the playtext. A critical commentary after the play opens with a discussion of Angela Carter's short story, then discusses critical reception of the play and Ford's reputation in literary circles of the nineteenth and twentieth centuries, commenting on how the reception of the play seems to depend on associating or disassociating it with Ford's moral stance. Barker includes a section on Ford and Shakespeare, especially *Romeo and Juliet*; a section on religion and morality, in which he draws on recent (late twentieth-century) criticism; and ends with the play as cultural history. Finally, Barker includes an excellent bibliography.

Bawcutt, N. W., ed., *'Tis Pity She's a Whore*, Regents Renaissance Drama (Lincoln, NE: University of Nebraska Press, 1966). This edition includes an introduction dealing with dates and sources, as well as an overview of critical reception, focusing on seventeenth-century views, as well as those of early editors, especially William Gifford's 1827 complete works. Bawcutt emphasizes incest, fate, revenge and justice, and includes character analyses of Giovanni, Annabella and Friar Bonaventura in the introduction. As is the Regents Renaissance practice, textual variants are included below the text on each page, just above the glosses and footnotes.

Ford, John, *'Tis Pity She's a Whore*, Kessinger Publishing's Rare Reprints. Touting its thousands of reprints of scarce and hard to find books, Kessinger's website (www.kessinger.com) offers several selections of Ford's works. This reprint has no notes, introductions or editing, nor is it clear which version of the text they are reprinting. This edition is also expensive relative to the other editions mentioned.

Hopkins, Lisa, ed., *'Tis Pity She's a Whore*, Drama Classics (London: Nick Hern Books, 2003). Hopkins's introduction includes a brief biography, a summary of 'what happens in the play' and sections on the title, incest, gender, bodies and souls, knowledge and faith, staging and further reading. The playtext is presented 'uncluttered', as is the practice of the Drama Classics series, with a short glossary at the end. This edition, though genuinely pocket-sized, is loaded with information.

Roper, Derek, ed., *'Tis Pity She's a Whore*, Revels Student Edition, based on the Revels Plays edition, ed. Derek Roper (Manchester: Methuen, 1975). Roper presents a very readable student introduction to Ford, his influences, the play and its context. He presents a reading that focuses on the love plot, and draws parallels between *'Tis Pity* and *Romeo and Juliet*. He then suggests, more briefly, other readings of the play that might be useful to students, giving references to some scholars who make use of Freudian, psychoanalytic and poststructuralist readings. Roper offers further readings in his introduction, and includes useful glosses and footnotes in the text. Some will surely be enticed by the cover.

Wiggins, Martin, ed., *'Tis Pity She's a Whore*, New Mermaids (London: A&C Black, 2003). Wiggins offers solid introductory material on the author, sources and early productions of the play, as well as on incest, intellectualism and secrets, among other things. He offers sources for further reading and surveys the major British productions of the play up to 1999. He also includes useful glosses and footnotes, and some photos of recent productions.

Film

'Tis Pity She's a Whore, filmed in Italy in 1971 (released in the US in 1974), directed by Giuseppe Patron Griffi. Having seen the theatre production at the Goodman Theatre the year before in Chicago, Roger Ebert commented in 1975:

> It's a good film to look at, filmed in warm earth colors and airy pastels. But it's not especially successful. Perhaps the acting is at fault. Nobody in the cast seems to have quite solved the problem of how to perform in a melodrama as violent as it is implausible, and still look believable on the screen. On the stage, this sort of material can be attacked head-on with theatrical gusto. But movies have a way of making even the most unlikely fantasies take on a photo-graphic reality, so Ford's story has to be played straight. The alternative, to ham it up, would be so out of scale on the screen we'd just laugh [...] The story involves an incestuous love affair, the pregnancy which is its exceedingly unfortunate consequence and a final act of wholesale bloodletting. There's nothing in the movie quite as dramatic as the bloody heart waved around onstage at the Goodman. But the closing scenes

are sufficiently tragic [...] All of this really looks a lot better on the stage. *'Tis Pity She's a Whore* still works as theater, especially when we can enjoy it in a period costume production. But as a movie it's hard to take seriously, and especially as seriously as Griffi takes it. 'Tis pity.

Mr Ebert's full review, from 1 January 1975, in the *Chicago Sun-Times* can be found at http://rogerebert.suntimes.com/apps/pbcs.dll/article?AID = /19750101/REVIEWS/501010369/1023.

Roland Joffé directed a televised version of *'Tis Pity* on BBC2 in 1980, but this is not presently available for purchase. The full cast and information are available at www.imdb.com/title/tt0295144/.

Conclusion

This chapter has focused on how to find materials on the internet and how to use internet sources to find materials in the library. The resources provided here are by no means exhaustive; in the case of the syllabi I have included, they are representative of the range that is available on the internet and of many more, I am sure, that are not so readily accessible. Search strategies will vary from person to person, and will change over time, but at the time of writing the internet seems to afford professors and students an excellent means of research, and makes available a vast array of digital and digitized sources hitherto found only in print, and many times only in research libraries and rare books' rooms. These blessings are mixed, though, as is the uneven quality of the materials that are posted on the internet. Proper research and citation methods need to be stressed continually and can be demonstrated rather easily in our brave-new-electronic-classroom world, but if we do not also convey to our students (at both graduate and undergraduate levels) the joys of print culture and the epiphanies and near ecstasies to be found in browsing the stacks of our libraries and at the act of opening a 400-year-old quarto (and I know that I'm preaching to the choir here), it really would be, well, a pity.

Selected Bibliography

Amtower, Laurel, ' "This Idol Thou Ador'st": The Iconography of *'Tis Pity She's a Whore'*, *Papers on Language and Literature* 34.2 (1998), 197–206.

Anderson, Donald, K. Jr, *John Ford* (New York: Twayne, 1972).

Artaud, Antonin, *The Theatre and its Double*, trans. Victor Corti (London: Calder & Boyars, 1970).

Bacon, Wallace A., 'The Literary Reputation of John Ford', *Huntington Library Quarterly* 2 (1947–48), pp. 181–99.

Banerjee, Pompa, 'The Gift: Economies of Kinship and Sacrificial desire in *'Tis Pity She's a Whore'*, *Studies in the Humanities* 29.2 (2002), pp. 137–49.

Billing, Christian, 'Modelling the Anatomy Theatre and the Indoor Hall Theatre: Dissection on the Stages of Early Modern London', *Early Modern Literary Studies*, special edition 13 (2004), online: http://extra.shu.ac.uk/emls/si-13/billing/index.htm.

Black, Cheryl, 'A Visible Oppression: JoAnne Akalaitis's Staging of John Ford's *'Tis Pity She's a Whore'*, *Theatre Studies* 40 (1995), pp. 5–16.

Boehrer, Bruce, 'Nice Philosophy: *'Tis Pity She's a Whore* and the Two Books of God', *SEL* 24 (1984), 355–71.

Boehrer, Bruce, *Monarchy and Incest in Renaissance England* (Philadelphia, PA: University of Pennsylvania Press, 1992).

Bolam, Robyn, 'Ford, Mary Wroth, and the Final Scene of *'Tis Pity She's a Whore'*, in *A Companion to English Renaissance Literature and Culture*, ed. Michael Hattaway (Oxford: Blackwell Publishing, 2000), pp. 276–83.

Brissenden, Alan, 'Impediments to Love: A Theme in John Ford', *Renaissance Drama* 7 (1964), pp. 95–102.

Bueller, Lois, 'The Structural uses of Incest in English Renaissance Drama', *Renaissance Drama*, n.s. 15 (1984), pp. 115–45.

Butler, Martin, *Theatre and Crisis: 1632–1642* (Cambridge: Cambridge University Press, 1984).

Butler, Martin, *'Love's Sacrifice*: Ford's Metatheatrical Tragedy', in *John Ford: Critical Revisions*, ed. Michael Neill (Cambridge: Cambridge University Press, 1988), pp. 201–31.

Champion, Larry S., 'Ford's *'Tis Pity She's a Whore* and the Jacobean Tragic Perspective', *PMLA*, 90.1 (1975), 78–87.

Clark, Ira, *Professional Playwrights: Massinger, Ford, Shirley and Brome* (Lexington, KY: University Press of Kentucky, 1992).

Clerico, Terri, 'The Politics of Blood: John Ford's *'Tis Pity She's a Whore'*, *English Literary Renaissance* 22 (1992), pp. 405–34.

Coleridge, Hartley, *The Dramatic Works of Massinger and Ford*, 2 vols (London: Edward Moxon, 1840).

Cushman, Robert, 'The Actors' Revenge', *Plays and Players*, (December 1972), 44–46.

Davril, Robert, 'John Ford and La Cerda's *Ines de Castro*', *Modern Language Notes* 66 (1951), pp. 464–66.

Defaye, Claudine, 'Annabella's Unborn Baby: The Heart in the Womb in *'Tis Pity She's a Whore*', *Cahiers Élisabéthains* 15 (1979), pp. 35–42.

Dente, Carla, 'Reading Symptoms of Decadence in Ford's *'Tis Pity She's a Whore*', in *Romancing Decay: Ideas of Decadence in European Culture*, ed. Michael St John (Aldershot: Ashgate, 1999), pp. 27–38.

Dessen, Alan, *'Tis Pity She's a Whore*: Modern Productions and the Scholar' in *'Concord in Discord', The Plays of John Ford 1586–1986*, ed. Donald K. Anderson Jr, (New York: AMS Press, 1986), pp. 87–108.

Diehl, Huston, 'The Iconography of Violence in English Renaissance Tragedy', *Renaissance Drama* X1 (1980), 27–44.

Diehl, Huston, 'Bewhored Images and Imagined Whores: Iconophobia and Gynophobia in Stuart Love Tragedies', *English Literary Renaissance* 26 (1996), pp. 111–37.

DiGangi, Mario, 'John Ford' in *A Companion to Renaissance Drama*, ed. Arthur F. Kinney (Oxford: Blackwell, 2004), pp. 567–83.

Ewing, S. Blaine, *Burtonian Melancholy in the Plays of John Ford* (Princeton, NJ: Princeton University Press, 1940).

Farr, Dorothy M., *John Ford and the Caroline Theatre* (Basingstoke: Macmillan, 1979).

Fehrenbach, R. J., 'Typographical Variation in Ford's Texts: Accidentals or Substantives', in *'Concord in Discord': the Plays of John Ford, 1586–1986*, ed. Donald K. Anderson Jr (New York: AMS Press, 1986), pp. 265–94.

Findlay, Alison, *A Feminist Perspective on Renaissance Drama* (Oxford: Blackwell, 1999).

Ford, John, *The Broken Heart*, ed. T. J. B. Spencer (Manchester: Manchester University Press, 1980).

Ford, John, *The Lover's Melancholy*, ed. R.F. Hill (Manchester: Manchester University Press, 1985).

Ford, John, *'Tis Pity She's a Whore*, ed. N.W. Bawcutt (Lincoln, NE: University of Nebraska Press, 1966).

Ford, John, *'Tis Pity She's a Whore*, ed. Derek Roper (London: Methuen, 1975).

Ford, John, *'Tis Pity She's a Whore and Other Plays*, ed. Marion Lomax (Oxford: Oxford University Press, 1995).

Ford, John, *'Tis Pity She's a Whore*, ed. Simon Barker (London: Routledge, 1997).

Ford, John, *'Tis Pity She's a Whore*, ed. Martin Wiggins (London: A&C Black, 2003).

Forker, Charles, *Fancy's Images: Contexts, Settings, and Perspectives in Shakespeare and his Contemporaries* (Carbondale, IL: Southern Illinois University Press, 1990).

Foster, Verna, *"Tis Pity She's a Whore* as City Tragedy', in *John Ford: Critical Revisions*, ed. Michael Neill (Cambridge: Cambridge University Press, 1988), pp. 181–200.

Gauer, Dennis, 'Heart and Blood: Nature and Culture in *'Tis Pity She's a Whore*', *Cahiers Élisabéthains* 31 (1987), 45–57.

Gibson, Colin, '"The stage of my mortality": Ford's Poetry of Death', in *John Ford: Critical Re-Visions*, ed. Michael Neill (Cambridge: Cambridge University Press, 1988), pp. 55–80.

Greenfield, Thelma N., 'John Ford's Tragedy: The Challenge of Re-Engagement', in *'Concord in Discord: The Plays of John Ford, 1586–1986*, ed. Donald K. Anderson (New York: AMS Press, 1986), pp. 1–26.

Hazlitt, William, *The Complete Works of William Hazlitt*, ed. P. P. Howe, 21 vols (London: Dent, 1931).

Hogan, A. P., *''Tis Pity She's A Whore*: The Overall Design', *Studies in English Literature 1300–1900* 17 (1977), pp. 303–16.

Homan, Sidney R., 'Shakespeare and Dekker as Keys to Ford's *'Tis Pity She's a Whore'*, *Studies in English Literature, 1500–1900* 7.2 (1967), pp. 269–76.

Hopkins, Lisa, *John Ford's Political Theatre* (Manchester: Manchester University Press, 1994).

Hopkins, Lisa, 'John Ford's *'Tis Pity She's a Whore* and Early Diagnoses of Folie á Deux', *Notes and Queries* 41.1 (1994), pp. 71–74.

Hopkins, Lisa, '*Close My Eyes*: A Modern Reworking of Ford', *Marlowe Society of America Newsletter* 14. 2 (autumn 1994), pp. 2–3.

Hopkins, Lisa, 'A Source for *'Tis Pity She's a Whore'*, *Notes and Queries* 41.4 (1994), pp. 520–21.

Hopkins, Lisa, 'Speaking Sweat: Emblems in the Plays of John ford', *Comparative Drama* 29.1 (1995), pp. 133–46.

Hopkins, Lisa, 'John Ford's Annabella and the Virgin Mary', *Notes and Queries* 42 (1995), p. 380.

Hopkins, Lisa, 'Marlowe, Chapman, Ford and Nero', *English Language Notes* 35.1 (1997), pp. 5–10.

Hopkins, Lisa, 'Knowing their Loves: Knowledge, Ignorance, and Blindness in *'Tis Pity She's a Whore'*, *Renaissance Forum* 3.1 (1998), online: http://www.hull.ac.uk/renforum/v3no1/Hopkins.htm.

Hopkins, Lisa, 'Incest and Class: *'Tis Pity She's a Whore* and the Borgias', in *Incest and the Literary Imagination*, ed. Elizabeth Barnes (Gainesville, FL: University Press of Florida, 2002), pp. 94–116.

Hopkins, Lisa, 'A New Source for *'Tis Pity She's a Whore'*, *Notes and Queries* 50.4 (2003), pp. 443–44.

Hopkins, Lisa, *Screening the Gothic* (Austin, TX: University of Texas Press, 2005).

Houlahan, Mark, 'Postmodern Tragedy? Returning to John Ford', in *Tragedy in Transition*, ed. Sarah Annes Brown and Catherine Silverstone (Oxford: Blackwell, 2007), pp. 248–49.

Hoy, Cyrus, ' "Ignorance in knowledge": Marlowe's Faustus and Ford's Giovanni', *Modern Philology* 57 (1960), pp. 145–54.

Huebert, Ronald, *John Ford: Baroque English Dramatist* (Montreal: McGill-Queen's University Press, 1977).

Ide, Richard S., 'Ford's *'Tis Pity She's a Whore* and the Benefits of Belatedness', in '*Concord in Discord': The Plays of John Ford, 1586–1986*, ed. Donald K. Anderson (New York: AMS Press, 1986), pp. 61–86.

Innes, Christopher, *Modern British Drama: The Twentieth Century*, 2nd edn (Cambridge: Cambridge University Press, 2002).

Jephson, Valerie and Boehrer, Bruce, 'Mythologizing the Middle Class: *'Tis Pity She's a Whore* and the Urban Bourgeoisie', *Renaissance and Reformation* n.s.18.3 (1994), pp. 5–28.

Kaufmann R. J., 'Ford's Tragic Perspective', in *Elizabethan Drama: Modern Essays in Criticism*, ed. Ralph J. Kaufmann (1961) (Oxford: Oxford University Press, 1970), pp. 356–72.

Kent, Assunta and Nellhaus, Tobin, '*'Tis Pity She's a Whore* by John Ford', *Theatre Journal* 42.3 (October 1990), pp. 373–75.

Lamb, Charles, *Specimens of the English Dramatic Poets who Lived about the Time of Shakespeare* (London: Edward Moxon, 1808).

Langbaine, Gerard, *An Account of the English Dramatic Poets* (London: 1691).

Leech, Clifford, *John Ford and the Drama of his Time* (London: Chatto, 1957).

Low, Jennifer A., ' "Bodied Forth": Spectator, Stage, and Actor in the Early Modern Theater', *Comparative Drama* 39.1 (spring 2005), pp. 1–29.

Luís-Martínez, Zenon, *In Words and Deeds: The Spectacle of Incest in English Renaissance Tragedy* (Amsterdam: Rodopi, 2002).

Madelaine, Richard, '"The Dark and Vicious Place": The Location of Sexual Transgression and its Punishment on the Early Modern English Stage', *Parergon* 22.1 (2005), pp. 159–83.

Marienstras, Richard, *New Perspectives on the Shakespearean World* (Cambridge: Cambridge University Press, 1985).

McCabe, Richard, *Incest, Drama and Nature's Law 1550–1700* (Cambridge: Cambridge University Press, 1993).

McLuskie, Kathleen, '"Language and matter with a fit of mirth": Dramatic Construction in the Plays of John Ford', in *John Ford: Critical Re-Visions*, ed. Michael Neill (Cambridge: Cambridge University Press, 1988), pp. 97–127.

Mintz, Susannah B., 'The Power of Parity in *'Tis Pity She's a Whore*', *JEGPh* 102 (2003), pp. 269–91.

Monsarrat, Gilles D., 'The Unity of John Ford: *'Tis Pity She's a Whore* and *Christ's Bloody Sweat*', *Studies in Philology* 77 (1980), pp. 247–70.

Neill, Michael, '"What strange riddle's this?": Deciphering *'Tis Pity She's a Whore*', in *John Ford: Critical Re-visions*, ed. Michael Neill (Cambridge: Cambridge University Press, 1988).

Neill, Michael, Issues of Death: Mortality and Identity in English Renaissance Tragedy (Oxford: Oxford University Press, 1997).

Nunn, Hillary M., *Staging Anatomies: Dissection and Spectacle in Early Stuart Tragedy* (Aldershot: Ashgate, 2005).

Oliver, H. J., *The Problem of John Ford* (Melbourne: Melbourne University Press, 1955).

Ornstein, Robert, *The Moral Vision of Jacobean Tragedy* (Madison, WI: University of Wisconsin Press, 1960).

Pepys, Samuel, Diary entry for 9 September 1661, online: www.pepysdiary.com/archive/1661/09/09/.

Powell, Raymond, 'The Adaptation of a Shakespearean Genre: *Othello* and Ford's *'Tis Pity She's a Whore*', *Renaissance Quarterly* 48.3 (1995), pp. 582–92.

Sanders, Julie, *Caroline Drama: The Plays of Massinger, Ford, Shirley and Brome* (Plymouth: Northcote House, 1999).

Sargeaunt, M. Joan, *John Ford* (New York: Russell & Russell, 1966).

Sawday, Jonathan, *The Body Emblazoned: Dissection and the Human Body in Renaissance Culture* (London: Routledge, 1995).

Schelling, Felix E., *The Elizabethan Drama 1558–1642*, 2 vols (Boston, MA: Houghton Mifflin, 1910).

Scott, Michael, *Renaissance Drama and a Modern Audience* (Basingstoke: Macmillan, 1982).

Sensabaugh, G. F., *The Tragic Muse of John Ford* (Palo Alto, CA: Stanford University Press, 1944).

Sharpe, Kevin, *Criticism and Compliment: The Politics of Literature in the England of Charles I* (Cambridge: Cambridge University Press, 1987).

Slights, William, E., 'The Narrative Heart of the Renaissance', *Renaissance and Reformation* n.s. 26.1 (2002), pp. 5–23.

Slights, William, E., *The Heart in the Age of Shakespeare* (Cambridge: Cambridge University Press, 2008).

Smith, Molly, *Breaking Boundaries: Politics and Play in the Drama of Shakespeare and His Contemporaries* (Aldershot: Ashgate, 1998).

Stanton, Kay, '"Made to write 'whore' upon?": Male and Female Use of the Word "Whore" in Shakespeare's Canon', in *A Feminist Companion to Shakespeare*, ed. Dympna Callaghan (Oxford: Blackwell, 2001), pp. 80–102, p. 95.

Stavig, Mark, *John Ford and the Traditional Moral Order* (Madison, WI: Wisconsin University Press, 1968).

Stoppard, Tom, *Plays Five* (London: Faber & Faber, 1999).

Strout, Nathaniel, 'The Tragedy of Annabella in *'Tis Pity She's a Whore*', in

Traditions and Innovations, ed. D. G. Allen and R. A. White (Newark, DE: University of Delaware Press, 1990), pp. 163–76.

Styan, J. L., *The English Stage: A History of Drama and Performance* (Cambridge: Cambridge University Press, 1996).

Warren, Roger, 'Ford in Performance', in *John Ford: Critical Re-Visions*, ed. Michael Neill (Cambridge: Cambridge University Press, 1988), pp. 11–29.

Wilks, John S., *The Idea of Conscience in Renaissance Tragedy* (London: Routledge, 1990).

Williamson, Audrey, *Theatre of Two Decades* (London: Rockliff, 1951).

Wiseman, Susan J., *''Tis Pity She's a Whore*: Representing the Incestuous Body', in *Renaissance Bodies: The Human Figure in English Culture c. 1540–1660*, ed. Lucy Gent and Nigel Llewellyn (London: Reaction, 1990).

Womack, Peter, *English Renaissance Drama* (Oxford: Blackwell, 2006).

Wymer, Rowland, *Webster and Ford* (Basingstoke: Macmillan, 1995).

Wymer, Rowland, ' "The Audience is Only Interested in Sex and Violence": Teaching the Renaissance on Film', *Working Papers on the Web* 4 (September 2002), online: http://extra.shu.ac.uk/wpw/renaissance/wymer.htm.

Zinman, Toby, '*Travesties, Night and Day, The Real Thing*', in *The Cambridge Companion to Tom Stoppard*, ed. Katherine E. Kelly (Cambridge: Cambridge University Press, 2001), pp. 120–35.

Notes on Contributors

Corinne S. Abate is the editor of *Privacy, Domesticity, and Women in Early Modern England* and has published articles on *Henry V*, *Measure for Measure*, *Tamburlaine* and *Perkin Warbeck*, among other Renaissance dramas. She holds a doctorate from New York University and teaches English at Morristown-Beard School in New Jersey.

Sandra Clark is Professor Emeritus of Renaissance Literature at Birkbeck, University of London, and deputy director of the Institute of English Studies at the University of London. She is currently editing *Macbeth* for the third series of the Arden Shakespeare. Her book *Renaissance Drama* was published in 2007.

Lisa Hopkins is Professor of English at Sheffield Hallam University and co-editor of *Shakespeare*, the journal of the British Shakespeare Association. Her publications include *John Ford's Political Theatre* and many articles and notes on Ford. She is currently editing *The Lady's Trial* for the Revels series and *The Broken Heart* and *The Fancies, Chaste and Noble* for the Oxford Complete Ford.

Mark Houlahan is Senior Lecturer in English at the University of Waikato, Hamilton, New Zealand. He has published numerous essays on Renaissance playtexts and is currently editing *Twelfth Night* for the ISE Shakespeare series (www.ise.uvic.ca).

Rhonda Lemke Sanford is an associate professor of English at Fairmont State University. Her first book, *Maps and Memory in*

Early Modern England: A Sense of Place, was published in 2002 by Palgrave-St Martin. She is currently working on a book on legitimacy and illegitimacy.

Catherine Silverstone is lecturer in drama, theatre and performance studies at Queen Mary, University of London. She has published several articles on contemporary performances of Shakespeare and is co-editor with Sarah Annes Brown of *Tragedy in Transition*. She is currently writing a monograph for Routledge entitled *Shakespeare and Trauma: Contemporary Performance on Stage and Screen*.

Kate Wilkinson is a research student at Sheffield Hallam University studying Shakespeare's history plays in performance. As well as numerous theatre reviews, she has published papers on films of *Richard III* and Kevin Spacey's *Richard II*. As well as her thesis, she is currently working on *1 Henry VI* for the Facts on File Companion to Shakespeare and a paper about ghosts in the history plays.

Gillian Woods is a junior research fellow at Wadham College, Oxford University. She has published articles on Renaissance drama and her current projects include a book-length study on Shakespeare, fiction and Catholicism, and a guide to criticism of *Romeo and Juliet*.

Index